A Pa
at Iwo Jima

M000252147

A Pacifist at Iwo Jima

*Rabbi Roland Gittelsohn
from Pulpit to the U.S. Marine Corps'
Bloodiest Battle*

Lee Mandel

McFarland & Company, Inc., Publishers
Jefferson, North Carolina

A previous version of this book was published
in 2014 as *Unlikely Warrior: A Pacifist Rabbi's Journey
from the Pulpit to Iwo Jima* (Pelican Publishing, 2014).

ISBN (print) 978-1-4766-8741-4
ISBN (ebook) 978-1-4766-4676-3

LIBRARY OF CONGRESS AND BRITISH LIBRARY
CATALOGUING DATA ARE AVAILABLE

Library of Congress Control Number 2022008068

On the cover: *inset* Roland Gittelsohn from his commissioning application
for the United States Navy, 1943 (St. Louis Personnel Records Center,
National Archives); photograph of flag raising on Iwo Jima,
Joe Rosenthal, photographer, Department of the Navy,
February 23, 1945 (National Archives)

Printed in the United States of America

*McFarland & Company, Inc., Publishers
Box 611, Jefferson, North Carolina 28640
www.mcfarlandpub.com*

This book is dedicated to all the chaplains who served
in our military forces in World War II and to all members
of the Greatest Generation who fought in that war.
We owe them a debt that we can only hope to repay.

Acknowledgments

There are several people and organizations without whom *A Pacifist at Iwo Jima* would not have been possible. I am greatly indebted to the archival staff of the American Jewish Archives at the Jacob Rader Marcus Center in Cincinnati for their assistance in helping me obtain Rabbi Roland Gittelsohn's private papers. I especially want to acknowledge archivist Michelle Detroit for her efforts on my behalf. David Gittelsohn and Judith Gittelsohn Fales were gracious enough to talk with me on several occasions and share memories of their father, as well as provide me with photographs. Stepson Gerry Tishler was also helpful providing his recollections of Rabbi Gittelsohn. Their recollections are priceless, and many of them are included in the book.

For this revised edition, I would like to especially acknowledge the assistance of two distinguished scholars. I am indebted to Rabbi Edgar Weinsberg, EdD, who carefully edited my manuscript and helped pinpoint various passages that needed clarification and revisions. In addition, he provided me with critical insights into the history of Judaism. Bryan Mark Rigg, PhD, a world-class military historian and author, has mentored me through the entire process, providing both historical materials and insights into the battle for Iwo Jima, as well as the United States Marine Corps in general. Last, but certainly not least, I would like to thank my wife Ann for her patience and support throughout the entire writing of this book.

Table of Contents

Preface

In the spring of 2012, I received an invitation from my alma mater, Washington & Jefferson College, to take part in the homecoming weekend scheduled for October. At each homecoming there is a Veterans Memorial Service, and I was asked to be the speaker at the ceremony. This was my 40th reunion and, knowing that maybe a dozen of us from the class of 1972 had served in the military, I was sure that at that point I was the only member of the class still on active duty. I was at that time currently serving as a captain in the United States Navy.

After studying several of the previous years' speeches, I was looking for some particularly inspiring words to frame my presentation. As a historian, I remembered reading about a famous speech—a sermon, actually—delivered by a Navy chaplain at the end of the Battle of Iwo Jima. I checked my sources and found out that his name was Lieutenant Roland Gittelsohn, U.S. Navy, a rabbi from New York. He was the first rabbi ever to be assigned to the United States Marine Corps.

His fellow Christian chaplains' strong objections nearly prevented Gittelsohn from delivering his sermon, which has come to be known as "The Purest Democracy." It made for very interesting reading to learn of the infighting behind the scenes leading up to the March 21, 1945, dedication of the 5th Marine Division cemetery on Iwo Jima, where Gittelsohn delivered his sermon. Within a month, most of the free world knew of "The Purest Democracy," a speech that in various circles has been referred to as "The Gettysburg Address of World War II."

I read his entire speech and was impressed by the power and passion of that Navy chaplain's words. I was intrigued by Gittelsohn and began researching his background. I quickly learned that he was an outspoken pacifist in the 1930s who opposed all wars and frequently preached against the United States' entanglement in future European wars. Yet, to my astonishment, Gittelsohn actively sought and received a commission in the United States Navy in 1943. It was amazing to me that a longtime outspoken pacifist who volunteered to join the Navy, became the first Jewish chaplain in the history of the United States Marine Corps, and would finally end up in combat on Iwo Jima. As the expression goes, "You can't make this stuff up!" My interest in the man only accelerated at that point.

Gittelsohn was a prominent rabbi both on Long Island, New York, and in Boston, Massachusetts. He was a leader in the Reform Judaism hierarchy and after the war served on President Truman's Committee on Civil Rights. He was a prolific writer, having authored over a dozen books. To my delight, I discovered that he was also a meticulous documenter and kept voluminous personal files.

In 2002, Gittelsohn's son David Gittelsohn and daughter Judith Gittelsohn Fales, donated all his personal papers to the Jacob Rader Marcus Center of the American Jewish Archives. The Marcus Center is located on the campus of the Hebrew Union College–Jewish Institute of Religion in Cincinnati, where Roland Gittelsohn attended rabbinical school. The Gittelsohn collection contains 64 boxes of his personal papers, each organized into multiple folders. It is a researcher's treasure trove. With the assistance of the staff at the American Jewish Archives, I was able to obtain many of Rabbi Gittelsohn's notes.

Gittelsohn was a brilliant man with strong opinions and was clearly one of the most well-read people of his generation. Studying him and his life provides not only insight into a truly remarkable individual, but also provides an excellent framework in which to study several world events and significant social movements during his lifetime. His papers help us understand Jewish immigration from Tsarist Russia around the turn of the century, the ever-expanding anti-war movement that followed World War I along with the so-called "lessons of the World War," the transformation of America with Franklin D. Roosevelt's New Deal, the rise of Nazi Germany, the entry of the United States into World War II, the chaplaincy in the United States military, the United States Marine Corps, and of course, the Battle of Iwo Jima. To tell Roland Gittelsohn's story is to tell the story of these events.

Gittelsohn was a product of this historic time, the events of which would ultimately transform a short, scholarly, pacifist rabbi into a highly effective chaplain serving with the Marines on Iwo Jima. To be certain, he would remain an outspoken opponent of war until he passed away in 1995. But from that point on, Gittelsohn would speak not as a theorist who was well-read about war, but with the authority of one who had lived through the horror of the bloodiest battle in the history of the U.S. Marine Corps.

Introduction

In the years between the world wars, many Americans were obsessed with what they perceived were the lessons of the Great War. Never again, they vowed, should the United States become involved in any wars, wars that often originated in Europe. Isolationism and pacifism became the watchword for many Americans. Paradoxically, it was during this time when anti-war sentiment in the United States was rapidly accelerating that Nazi Germany and Imperial Japan had begun their quest for world domination.

Roland Gittelsohn was one of those pacifists. A scholarly rabbi and an extremely well-read student of history, he was active in the anti-war movement. His sermons frequently decried the policies of Franklin D. Roosevelt, which he felt were hypocritical and would lead the country to war. He also opposed the military which he felt was an "undemocratic" organization and its bellicose behavior would entangle the country with future conflicts. He was a member of the War Resisters League and had solemnly taken the Oxford Pledge, declaring he would never go to war for any reason.

How, then, did this short, professorial-looking man, an outspoken opponent of all forms of warfare, end up at the site of the bloodiest battle in U.S. Marine Corps history? What compelled this avowed pacifist to volunteer for military service with the United States Navy, where he became the first rabbi ever assigned by the Navy to serve with the U.S. Marine Corps? Last, how did it come about at the end of the Battle of Iwo Jima that he would deliver one of the most famous speeches in American history at the dedication of the 5th Marine Division cemetery, despite the anti–Semitic actions of some of his fellow chaplains?

The answers to these questions provide the framework for *A Pacifist at Iwo Jima*, the story of a remarkable man living during remarkable times. Roland Gittelsohn was a member of the Greatest Generation and like all members of that remarkable group his story needed to be told. It is now possible to study this complex man, a man who was a typical representative of the American clergy in the 1930s that was largely opposed to any wars. Yet when the United States was plunged into World War II, many of the clergy joined the military to serve with their fellow citizen soldiers. The contribution to the war effort by these clergymen cannot be overstated. Many of these men were older and had spent their lives preaching pacifism and, prior to December 7, 1941, declared they would never serve in future wars in any capacity.

Men like Rabbi Roland Gittelsohn...

Prologue

In a world of pain and horror, a message was sent that provided a rare moment of joy. It arrived just before darkness, as mortar shells exploded around the recipient and rifle and small arms fire crackled overhead. Chaplain Roland Gittelsohn read the telegram that had been sent by the wife of Herman, one of his fellow Marines in the 5th Marine Division. Because the Red Cross was unable to clear cables to men in active combat, she had arranged for the telegram to be sent to his chaplain so he could convey the joyous news that she had given birth to a baby girl. There in the carnage that was Iwo Jima, Lieutenant Gittelsohn actually felt a glimmer of hope as he reread the telegram. Maybe, just maybe, they would survive to go home and resume the lives they led before the war. That next morning, he would track Herman down and deliver the wonderful news from home.

Nine months earlier in May 1944, Gittelsohn had reported to the 5th Marine Division and learned that because he was the division's only Jewish chaplain, he was being assigned as the assistant division chaplain. Like all military chaplains, he ministered to men of all faiths while in the field, and like all effective chaplains, he became a counselor, mentor, and father-figure to many young Marines like Herman. A short, balding, scholarly-appearing man, Gittelsohn was somewhat older than many of the Marines in the division and, at the age of 34, he no doubt reminded many of the young men of their high school teachers and college professors. In the same vein, he forged a bond with many of his fellow Marines through the weekly discussion groups that he established in Hawaii to foster discussions on war goals and visions for the peace after the war ended. While they were still training in Hawaii, Herman had learned that his wife was pregnant with their first child and had shared the news with Chaplain Gittelsohn.

Since landing on February 19 on the beaches at Iwo Jima, 70,000 Marines were pitted in mortal combat against 21,900 well-entrenched Japanese defenders. Each Japanese soldier was under orders to fight to-the-death and to each kill at least 10 Americans before dying. On a daily basis, Gittelsohn and his fellow chaplains ministered to Marines in combat and comforted the dying. In addition, Gittelsohn was in charge of the 5th Marine Division cemetery. Each day, scores of young Marines killed in combat were brought to the cemetery for identification and burial. It was emotionally devastating work. The telegram Gittelsohn had received from Herman's wife was therefore like a ray of sunshine on an overcast, stormy day. To the young rabbi, it represented an affirmation of life over death, despite the hellish environment that was Iwo Jima.

Gittelsohn set out the next morning on his mission to find Herman and deliver the joyous news. But his mission would prove to be more difficult than he could imagine.

PART I

PACIFIST

And he shall judge among the nations, and shall rebuke many people: and they shall beat their swords into plowshares, and their spears into pruning hooks: nation shall not lift up sword against nation, neither shall they learn war any more. —Isaiah 2:3–4

I will fight no more forever. —Chief Joseph of the Nez Perce

ONE

Family Origins

Roland Gittelsohn was able to trace back his family heritage with certainty only as far back as his grandparents. His grandfather, Rabbi Benjamin Gittelsohn, was born in Russia in 1852 or 1853. A few weeks before he died, Benjamin shared his family's earlier history with his son Reuben, Roland's father. His research indicated that the family was descended from Rabbi Isaiah Horowitz, a renowned sixteenth-century rabbi who lived in Poland. Rabbi Horowitz was known for his scholarship and, like most great rabbis of those times, he was identified by the name of one of his books which had made him famous. This major work was entitled *Sh'nay Luchot Habrit*, or *Two Tablets of the Covenant*. Horowitz's contemporaries took the first letter of the three-word title and created an abbreviated title: *Shelah*. When they referred to the author himself, they called him *Shelah Ha-kodosh*, or the Shelah. Reuben Gittelsohn would note of his ancestor, "From such titles you could see that he was considered a great and holy man."[1] This familial linkage was impossible to corroborate, but it remained a part of the Gittelsohn family tradition on his father's side.

Further research showed that the Gittelsohn family name extended back only as far as Benjamin. Reuben would recall that, like most European Jews of the era, Benjamin Gittelsohn's father probably didn't have a family name at all. The draft law promulgated by Tsar Nicholas I in 1827 for the first time allowed male Russian Jews to serve in the army and this would lead to the creation of many family names in the Jewish community. Among the stipulations of the law was the requirement that all Jews must adopt family names. This bureaucratic requirement was likely enacted for the government's record-keeping purposes.

Permitting Jews to serve in the army may, at first glance, appear to have been a new measure of social equality, but it was in fact an effort to detach Jews from their own society and force them to convert to Christianity. The law required all Jewish males between the ages of 12 and 25 to be

9

drafted into the army and to serve for 25 years. One of the results of the law was a scramble among Jews to acquire created family surnames.

Some of them adopted the plan of using their father or mother's name, in the form of Abramson, Isaacson, Jacobson, Gittelsohn, etc. Some adopted the names of well-known cities such as Berlin, Manheim, Hamburger, or Frankfurter. Others adopted names of certain birds or animals, or of professions or businesses that they were engaged in at the time. Examples of the latter category include such well-known names as Gold, Goldsmith, Goldstein, Goldman, Goldberg, etc.[2]

The draft law also had a loophole that many families took advantage of to avoid the draft. According to the law, an only son was exempt from the draft. In a family that had several sons, each one would adopt a different name and register as the only son of another family, real or fictitious.[3] This was the method used by Benjamin Gittelsohn; his other two brothers had different family names—Kaplan and Cohen. Reuben confirmed this after consulting another family member who also concurred that he changed his name on account of the draft. Reuben would later write to his son Roland, "Why he assumed the name Gittelsohn, we don't know. It is funny that we never discussed the matter with him. At any rate, the consensus of opinion is that there are no other Gittelsohns in the family."[4]

• • •

Benjamin Gittelsohn was born in the northwestern part of Lithuania, then part of Russia, in the area known as Samogitia—or as he referred to it in Yiddish, Zamet. The area was part of the Pale of Settlement, the only part of Russia where Jews could legally live. Established by Catherine the Great in 1791 as an area to which Jews could be exiled to rid cities like Moscow of Jewish business competition and to shield Russians from "evil" Jewish influences, the area was comprised of parts of present-day Latvia, Poland, Lithuania, Ukraine, and Belorussia.

Benjamin was only eight years old when his father died. As Benjamin was the oldest child in his family, he went out on his own. He traveled around the area, spending a few years in different Orthodox Jewish schools—*yeshivas*—and eventually ended up in the town of Slonim, in the Grodno Province of Lithuania. As a young man in Slonim he met Celia "Sippa" Alenik, whom he married shortly after. The newlyweds settled in with Sippa's family who supported the couple while Benjamin continued his Talmudic studies. This arrangement, known as *kest*, was a common practice of the times. During this time, Benjamin and Sippa began their own family, eventually having 12 children. After several years of Talmudic studies, Benjamin was confirmed as a rabbi and the Gittelsohn family moved on from Slonim.

In 1878, Benjamin and Sippa settled in the town of Avanta, located in the Kovno province of Lithuania. It was there that their son Reuben was born. After serving as the town's rabbi for several years, Benjamin relocated his family to another town in the Kovno Province, Trashkun, in 1883. The family would remain in Trashkun until they immigrated to the United States several years later. Their life in Trashkun was typical of the lives of the Jews in the Pale of Settlement; grinding poverty and discrimination from other parts of Russian society were parts of the daily norm. In addition, a somber fact of life for Jews living in the Pale was the government's frequent instigation and approval of *pogroms*, or anti–Jewish riots.

Reuben Gittelsohn would carry memories of his youth in Trashkun with him for the rest of his life. In the frequent letters he would write to his son Roland and his daughter Natalie, he would vividly describe what their life was like, while contrasting it to the comparably wonderful life that they were living in the United States. He urged them to remember his reminiscences of his youth in Trashkun and to not forget their family roots. He hoped that they would someday travel to the region and when they did go there, they visit the small towns further away from the railroad stations in order to get a true picture of their roots. "The further away they are from a railroad station," he noted, "the further away from civilization, the better; because it is there that you will find the real old-fashioned Jewish life, the kind of life that has been lived in the same rut for centuries."[5]

Each little village consisted of about two hundred houses. The houses would be built adjoining two major intersecting streets, and each house featured a small fenced garden in the back where the owners would grow vegetables. Most of the houses were built of rough, rounded logs, "on the order of the log cabin where Abe Lincoln lived."[6] The ceilings were flat wooden boards covered with straw. The difficult task of constructing the roof was done by the *goyim*, non–Jews from neighboring villages. There might be three or four windows in the house and Reuben would recall never seeing a clean window. Attempting to keep windows clean in that environment was an exercise in futility. In addition, the grime on the windows cut down on the brightness inside of the house and was easier on the residents' eyes.

A wood-burning brick oven took up a large part of the floor space. The oven served two purposes—cooking as well as providing heat. Hence, there were piles of wood alongside the house all year round. The floors were bare dirt.

Benjamin Gittelsohn was one of two rabbis who led the *Misnagdim* congregation in Trashkun, Lithuania. As such, he and his family lived in the rectangular synagogue building itself. About one-sixth of the room on the left of the entrance corridor was partitioned off as the rabbi's family residence. An equal sized room was partitioned off on the other side of the entrance corridor to serve as the *Beth Hamidrash*, or study hall, that was also used for daily services. The small rabbi's residence that Reuben would jokingly refer to as their "mansion" was home to the rabbi, his wife, and their 12 children. In addition, on cold nights, the goat belonging to the family would be brought into the residence to sleep next to the oven.

About one third of the rabbi's residence was partitioned off into a second room. This smaller room "…served as my father's office, study, library, Beth-Din (rabbinical court), meeting place of the town nobles, reception room for out-of-town rabbis who visited us occasionally and … my bedroom!"[7] Reuben once wrote, in this room, he would have access to all of his father's books in a library which was considered immense by the town's standards. In this library he would discover a book on Kabbalah and, much to his astonishment, a copy of the New Testament. This was unheard of in the Russian Jewish community, but Roland Gittelsohn would later write about the incident when reflecting on his grandfather, stating, "…his incisive mind insisted that he could not defend Judaism, could not protect it against hostile invasion, unless he knew and understood the source of such invasion."[8]

Like all young boys in Trashkun, the whole focus of Reuben Gittelsohn's life was the study of Judaism. In numerous letters to his children, he would describe the stress of those days, although he would often look back with nostalgia on his childhood. He would attend school at the local *cheder*, or elementary Hebrew school. He and his friends would attend school at the *cheder* for up to 10 hours a day, six days a week, for 48 weeks a year. There they would study Hebrew, Yiddish, and Aramaic. In addition, as Reuben wrote, the curriculum contained study of the "Bible, Midrash, and the Talmud; rabbinical commentaries and codes; probably a smattering also of modern Hebrew literature. None of their education was secular, for intellectually and culturally, their world was limited to Judaism and Jews. Russian government authority dictated it that way; the Jews of Trashkun acquiesced."[9]

Although he would grow up to become a man of science and medicine, it was during his childhood in Trashkun that Reuben developed his lifelong belief in the supernatural—a belief in ghosts and spirits. In several of his letters to his children, he told of the ghosts from his days in Russia. Describing the dark dreariness of Trashkun, he stated as fact that the town was literally infested with hordes of spirits, ghosts and devils, calling them in Yiddish *shaydim*. "They used to roam around freely through our crooked streets and narrow alleys, making all kinds of weird noises to scare the life out of us poor kids."[10] Knowing the cynicism that this would elicit from Roland and Natalie as they read the letters, he told them he would expect "doubting-Thomas" snickers from them, expressing their disbelief. "Well, you can take my word for it," Reuben insisted. "I really have seen it with my own eyes. I have seen it again and again on those dark, cold, wintry nights as I used to run home from the cheder."[11]

In a letter written nearly two years later, Reuben described an incident that might have been the genesis of his belief in ghosts. On that night, Reuben stayed in the synagogue with the Shamos, the assistant synagogue manager. One of the Shamos' duties during the beginning of the High Holiday season was to arise at 3 o'clock in the morning and to awaken all the Jews in the village from their slumber to prepare to go to synagogue. The Shamos was afraid he would fall asleep and not complete his task, so he invited young Reuben to spend the night in the synagogue with him to prevent this from happening. Reuben gladly accepted.

They each brought books to study, but soon tired of this and began to talk. The Shamos talked mainly about the dead and the ghosts that were all about in Trashkun. He explained to his young colleague that dead people don't stay in their graves all the time and, in particular, at night they come out to the synagogue and pray until dawn. The ghosts (*shaydim*) would roam around in all the dark streets and alleys. They would usually appear in the form of a large black goat with a long beard and long twisted horns, but sometimes they would disguise themselves and appear as a black dog or an old woman dressed in black, standing in a dark corner and talking to herself incoherently.

"The Shamos lit his lantern," recalled Reuben, "picked up his cane and went out into the dark night. Meanwhile, I—the only living, wide-awake person in the whole dark and slumbering world—was left alone in my room, with all the stories about *maysim* [dead people] and *shaydin* [demons] dancing before me...."[12] Again, as if to ward off the skepticism of his children, he added:

> You children, products of a modern, unbelieving world, who were born and educated in this country, may not believe these stories. But I am talking about "facts": things that I have seen with my own eyes and heard with my own ears.... On such nights as I happened to lay awake on my bed near the wall that separated me from the synagogue, I could hear the dead people come in, one by one; I could hear them open the Ark, I could hear them pray in mournful, crying tones. I could hear their voices rise and fall, synchronous with the howling of the wind and the barking of the dogs, and on one or two occasions I could even discern the voices of somebody who had died a short time before and whose memory was still fresh in my mind.[13]

Reuben, a scholar who would go on to become a successful physician, attempted to keep his "old world" memories, including those of ghosts and devils, alive as he described the world of his youth to his children. All the while he freely acknowledged that his children, as native-born Americans, would be highly skeptical of his stories of the *shadyim* and *maysim*.

• • •

The first Jewish settler in Cleveland was Daniel Maduro Peixotto, a physician who joined the faculty of Willoughby Medical College in 1836. The next year, Simson Thorman, a hide trader from Unsleben, Bavaria, settled in the area. With the expanding economic opportunities being offered by the opening of the Ohio and Erie canals, 19 residents of Unsleben departed for the United States aboard the S.S. *Howard*, to live in New York City. Later 15 of these immigrants settled in Cleveland. The group brought with them a message and a prayer, written by their teacher Lazarus Kohn, imploring them to remember their heritage and not to abandon their religion in their new country.[14] They brought with them a *Sefer Torah* (a hand-written Torah) and one of the men, Simson Hopferman, served as a *hazzan* (cantor) and a *shohet* (kosher butcher).

By 1839, they had enough men to form a *minyan* (prayer quorum) and proceeded to establish the Israelitic Society. Within two years, internal bickering led to the formation of a second temple, Anshe Chesed. After reuniting briefly, the groups split again in 1850 and a new congregation was formed, Tifereth Israel. In addition, six communal organizations were formed before the Civil War. By the time of the war's outbreak, the Jewish population of Cleveland was approximately one thousand, with 78 percent of them from the German states (primarily Bavaria) and 19 percent from the Austrian empire (primarily Bohemia). During this first period of Jewish immigration to Cleveland, known as the German era (1837–1900), the immigrants were businessmen and shopkeepers who prospered in their adopted country. They embraced Reform Judaism as they attempted to minimize the difference between them and their Christian neighbors. During this first immigration period, Cleveland became the second largest garment manufacturing area in the country behind New York City, with many firms making uniforms for the Civil War soldiers.[15]

This period contrasted with a second, overlapping immigration period known as the East European era that ran from 1870 to 1924. Compared to the earlier German era of Jewish immigration, the new arrivals were primarily from Russia, Poland, and Romania. Unlike the immigrants from the German era, immigrants of the East European era were generally East European Jews who were fleeing pogroms and dire poverty. They arrived in America to find that their German Jewish predecessors were often affluent and had more in common with their Protestant neighbors than with their newly arrived co-religionists. In Cleveland, the differences between the two groups embarrassed the German Jewish leadership and enraged the new immigrants.[16]

While the exact date of his arrival from Lithuania is unknown, it was during this period of religious turmoil in the Cleveland Jewish community that Benjamin Gittelsohn came to America. Different sources provided different dates for his arrival to Cleveland. The United States Federal Census Record of 1900 lists 1890 as the year that he arrived in the United States. That census record lists 1891 as the year that his wife Celia and the children, including Reuben, arrived in America. In subsequent census reports, the years of their arrival would vary slightly from the 1900 report. Their home was listed as Cleveland Ward 16, Cuyahoga, Ohio.[17] Despite the discrepancy in dates, it is known that Benjamin was a highly regarded Orthodox Jewish scholar and was asked to immigrate to Cleveland to become a leader in the Orthodox Jewish community.

There are somewhat conflicting records of the synagogues where Benjamin served as rabbi. Records of Congregation Oer Chodosh Anshe Sfard state that this Orthodox Jewish synagogue was founded in 1894 and "The founding rabbi was Benjamin Gittelsohn."[18] The *Encyclopedia of Cleveland History* records that in 1890, Gittelsohn was asked to settle in Cleveland by the growing community of Lithuanian Jews in the city and became the rabbi at Beth Hamidrosh Hagodol, serving that congregation until 1901. He then assumed the pulpit at Oer Chodosh Anshe Sfard and remained its rabbi until his death on January 7, 1932.[19] Rabbi Benjamin Gittelsohn's religious knowledge as Cleveland's first rabbinic scholar soon led him to become the spiritual authority for a number of other small congregations in Cleveland, such as Shaare Torah and Agudath Achim.[20]

From his earliest years, Roland Gittelsohn would have fond memories of his grandfather. Benjamin never learned to speak English, instead conversing only in Yiddish. Roland spoke English and had also learned to speak Hebrew. His grandfather, however, would not converse in Hebrew because for most Orthodox Jews of that era it was a tongue for sacred conversation with God in the Bible and prayer books, not for ordinary discourse with people. Despite this barrier, Roland recalled how Benjamin would listen to his grandchildren speak to him in Hebrew with undisguised pride. Remembering the smell of his grandfather's beard when he kissed him, as an adult Roland would recall when he closed his eyes he could "… still see the combination of regal dignity and paternal love on his face as he conducted the yearly Seder. My heart is tempted to beat wildly again today as I recall standing next to him on the pulpit of his synagogue for my Bar Mitzvah."[21]

Shortly after his arrival in the United States, Benjamin was quoted as saying, "Here too I found no ease or repose, nor did I have joy or pleasure, (but) thank God who brought me here, I have just a little bit…."[22] Roland would theorize that the reason for his grandfather's initial lack of joy may have been the fact that he perceived that very little attention was given to his learned accomplishments.[23] This perception would soon be altered because in Cleveland, Benjamin Gittelsohn's prominence as a scholar would soon be widely acknowledged. A distinguished writer, he published two renowned works of Hebrew scholarship after he immigrated to the United States. *Ha-Poteah ve-ha-Hotem* was a collection of Talmudic discourses, most of which he had delivered to his congregations, and *Seder Haggada shel Pesah 'im Be'ur Nagid ve-Nafik*, a detailed commentary on the Passover Haggadah.

Despite his exalted status for his scholarship and his spiritual guidance, he remained a modest and grounded man. On multiple occasions he was urged by his followers and admirers to assume the title of chief rabbi in Cleveland. Each time he refused. Titles meant little to him. He was happy to accept the authority earned by his courageous leadership and several brilliant books, but wanted no other titles or positions of respect.[24]

Orthodox rabbis of that era were scholars, teachers, and judges; they rarely preached in synagogue. Rabbi Benjamin Gittelsohn only preached about four times a year, but he was a very mesmerizing and powerful orator. His son Reuben described the power of his father's sermons: "You have never seen or witnessed such a sight. Imagine a large group of men, old and young, breathing heavily, sobbing, with tears running down their cheeks into their beards; and the women upstairs crying so loud that one could hear them across the street. That was a sight never to be forgotten, and an art on my father's part that very few preachers could have equaled."[25]

Benjamin had one fervent belief that set him apart from his fellow Orthodox rabbis. His arrival in America coincided with the beginnings of modern Zionism. Most of his peers strongly opposed the concept of a Jewish homeland being championed at that time by Theodore Herzl. They believed that in His own good time God would reconstitute the Jewish commonwealth through the agency of the Messiah. To "push the end" by human means was to be guilty of utmost arrogance.[26] While he believed in the Messiah, Gittelsohn believed that the partnership of God and man would be the best means for fulfilling God's purpose for the Jewish people. Hence, he became one of the first Orthodox rabbis to wholeheartedly embrace the concept of Zionism. Years later, Roland Gittelsohn's autobiography proudly cited a Zionist historian's note about Benjamin, stating, "On October 20, 1897 Herzl was told that at a Zionist meeting in Cleveland, where Rabbi Gittelsohn and S. Rocker spoke, many members were signed up."[27]

• • •

The exact date of Reuben Gittelsohn's birth is unknown, as was his father's. The 1900 census report lists his date of birth as "August, 1876." His draft card, issued during World War I, lists his birthday as August 15, 1878. Roland Gittelsohn was only able to estimate that his father was about 18 or 19 years old when he came to America. Even the date of his emigration from Russia is a source of conflict. The 1900 census reports his arrival to America as taking place in 1891, whereas the 1910 and 1930 census reports state he arrived in 1893. Arriving in Cleveland as a shy teenager who spoke no English proved to be a very difficult transition for young Reuben.

The years of living in extreme poverty with constant threats of pogroms and discrimination no doubt took a toll on the development of Reuben's personality. His shyness and lack of assertiveness, coupled with his small physical stature, served to greatly diminish his self-confidence. Writing to his son, Reuben lamented his lack of a proper public school education, noting that if he had attended public school, he would perhaps be a different man and possibly followed a different vocation. "Not that I would have been more of a success than I am, because to be truly successful one must have those all-important qualities, 'push and pull,' born into him; and I am rather lacking in them...."[28]

Reuben went on to profess his admiration for people who could stand up in front of an audience and inspire them to noble causes. This is where Reuben's inferiority complex stands out: "I know my shortcomings. I could never be a leader because I wasn't born to be one. I could never be a shepherd because I wasn't trained to be one. I was born to be a poor sheep, a member of a large flock, a follower, that's all."[29] Although he would go on to a successful career in medicine, he would always regret that he didn't have the personality or the oratorical skills to become a rabbi. When Roland eventually decided to become a rabbi, his father Reuben lived vicariously through him as if he himself had entered the rabbinate.

Determined to build a new life for himself while at the same time proudly maintaining his Jewish heritage, Reuben went to work in a cigar-making factory in Cleveland. Knowing the critical importance of language skills, he was determined to learn English. Accordingly, he attended night school for a year and supplemented his studies with private lessons in English twice a week for at least a summer.[30] All the while, the only language spoken in the Gittelsohn household was Yiddish, a Germanic language spoken by eastern European Jews. He would admit to his children that he was always self-conscious that he had not attended a liberal arts college where he could have obtained the skills he so desired in language, writing, and literature. As he would note with a mixture of regret and pride, "I acquired all my preliminary education through my own plugging."[31]

Reuben would eventually become the only one of the 12 Gittelsohn children to become a professional. Realizing that he had neither the personality nor the oratorical skills to become a rabbi, he set his sights on a career in medicine. At the time, the requirement to enter medical school was either to have obtained a high school diploma or the ability to pass a rigorous official entrance examination that covered certain high school subjects. Reuben arranged to take the entrance examination with Professor John White, principal of Central High School on East 55th Street. There was only one problem—the exam was scheduled to be given on Yom Kippur, the holiest day of the year.

It would be scandalous for the son of the Orthodox synagogue's rabbi not to be in the synagogue all day on Yom Kippur, the Day of Atonement. Somehow, Reuben managed to leave the service without attracting his father's attention, or, as Roland would explain, "…perhaps Grandpa noticed this as he did so many things of which he pretended to be oblivious."[32] Reuben did manage to get away to Central High School, took his examinations, and return to resume his worship several hours later.

At Central High School, the first test that Reuben had to complete was a lengthy essay chosen from any topic on a list that was given to all the prospective medical students. He selected "Why I Want to Study Medicine." He was pleasantly surprised that he did quite well, receiving a compliment from Dr. White that his "composition was excellent."[33] While recalling this moment of achievement to his grandchildren, Reuben again bemoaned his lack of a better education, stating, "I deplored the fact that I didn't have the opportunity of getting a proper preliminary education, in which case I might have selected a different profession altogether, with somewhat greater success."[34]

Reuben did well enough on his entrance exams to be accepted into Ohio Wesleyan University's Cleveland College of Physicians class of 1905. His junior year class roster lists his birthplace, along with two other students, as "Russia." To afford the tuition for his studies, he continued to work at the cigar factory until he graduated. He became a general practitioner, making frequent house calls and serving his community with devotion. Reuben would continue to practice into his eighties. Roland would recall the type of physician his father was, thusly:

> He never failed them. Not any of his patients. A general practitioner, he made house calls at the most ungodly hours, responding from his badly needed sleep to those who hadn't paid their bills, even to those whom he knew to be hypochondriacs. His purpose in life was to help people, not to tell them from some lofty perch that they didn't really need help.[35]

Reuben had taken the Hippocratic Oath and he took his obligation to serve and heal his fellow man with utmost seriousness. Roland's pride and admiration for his father was evident and this ethos of service to one's fellow man was a trait that was passed down from father to son.

Despite his important and satisfying medical practice, Reuben's heart never drifted far from his probable first career choice: to become a rabbi. He never stopped studying Judaism and was a voracious reader in English, Yiddish, and Hebrew. He began every day the same, reading six or more chapters from the Hebrew Bible right after finishing his breakfast. His self-imposed schedule called for completion of the entire biblical text once each year.[36] This routine continued into his later years, and his joy of reading the Bible never diminished. Roland would recall visiting him when he was living in a nursing home towards the end of his life. Invariably, he would pick up his Hebrew Bible, read Roland a few verses and say: "You know, Roland, I must have read these words a thousand times, but when I encountered them yesterday a new interpretation came to me."[37]

Roland would inherit certain passions from his father, in addition to his love of Judaism. One was his passion for the underdog and for the equality of all men. After Reuben's medical practice began to flourish, he took his first trip to Washington, D.C. He had developed a great love and sense of patriotism for America, his adopted country, that had given him the opportunities he could only dream of as a boy back in Russia. On the first day of his visit to the nation's capital, he took his first trolley ride and made an unknowingly innocent mistake that would have a profound effect on him. He took a seat in the back of the trolley car.

As he sat, looking out the window, he was approached by the conductor. He was informed that he was sitting in the rear of the trolley car where only Blacks were supposed to sit. He was invited to move up to the front section which was, of course, restricted to White trolley riders. Reuben was stunned—this was his first experience with discrimination against another minority. It surely must have immediately recalled to him the years of discrimination and maltreatment that he had experienced as a young Jew during his childhood in Russia. He did not move to the front of the car. Rather, he got off the car entirely.

For the remainder of his visit to Washington, he would walk to his destinations rather than ride the streetcar. Roland inherited this sense of outrage against discrimination toward all minority groups, especially Black Americans. His outspokenness on this issue would cause much turmoil in his life in later years, but Roland would never retreat from the controversy or tone down his strong feelings on the subject.

Another topic that Reuben was passionate about was Zionism. As Roland would recall, "My sister and I were weaned on Zionism. *Palestine* was a sacred word in our household. Dad read or told us stories about the destruction of the Temple in Jerusalem—how the birds carried the burning embers in their effort to quench the conflagration, how the priests threw the Temple keys heavenward as they apologized to God for having failed to protect the Holy Place, returning the responsibility to Him."[38]

Reuben truly saw Zionism as the ultimate culmination of Jewish nationalism.[39] In Roland's first year as a rabbinical student, Reuben charged his son "to spread the holy gospel of Jewish nationalism." Writing to Roland in 1931 on the eve of *Tisha B'Av*, the holiday that commemorates the destruction of the ancient Temples of Jerusalem, Reuben wrote, "We never forgot Jerusalem. We always remembered Palestine. And now, after the long night of exile, we of the present generation have the greatest privilege of witnessing the beginning of the fulfillment of our sweet dream."[40]

Roland would recall in his autobiography that next to the birth of his children, May 15, 1948—the day that the State of Israel was proclaimed a nation—was the most glorious day of his father's life.[41] The desire for an independent Jewish state was a dream shared by the three generations of Gittelsohn men—from the poverty stricken Russian-born rabbi; to his son, the struggling immigrant who became a doctor; to his grandson, a scholarly, outspoken, and prominent rabbi. The dream became a reality in 1948.

In later years, Roland Gittelsohn would recall his mother, Anna Manheim Gittelsohn, as a unique and somewhat troubled woman. Like Reuben, she was born in Russia, around 1887. Her family immigrated to the United States when she was only six months old and, in a very unusual move for Jewish immigrants of that era, they settled in Montana. Her father became a merchant in both Washington and Montana.

Anna's childhood was unique. The Manheim family household kept kosher, which was not an easy thing to do in Missoula, Montana, a city that had only seven Jewish families. Anna had an Orthodox Jewish upbringing. In later years, she would share with her son Roland how lonely and insecure she was as a child. There was no Jewish community in Missoula and Jews were largely ostracized from society.[42] She was so desperate in her need for companionship and acceptance that at one point—with no perception at all of its theological significance—she secretly joined the Salvation Army. As Roland recalled, "When her parents discovered what she had done, their punishment must have painfully reinforced her innate sense of loneliness and alienation."[43]

In 1905, Anna traveled to Cleveland to visit a cousin. It was there that she met a scholarly, shy medical student named Reuben Gittelsohn. It was pretty much a case of love at first sight. Reuben and Anna got engaged and several months later were married in Cleveland on March 27, 1906. His age was listed on the marriage certificate as 28, hers as 19. Rabbi Benjamin Gittelsohn performed the wedding ceremony. Interestingly, on Cuyahoga County wedding license application number 46063, dated March 24, the bride-to-be's name was listed as "Emma E. Manheim." On the wedding certificate portion at the bottom of the application confirming the wedding on March 27, it lists the bride's name as Anna E. Gittelsohn. All other census documents in existence list her name as Anna.

Being married to a dedicated young physician who was busy making house calls at all hours and was frequently missing meals at home soon proved to be stressful for the young bride. Roland would describe her as an emotionally frail person who was quite incapable of carrying the full responsibilities of marriage and family. It was not long after she and Reuben were married that she suffered the first of a series of mysterious "breakdowns" and went off to live for a few weeks with her married sister in nearby Canton, Ohio. Observing these episodes throughout his youth would, in a sad sense, prepare Roland for the trials and tribulations that a rabbi must deal with in his role as a counselor and mentor to his congregants. It was also a harbinger of things to come in his own married life.

Reuben would find it difficult to deal with his wife Anna's breakdowns, vacillating "between tender patience and peevish irritation. Depending on the season, he would brood silently in the living room easy chair or on the porch swing." Seeing a glimpse of the positive in his father's marital stress, Roland then noted, "I suspect that his problems at home probably made him more sensitive to the emotional ills of his patients, more ready to empathize with their families."[44]

Anna Gittelsohn did have many positive influences on her husband's life, in spite of her emotional instability. Having come to their adopted country as a baby, she was certainly more "Americanized" than her husband. Roland would note that his father was the most urbane and Americanized of all of the 12 Gittelsohn siblings and he attributed this fact largely to his mother's influence. It was Anna who insisted that their children be allowed to go to summer camp and that they be exposed to many cultural opportunities, such as piano lessons.

Perhaps her greatest influence on Reuben was her religious sway. Both Reuben and Anna were raised as Orthodox Jews. However, having grown up in Montana, Anna had no sense of Orthodox community roots. Despite his Orthodox upbringing, Reuben was now an American and was taking advantage of all that his new country was able to offer him. He remained a devout Jew until the day he died, but he was no longer in the *shtetl* in Russia—he was in Cleveland, Ohio, an up-and-coming American physician. Roland felt that his father was ready to depart from Orthodoxy on his own, but clearly his mother accentuated his religious restlessness.[45] It was Anna who encouraged him to join a Reform synagogue and to send their children to a Reform religious school.

Roland would look back on the type of parents that Reuben and Anna were to him and his sister Natalie and reflect on both their parenting skills as well as perceived weaknesses. He was much more reflective about his father. Despite his obvious love and admiration for his father, Roland noted that he was not a perfect parent. Both Roland and his sister bitterly resented the times when family plans were aborted at the last minute due to medical emergencies for which Reuben got called away. "Many times I wished he had been interested in baseball, as my friend's fathers were."[46] By contrast, one of the joys of his childhood was accompanying Reuben on his house calls, "relishing his company and conversation as we drove from house to house, reading in the car while he attended to a patient."[47]

One area in which Roland found his father most lacking was sex education. In his autobiography, he specifically mentioned that Reuben provided no parental guidance to him when he was an adolescent. At Anna's insistence, he simply gave Roland several pamphlets on sex to read while he waited in the car for him to finish his house calls. When he returned, he asked if his son had any questions. That was the sum total of information on sex that Dr. Reuben Gittelsohn provided to his young son.

In his autobiography, Roland would ponder if his father lived a happy life. His thoughtful analysis attempted to answer that difficult question:

> Through placidity and peace, no. Through the achievement of either psychological or financial security, no. Through his children and grandchildren, yes.... Above all, through the satisfaction of knowing that he as an individual had substantially served purposes larger than himself, yes, in that respect too, my father was happy.[48]

In his autobiography and his personal notes, Gittelsohn frequently expressed his thoughts and memories of his father. On the whole they conveyed admiration for the humble, shy and learned man who dedicated his life to serve others. His recollections of his mother were much more limited and restrained. As mentioned, she had some positive influences on Reuben and was a dedicated homemaker to the Gittelsohn family. However, Roland would summarize his feelings thusly: "Mother did her best. At times she succeeded, but mostly failed."[49]

From his grandfather and his father, Roland Gittelsohn developed a thirst for knowledge and a desire to serve his fellow man. He would achieve great success with these attributes that he inherited from these scholarly, dedicated men.

Two

Gifted Student

On Friday, May 13, 1910, Anna Gittelsohn gave birth to their first child. Their new son arrived prematurely; they named him Roland Bertram Gittelsohn. In accordance with Jewish tradition, he was given a Hebrew name to sustain the memory of a deceased relative, in this case his maternal grandmother.

Interestingly Roland Gittelsohn would claim, "I have very few memories of early childhood, almost none."[1] Most significantly, what childhood memories he did harbor centered on humiliation and failure. He was in many ways like his father. Small in stature and abnormally thin, he felt himself to be a homely child. But unlike Reuben, he was a native-born American and was an eloquent individual. He differed substantially from his father in yet another way: He was an outspoken boy who grew up to be an outspoken adult. Never afraid to speak his mind, Roland would become the leader that his father never could dream of becoming. Like both his father and grandfather, he also became a first-rate scholar with a brilliant analytical mind.

After a lifetime of counseling congregants and serving numerous organizations as a compassionate clergyman, he would reflect on his childhood and realize that his selective recall of only episodes of failure or humiliation bespoke a great deal about his youthful insecurity.[2] He was conscious of his perceived shortcomings. Young Roland was a clumsy boy with little athletic prowess. When he was 11 years old, he had an appendectomy. In high school, he would still use the appendectomy as an excuse to get out of gym activities that he despised. So great was his insecurity that before he would telephone a girl for a date, he would prepare an outline of what he would say, lest there be an embarrassing silence. If a girl should turn down his invitation, he would "suffer a severe sense of rejection."[3]

In his youth and early in his professional career, Roland suffered from many recurrent dreams involving stressful, embarrassing situations. A typical dream would find him standing at the pulpit getting ready to deliver a sermon—and then realizing he forgot his notes. A variant would be his attending a convention and being unable to find the room where an important meeting was supposed to take place.[4] Any psychologist would note that dreams such as these are fairly typical for driven, intellectual achievers. With the passage of years Roland would come to realize that these dreams and his accompanying insecurities were not unusual. He recognized his dreams could be attributed to the nature of his youth and adolescence. Those experiences would add considerably to his personal skills in dealing with young people when he became a rabbi. As he once noted, "Openly sharing with them in retrospect my own adolescent turbulence has probably helped more of them than any other technique I might have used."[5]

Roland Gittelsohn, age 13, with his mother Anna and sister Natalie (courtesy David Gittelsohn and Judith Gittelsohn Fales).

At an early age, Roland demonstrated the verbal prowess and outspoken nature that he would become known for. When he was 14 years old, he was attending the Hebrew School at Euclid Avenue Temple, a Reform synagogue. As always, he was a superb student with a flawless attendance record, and his behavior was exemplary. Yet he was nearly thrown out of his confirmation class: "Because then, as now, I was given to vehement argumentation. Alone among my fellow students, I disputed Rabbi Louis Wolsey's views on Zionism."[6] Displaying the typical attitude of Reform rabbis of the time, Rabbi Wolsey was opposed to Zionism. He was quite taken aback when his ninth-grade star student, the son of a prominent member of the synagogue, a respected physician in the community, and, likely unbeknownst to Rabbi Wolsey, the only avowed Zionist in the congregation— proceeded to debate him in front of the class. This was possibly the first public exhibition of Roland Gittelsohn's considerable debating skills, a talent for which he would become well known.

It is not clear whether it was his academic excellence or his outspoken nature that first attracted the attention of one of his classmates. She was a shy girl who also did well in school. In addition, she had an artistic nature that attracted young Roland. Her name was Ruth Freyer, and they would become sweethearts during the rest of their school years. Graduating in the same confirmation class, they were destined to go to the same university where their futures would ultimately be entwined.

Roland's childhood stood in marked contrast to both his father's and grandfather's. He would never experience the grinding poverty of Russia as they did. He was supported by a strong, loving family unit that was augmented on August 13, 1914, with the birth of his sister Natalie. He was close to his parents and grandparents, who encouraged his academic pursuits and his interest in the rabbinate. His father was a busy physician and although the obligations of the medical profession frequently had an intrusive effect on the family, Reuben was apparently a financially successful general practitioner. This was reflected in a 1920 federal census report listing 19-year-old Eva Curni from Hungary as living at the Gittelsohn household as their servant.

Youthful insecurities aside, Roland had many strengths that he was blessed with and utilized them to the utmost. While dealing with his youthful angst, he was balancing these youthful tribulations with the God-given talents he possessed. He was a superb student and his intellectual prowess made it possible for him to skip an entire year of elementary school. To a degree, this laudable achievement further fueled his insecurity. From that point on, he was a year younger than his classmates, which all the more accentuated their differences in physical size and athletic prowess. "I would have given almost anything," he later wrote, "to exchange my talents for those of the school's most acclaimed athletic star, who quite probably felt as inadequate in my arena as I did in his."[7]

At Cleveland Heights High School, Roland was elected to the National Honor Society. The skinny, homely boy obviously made quite a positive impression on his high school classmates because they elected Roland president of the senior class. In addition, he was captain of the debate team and was winner of a statewide extemporaneous speaking contest. "Looking back," he would recall, "it all seems silly. In terms of long-range values, the areas in which I was clearly superior far outweighed those in which I was lacking."[8]

Beginning with his junior year of high school, debating became a major part of Roland's life. At Cleveland Heights High School, he was coached in speech and debate by Clarence P. Drury who was a former intercollegiate debater at Bates College in Lewiston, Maine. Drury was a disciple of Professor Howard Woodward, a leader in the field of speech and the former president of the National Association of Teachers of Speech.[9] Later on Professor Woodward would become Roland's debate coach in college. Both coaches stressed the importance of evidence and logic, and neither allowed their debaters to write out their speeches for memorization.[10] "We were forced to think on our feet, to scrap what we had prepared, if necessary, in order immediately to counter an opponent's argument."[11]

Roland would look back years later and realize that although he had a passion for debating and loved the intellectual challenge that it always presented to him, it probably had a negative effect on his personality development. Debate encouraged him to see issues as absolutes—as black and white, as right and wrong, or true and false. A debater either won or lost the argument; compromise indicated defeat. "In later years I had to discipline myself severely to recognize that in most controversies neither extreme view is wholly correct, that an aspect of truth inheres in each."[12]

Roland would also perceive a second disadvantage that resulted from his debate training: He came to depend too exclusively on reason and logic and too little on emotions. Always considering himself a rationalist, he viewed emotion without the control of reason as "a terrible danger." On the other hand, he felt that reason without emotion was too sterile. In his future counseling work, he became fond of saying that the longest distance in the universe is that which separates the heart from the mind. "In the human search for God, too, reason and fact, while indispensable, are by themselves not enough. To experience human life in its fullest dimension, we must think and feel together."[13]

• • •

After graduating from high school in 1927, Roland stayed in Cleveland to begin his college studies at Western Reserve University, now Case

Western Reserve University. He would continue to excel in his academic studies in college. As he did in high school, he joined the debate team and soon became its captain. At Western Reserve Professor Howard Woodward continued to hone his student's debating skills. At graduation Roland would be acknowledged for his debating skills with a Delta Sigma Rho key for forensic excellence.

While at Western Reserve he earned his tuition money mainly by giving private Hebrew lessons. By all accounts he thrived at college, excelling in virtually everything he attempted. By the end of his third college year, he had all but officially decided on his life's work. When Roland was a teenager, his father Reuben once asked him if he would ever consider becoming a physician. His answer was an emphatic "No!" At the time he was unsure of his career plans, but as he informed his father, "I'll tell you one thing for sure: it's going to be an occupation where my time will be my own, not like your life!"[14]

His career choice was not what he had originally planned on. When he was younger, Roland imagined he would become a lawyer. Given his eloquence and debating skills, this is not surprising. However, he was interested in becoming a crusading attorney along the lines of one of his heroes, Clarence Darrow. But much to his chagrin, he learned that most lawyers sat at their desks for hours busied with dull paperwork.[15] In time, when he became a rabbi, he realized that he had entered a career that would cut into his time probably as much as his father's work did.

He did not choose to join the rabbinate to please his father and grandfather, although they were delighted with his career choice. In addition, there was nothing explicitly theological about his decision to become a rabbi. As he explained, "I received no 'divine call'; neither, so far as I knew, did any of my classmates. We would have laughed uproariously had any of them made such a claim."[16] To Roland, Judaism's uniqueness accounted for his decision to join the rabbinate. He noted, "Strands of ethnicity and culture, of peoplehood and nationality, are woven—together with those of religion—into the total fabric of Judaism. To pull out one color or thread would unravel the entire tapestry."[17]

His love of God, his love of Judaism, and his love of people, coupled with the desire to help his fellow man, all factored into his career decision. It is not surprising then, to learn that during his first interview for admission to rabbinical school, when he was asked why he wanted to become a rabbi, he replied that he loved the Jewish people and felt that becoming a rabbi was the most constructive way he could serve them.[18]

As he began his senior year, word began to spread in Cleveland's Jewish community that Rabbi Benjamin Gittelsohn's grandson would be following in his footsteps and would enter rabbinical school. Reuben

Gittelsohn was absolutely delighted with his son's decision and the realization that he would be able to live out his repressed desire to become a rabbi vicariously through his son. However, Rabbi Gittelsohn's Orthodox congregation was very upset when they learned Roland's plans. Roland would be enrolling at the major school for educating Reform rabbis in the country—the Hebrew Union College in Cincinnati. Certainly, they felt, that as the pillar of the Orthodox community, Benjamin Gittelsohn must also be outraged that his grandson was planning on entering what they called "the rabbi factory."[19] They demanded to know what he intended to do about it.

Benjamin had total faith and trust in his grandson's decision to attend Hebrew Union College. As recreated by Roland, Benjamin acknowledged to his scandalized congregants that Orthodox Judaism was the only kind possible for them and for him. However, he continued, "Knowing my grandson's home background and education, if he were to tell me he planned to become an Orthodox rabbi, I would suspect him of hypocrisy. I want him to become the kind of rabbi he can honestly be."[20]

In the spring of 1931, Roland Gittelsohn graduated with a bachelor of arts degree from Western Reserve University with honors. In recognition of his academic achievements, he was elected to Phi Beta Kappa. That fall, he began five years of graduate study at Hebrew Union College in Cincinnati.

Throwing himself into his studies, young Roland continued to excel academically. After he wrote to his parents that he successfully completed his first set of examinations, Reuben wrote back to his son, expressing both pride and lack of surprise in his son's accomplishment. In his letter Reuben also expressed his future expectations for his son in reference to the seminary's president:

> I hear Dr. Morgenstern told you that you came highly recommended and that he expects a lot from you. Well, son, to us you came highly recommended twenty-one years ago, and we also expect a lot from you. Only our expectations embrace a much wider field than those of Dr. M. Whereas he expects you to become a successful rabbi, we expect you, in addition to all that, to also be a good man and a good Jew. Our people need you, son. Our people need new blood, the kind of blood that flows through your veins and in the veins of your colleagues at H.C.C. I hope that the small group of intelligent young men with whom you will live for the next four or five years will blossom forth into a group of Jewish leaders who will exert all their energies to reawaken the Jewish self-consciousness, and who will go out into the world with a strong determination to spread the holy gospel of Jewish nationalism.[21]

Reuben's pride in is son was evident in his note and once again, he instilled into Roland a sense of obligation, not only to be a good person, but also a good Jew. Expressing joy over his son's chosen field for his life's work as well as admiration and perhaps a bit of vicarious projection, Reuben felt that he and Anna had been successful in instilling into their children a love for everything Jewish. He wrote, "If that should happen to be my only achievement during my short stay on this planet, I shall be satisfied."[22]

• • •

World War I was supposed to be the "war to end all wars." In the United States it was said that the country entered the war "to make the world safe for democracy." When the armistice was signed in November of 1918, it quickly became apparent that the world was in many ways worse off than before 1914. The price worldwide in blood and treasure was enormous. Over 16 million people were killed and nearly 22 million people were wounded. The economy of Europe was wrecked, and Russia descended into a civil war that ended with the Bolsheviks taking control of the government. Worldwide, many people looked back with bitterness over what was perceived as the futility of the entire war and the futility of war in general. Many came to the conclusion that there must never be another war, and in its place, there had to be a rational alternative to resolving nation's disputes.

While not new, the concept of pacifism started to take hold around the world, including in the United States. In 1923, the War Resisters League was founded in New York City by Jessie Wallace Hughan, an educator, socialist activist, and radical pacifist. The War Resisters League was an offshoot of the London-based War Resisters International. The organization's core principles were opposition to the military and total opposition to war. It preached a radical brand of pacifism condemning

Roland Gittelsohn as a rabbinical student, approximately 1932 (courtesy David Gittelsohn and Judith Gittelsohn Fales).

all forms of violence, and activism in renouncing war as a means of resolving international disputes.

Their strident message of active resistance to war started to make an impression on a young teenager in Cleveland, Ohio, by the name of Roland Gittelsohn.

Gittelsohn would write, "Through my years of high school, college, graduate study and even into the initial stage of my professional life, absolute pacifism was one of my most cherished—and I thought inviolate—ideals."[23] Granted he was small in stature, and he was able to fight with words, but he truly believed that pacifism represented one of Judaism's highest ideals, quoting Zechariah: "Not by might, nor by power, but by My spirit—says the Lord of Hosts!"[24]

Born shortly before the Great War had begun, Roland would recall that he was too young during World War I to sense much of what was going on. But he would recall his fascination and pride with which he listened later to his two closest uncles telling of their experiences in the army and navy. "What would I do if ever I had to be a soldier or sailor? This dread was reinforced a few years afterward when I was repulsed by gory photographs of battlefield atrocities. In any event, for whichever reasons, war became for me the ultimate immorality, to be shunned at all cost."[25]

Several leaders in the world pacifist movement would have a great effect on young Roland. One of them was the famous physicist Albert Einstein. Living in Berlin when the war broke out in 1914, Einstein was shocked by the development. "Europe in her insanity has started something unbelievable," he wrote. "In such times one realizes to what a sad species of animal one belongs."[26] He helped draft an anti-war statement, "Manifesto to Europeans," that condemned the war, arguing that "national passions cannot excuse this attitude which is unworthy of what the world has heretofore called culture."[27] Einstein would continue with his anti-war, anti-military message throughout the 1920s and the 1930s.

Einstein emigrated from Nazi Germany to the United States in 1930. Later that year he was invited to address a meeting of New York's New History Society, an offshoot of the pacifist Baha'i religious movement. On December 14 he delivered an address that became known as the "Two Percent Speech." In it, he suggested the means to end future wars was to refuse to serve in the military under any circumstances. Einstein went on to make a key point: "…even if only two percent of those supposed to perform military service should declare themselves war resisters … the government would be powerless—they could not put such masses into jail."[28] These words would resonate with young Roland. For years he would wear a "2 percent pin with pride, almost defiantly."[29] In addition, he became a member of the War Resisters League.

Another great influence on Roland's pacifist beliefs was the Rev. Harry Emerson Fosdick. Emerson was a Baptist minister who in earlier years had been a staunch supporter of America's entry into World War I. Speaking in pulpits around the country, he exclaimed, "Sad is our lot if we have forgotten how to die for a holy cause!"[30] Later on, after the United States entered the war, he toured the trenches in Europe and observed firsthand the horrors of the war. Within a short time, he became increasingly disappointed in war's inability to unite the world.

By 1921, Fosdick had started to change his views. Ruefully, he concluded, "We cannot reconcile Christianity with war any more."[31] By 1923, he had completely embraced a commitment to peace. Preaching at the Christian interdenominational Riverside Church in New York City, on November 12, 1933, he delivered a sermon entitled "Apology to the Unknown Soldier." In it, he articulated his pacifist position that had been evolving since the end of World War I. With the passion of a true believer, he concluded his sermon by saying, "I renounce war and never again, directly or indirectly, will I sanction or support another!"[32]

Roland Gittelsohn would find much inspiration in the words of Pastor Fosdick. In his future sermons and writings, he would reference and cite Fosdick's example of active pacifism. Fosdick's opposition to a military draft, and to allowing ROTC units on college campuses—as well as his belief in disarmament, even if unilateral—were perfectly in consonance with Roland's own evolving beliefs. He also shared Fosdick's vision that eschewed isolationism and advocated a spirit of international cooperation.

Such views just explored of Fosdick, Einstein, and other peace advocates influenced the pacifist beliefs of young Gittelsohn. By the early 1930s, during his seminary years, he described himself as an avowed pacifist. He embellished on his pacifism, stating, "Not just a peace-lover who misunderstood or misused the word, but a complete pacifist,—a complete, convinced, literal, unreasonable, dogmatic, unchangeable pacifist! If there was one 'absolute' in my personal credo, it was the 'absolute' of pacifism."[33] He would also state, "I read Harry Emerson Fosdick's magnificent 'Apology to the Unknown Soldier' regularly from my pulpit, and felt as if Dr. Fosdick had written it especially for me."[34]

THREE

War No More

Roland Gittelsohn embraced the causes of social justice and pacifism as a young college student. His idealism stood out compared to others in his age group. Throughout the 1920s and into the early 1930s, the student bodies on virtually every college campus in the United States were on the whole both conservative and apolitical. The major issues that concerned students were football, fraternities, and parties. Before and during the first two years of the Great Depression, most college students had been middle to upper class and were shielded from the effects of the Depression. All this began to change in 1931, and the change began in New York City.

The birthplace of student activism was the City College of New York. In the fall of 1931, the New York Student League, soon to be called the National Student League (NSL), was founded at CCNY, and one of the first scathing editorials to be featured in its newsletter *Frontiers* was a call to ban Reserve Officer Training Corps (ROTC) from the campus. University President Frederick C. Robinson responded by attempting to confiscate all copies of the newsletter and then suspending ten of the members of the NSL. The NSL proceeded to organize a city-wide protest over the attempt at censorship, forcing Robinson to yield to public opinion and back down. In addition, all of the suspended students were reinstated.[1]

The NSL held its first convention in March of 1932, and 25 colleges, all of them from the East Coast, sent delegates. The League quickly attracted members from other New York City schools, as well as from schools in the Deep South. Drawn to the NSL were members of the Young Communist League (YCL), who were attracted to its overall agenda of social justice and pacifism, and many of them assumed leadership positions in the various chapters. The YCL "factions" became highly influential in the NSL. The NSL national plank praised the Soviet Union and called for emulating the Soviet Union as an example of an "inspiration and guide to us in other parts of the world who are witnessing the social and economic evils which accompany Capitalism."[2] As a communist-influenced organization, the NSL was unusual in that its birth was not dictated from above—by the Communist Party or by national Young Communist League leaders—but rather it evolved from below, out of the agitation of the Communist Party's rank-and-file and communist sympathizers in the wake of the CCNY free speech fight.[3] The NSL, especially its YCL faction, was initially opposed to any dealings with the rival League for Industrial Democracy (LID).

The LID was founded in 1905 and was a socialist movement, embodied by the leadership of its founder, muck-raking journalist Upton Sinclair. By the 1920s, the LID had become somewhat moribund, despite the leadership of national figures such as Norman Thomas, who would run for the presidency in 1932 as the Socialist Party candidate. Their movement initially had no student involvement. Rather, their philosophy was that of educating young students, resulting in an almost paternal relationship where the students were expected to learn from their teachers and then go on to become educators themselves, spreading the gospel of socialism. The LID leadership quickly realized that its relevance was being supplanted by the burgeoning student movement created by the NSL.

By the spring of 1932, students on many campuses shook off their apathy and became involved in social causes. This involvement was exemplified by Columbia University students who traveled to Harlan County, Kentucky, twice that spring to show support for the striking coal miners. The students were harassed and beaten by Kentucky law officials, and while they were unable to provide any real aid to the striking miners, the national news coverage of the brutal treatment of the students struck a chord with many readers nationwide.

Realizing the great unifying potential of the anti-war issue, the student activists in both the NSL and the LID joined forces in December of 1932. Meeting in Chicago, they convened the Student Congress Against War. It was the largest national meeting of student activists since the beginning of the Great Depression: It attracted 680 delegates from 89 colleges and universities in 30 states.[4] The inspiration for the meeting came from overseas. In August of 1932, the NSL sent a delegate to Amsterdam to attend the communist-sponsored World Congress Against War. Leaders of the American delegation such as novelist Sherwood Anderson were so impressed that they contacted the NSL, asking it to organize a similar conference in the United States, directed at the student movement.

The meeting of the Student Congress Against War did not go smoothly. The communist factions of the NSL, already wary of the socialists of the LID, felt that the NSL was too accommodating to the socialists. The communist leadership was very vocal in its criticism of both the socialists and the NSL members whom they felt were too compliant. In the end, the NSL's official account of the World Congress boasted that the meeting

had established a "basis of united action of all students and groups represented at the Congress." The account also mentioned that the Socialists
and the LID were part of this united front.[5] These organizations influenced
Roland Gittelsohn's thinking, but he was not affiliated with these groups.

A crucial schism developed at the Congress that would go far in defining pacifist core values in the coming years in a way that none of the delegates could have anticipated. The conflict was not between the socialist
and communist delegates, but between the leftist and pacifist delegates.[6]
The pacifists had embraced the anti-war movement largely because of their
religious principles. They opposed all forms of war and violence. The leftist delegates, while opposing war in general, had no problem with class
warfare and anti-colonial wars. This schism produced intense and heated
debate and was never truly reconciled. In the end, the pacifists issued a
minority report stating that, "We believe that war is not right, even if used
in trying to reach a worthy goal."[7]

Despite the frequent and stormy disagreements, the Congress was a
success, and a unified program was issued as a result of the debate. The
opposition to an American military build-up and opposition to the inter-
ventionist policies leading to the First World War were key position points.
The Congress also called for a nationwide campaign on college campuses to
promote anti-war meetings and regular college peace meetings, while abol-
ishing ROTC units. The goals of the Student Congress Against War were
about to get a major boost in the United States as a result of a debate that
was held two months later in Great Britain.

• • •

On February 9, 1933, a debate was held at the Oxford Union, the debating society of Oxford University. At the conclusion of the debate, the students voted 275 to 173 in favor of a motion stating "...that this house will
in no circumstances fight for its King and country."[8] The motion produced a firestorm of criticism and controversy around Great Britain, but
shortly after, students from all over the kingdom were adopting the "Oxford
Pledge." During that same semester an Americanized version of the Oxford
Pledge swept campuses across the United States.

It was during his first year of rabbinical studies at Hebrew Union College when Roland Gittelsohn, along with thousands of other American students, first heard of the Oxford Pledge. The influence of the First World
War on American student supporters of the Oxford Pledge was so strong
that they seemed unable to give a speech or make an argument about foreign affairs without referring to that war and its "lessons."[9] Those "lessons"
would figure prominently in Gittelsohn's future sermons.

The Oxford Pledge became a major factor in promoting the

American anti-war movement on college campuses, but the wording had to be retooled for use in America to accommodate both the pacifist and leftist branches of the movement. As previously noted, the leftist members of the anti-war movement had no problem with anti-colonial wars, and this went against the spirit of the Oxford Pledge, which espoused total pacifism. Accordingly, the wording of the Americanized version declared their intention to "refuse to support the government of the United States in any war it may conduct." Since the Marxist position maintained that the only type of war the American government could wage would be an imperialist war, members of the NSL and other leftist students felt they could support the pledge because it was a rejection not of all war, but only imperial war.[10]

The NSL would soon organize national student strikes against war. The first, held on April 13, 1934, drew 25,000 students, mainly from the East Coast. The second Student Strike Against War in 1935 was far larger, drawing about 175,000 students, this time from all around the country, including students from Ohio State and Oberlin College. The year Roland took the Oxford Pledge is not clear, but he certainly embraced it completely. He appeared to support the religious pacifist view that all war is evil and cannot be supported. However, in later years, he would embrace a position consistent with that of the leftists in the anti-war movement, which justified some wars. Ironically his change of mind was due largely to Jewish religious principles, which in the early 1930s may have appeared wildly inconsistent. His conversion would involve his "spiritual schizophrenia" that he would later write about.[11]

Like virtually all of the young anti-war activists of the 1930s, Gittelsohn believed the United States' involvement in World War I in 1917 was motivated primarily by economic factors despite President Wilson's lofty rhetoric that we entered the war to "make the world safe for democracy." Students like Roland believed that war served to protect the profit margins of American capitalists.[12]

Another "lesson" many students learned was to be wary of propaganda produced by the government to generate the support of war. They believed the demonization of the German people was largely the work of the media supporting the country's entry into the war. Convinced that history tends to repeat itself, student anti-war activists took these lessons about economics, war guilt and the origins of Worlds War I and applied them to the turbulent international scene of the 1930s.[13] They thought that their understanding of these "lessons" learned from the First World War would help them understand and appropriately respond to the world issues developing in the 1930s. The cliché about generals always fighting the last war was applicable here to the campus peace movement and to the pacifist movement in general. The student anti-war activists in 1933–1935 still had their minds on 1917; and in a sense, as NSL leader Joseph Clark recalled, they "relived an era ... which no longer existed."[14]

Activists such as Gittelsohn would bemoan the growing size of the military and increasing defense budgets as an indication of the country's expansionist tendencies and willingness to be embroiled once again in foreign conflicts. In fact, in the early and mid–1930s, there was a strong isolationist movement in the country and an overall disinclination to once again to be drawn into a foreign conflict. This was clear given the relatively small size of the America military on the eve of World War II in 1939, when the United States had the 19th largest army in the world, behind such countries as Portugal and Belgium.

By honing in on the largely economic "lessons" gleaned from their study of World War I, student pacifists failed to assess the nature of the coming storm in Europe, a conflict not defined by capitalist protection but for the sake of combating Nazi totalitarianism.[15] While American students were taking the Oxford Pledge, students in Nazi Germany were burning pacifist books. Meanwhile American students went on strikes for peace on successive anniversaries commemorating World War I. They also marched against pro-war Wilsonian slogans of 1917, such as making the world safe for democracy, while championing anti-interventionalism. These students, including Roland Gittelsohn, remained captives of the past: opposing the wrong war at the wrong time.[16]

As he continued his studies at Hebrew Union College, Gittelsohn vigorously embraced the growing pacifist movement. For years he had believed in the tenets of total pacifism long before the average student had embraced it. He had established his bona fide credentials by proudly wearing his two percent pin and maintaining his membership with the War Resister's League. While still a rabbinical student, he would greatly refine his credentials and become a well-known, outspoken advocate of peace throughout the Jewish community.

• • •

In the latter half of 1931, during the first year of his rabbinical studies, Roland and his longtime sweetheart Ruth Freyer decided that they would marry. Ruth was the same age as Roland and was a student at Flora Stone Mather College—the women's school of Western Reserve University. Born in Cleveland like Roland, she was the daughter of Solomon Freyer and Eva Cohen Freyer. Solomon was a garment worker who was born in New York City in October of 1872. Her mother Eva was born in England in September of 1879. The Freyers moved to East Cleveland, while the Gittelsohns resided in Cleveland Heights.

After getting engaged, Roland approached his grandfather, Rabbi

Benjamin Gittelsohn, and posed a potentially awkward dilemma for him. Both Roland and his family, and Ruth and her family were members of the Euclid Avenue Temple, a Reform synagogue. Would Orthodox Rabbi Benjamin Gittelsohn be willing to officiate at their marriage ceremony along with their rabbi, Barnett R. Brickner of the Euclid Avenue Temple affiliated with Reform Judaism? His answer was, "We'll see." Roland clearly understood that his grandfather was telling him, "If you observe such essential Orthodox marriage rites as covering your heads and reciting the appropriate formulae and including the traditional seven wedding blessings, yes."[17]

Regrettably, Rabbi Gittelsohn was never able to co-officiate at his grandson's wedding. By late 1931, he was in failing health and was living in a nursing home. On January 7, 1932, he died at the approximate age of 90.

On September 25, 1932, Roland Gittelsohn and Ruth Freyer were married at the Euclid Avenue Temple. Rabbi Barnett Brickner performed the wedding rites for the young couple. Both of the newlyweds resumed their studies after the wedding. In 1934, Gittelsohn received his bachelor of Hebrew studies degree from Hebrew Union College. Ruth Gittelsohn would receive her Bachelor of Arts Degree from Western Reserve University on June 12, 1935. The following year, after additional postgraduate work, Roland would be ordained as a rabbi.

• • •

Roland's early views on pacifism and social justice were two subjects that would dominate his thinking and action throughout his rabbinical career. The first airing of his views took place in the years between the completion of his bachelor's degree and his ordination. Over the next decades the pulpits of various synagogues where he would preach provided the forum for his views on war, pacifism, injustice, and the world's situation in general.

In 1934, when Roland was 24 years old, he delivered a Jewish New Year sermon that he entitled "More Human Bondage." This sermon, expounding his views on war and pacifism, was one he would deliver several times with modifications in the near future—on November 16, 1935, and again after his ordination on Rosh Hashanah eve in 1936.

That night he began his speech by relating the story of Abraham on Mt. Moriah. God had called to Abraham, asking that he sacrifice his only son Isaac, the boy whom his entire life was centered around. This was not an unusual request, as in the religions of antiquity human sacrifice was the noblest and highest of all rites.[18] Dutifully, Abraham obeyed God's request and he prepared to sacrifice Isaac. Just as Abraham raised his knife, preparing to take Isaac's life, an angel called out, crying: "'Abraham, Abraham, … Lay not thy hand upon the lad, neither do thou anything to him.' Lay not thy hand upon human life, said the voice to all mankind. The days of human sacrifice were to be ended."[19]

Gittelsohn then related a question that ancient rabbis had debated: Why had the angel called out Abraham's name twice?:

> Wouldn't one [call to] Abraham have been enough, asked the rabbis? Their answer is important. The first Abraham was for that very one who stood there, knife raised aloft, ready to slay his son. The second Abraham, said the wise old rabbis, was for all the Abrahams to come. In other words, the great message given to Abraham on Mt. Moriah was not intended for him alone. It came, through him, to Jews of all time.... What about those to whom the second Abraham was addressed? ... Have we too heeded the message and stopped sacrificing human life [in wars]? Oh, if only the answer in our case could be the same! ... What we do in war speaks too loudly for any sane answer to the question of human sacrifice to be heard.[20]

Gittelsohn deftly used the story of Abraham and Isaac on Mt. Moriah as a metaphor for mankind and the Jewish people. Stating "...we might go on and see that almost every incident in the life of Abraham is symbolic of some great advance in the life of his people,"[21] he then compared the potential sacrifice of Isaac with the senseless killing of thousands of human lives in warfare. Human sacrifice was ended on Mt. Moriah, Gittelsohn noted, advancing the concept of the sanctity of life. And yet mankind continued to sacrifice human lives in senseless wars.

Gittelsohn then spoke about one of the exhibits currently being displayed at Chicago's Century of Progress International Exposition. Describing a miniature model of the United States Treasury Building, he noted that it had a long conveyor belt in lieu of steps, down from which came a continuous stream of gold coins. A sign above the belt explained the meaning of the coin display: It showed that of every dollar taken in taxes by the federal government, 82 cents went for war. One can envision the rising anger in Gittelsohn's voice as he urged his congregation to consider the sad and pathetic irony. People were starving, searching for work, misery was widespread, "and still our government spends 82 cents out of each dollar to pay for the last war, which nobody admits starting, and the next war, which nobody admits wanting."[22]

Imagine, asked Gittelsohn, how much more terrifying the exhibit would be if, instead of coins being displayed on the belt, there were instead the ten million bodies of the men killed in the last war.

Reflecting on those millions killed in World War I, he rhetorically asked, "And for what? At least primitive man, in sacrificing his own flesh and blood to a god, expected some benefit in return."[23] Riches? Freedom? Democracy? Roland asked cynically. Had any of these things been achieved? "We sacrificed ten million souls in a war to end war, and what have we today? More war, more hate, more suspicion, more death," he passionately declared.[24]

It was clear to Gittelsohn that greater than the cost in blood and treasure was his belief that these men had died in vain. This was the ultimate mockery; that they may have died for nothing. This was intolerable to him. To his congregation he posed the question: What are we going to do about it?

Gittelsohn believed the first concrete step to be taken was to disarm. He proceeded to reference a speech that President Franklin D. Roosevelt made the year before, when Roosevelt stated "...that the invasion of any nation or the destruction of a national sovereignty can only be prevented by the complete elimination of the weapons which make such a course possible. The only way to disarm is to disarm."[25] Yet a year later, Gittelsohn pointed out, a leading periodical commented on the legislation that Roosevelt promoted, contradicting the President's statements of the previous year. The source stated, "After President Roosevelt took office, building of warships began on such a scale as the Navy had never before known in peacetime."[26] This, noted Gittelsohn, from that man who said: "The only way to disarm is to disarm." To him the hypocrisy was thoroughly distasteful.

Like many of the pacifists of the era, Gittelsohn pointed to the real possibility of disarmament by citing the example of the United States–Canadian border. He specifically noted the efforts of Acting Secretary of State Richard Rush after the War of 1812, resulting in the Rush-Bagot Treaty, effectively demilitarizing the border between the two nations. With admiration, Gittelsohn pointed out that for a century there hadn't been a single piece of armament on the 3,000 mile border between the United States and Canada, "and in all that time, not one single war! Isn't it about time for the rest of the world to sit up and take notice?"[27]

Quoting the French philosopher Edmond Fleg, Gittelsohn claimed, "Peace will not be achieved by conferences nor by treaties. There will be peace when men are willing to die for peace."[28] There can be no compromise, Gittelsohn insisted. To him, that was the trouble with most pacifists. Even they were willing to fight just one more war. "Communists want one more war for Communism. Fascists want one more war for Fascism. But if we are ever to reach peace, then we must sacrifice Communism and Fascism and every other 'ism' to the greatest of all, Pacifism."[29]

How many of us in the synagogue, he asked, have ever done anything to truly oppose war? How many of them had questioned candidates for office on their positions on peace? How many of them protested when Congress appropriated billions of taxpayer dollars to build more warships? After noting that it took a long time for religion to grow out of human sacrifice, he cautioned that it may well take a long time for people to achieve peace. But he reminded his listeners that everyone in attendance that day could do something, be it ever so humble, in the fight for peace:

> If we do, men will tell how we were commanded by the Great God of War to sacrifice millions of our sons on his altar.... And they will tell how a voice came forth from the heavens and said to us: "Abraham, Abraham, lay not thy hand upon thy son, neither do thou anything to them, for I the Lord thy God am a God of peace."[30]

Here Gittelsohn's passion for peace and conviction that it was everyone's obligation to work for peace shone through. However, his convictions also revealed a naivety that was common to pacifists throughout that era. They assumed that all nations were rational and acted with reason and honesty. The reality was that this was an era that gave rise to Hitler, Mussolini and Stalin.

Gittelsohn delivered "More Human Bondage" again the next year on November 16, 1935. On that occasion he had embellished several points of his earlier sermon, making his message more urgent and more strident in its tone. Once again, he began with the story of Abraham and Isaac on Mt. Moriah. Abraham, he reasoned, was willing to give up the most important thing in his life—his son Isaac—in support of his beliefs. To his congregation he posed the question: how about ourselves? "How much are we really willing to sacrifice, if need be, to achieve that peace?"[31] Sure, people may protest and preach, but how many people would be willing to sacrifice "their Isaac?" How many of them would give up their wealth, social standing, and approval—and perhaps even life itself? This, he stated, was the key to all of their failure.

The soldier is often willing to die for his beliefs, so he asked, "How can we, who pretend to love peace, do less than the soldier who is willing to go forth into battle and possibly lose his life in support of that in which he believes?"[32] Once again quoting the French philosopher Edmond Fleg, Gittelsohn claimed, "Peace will not be achieved by conferences nor by treaties. There will be peace when men are willing to die for peace."[33]

To those who might wonder why his rhetoric was so strident and so urgent, Gittelsohn exclaimed that they could not afford to be patient any longer. "We cannot afford to wait patiently for peace. We have no other choice than to be extreme.... We have no time for patience."[34] Comparing everyone to passengers in a car being driven by a drunk driver, he pointed out that they had to take the wheel from such a driver, as they had no time to attempt to teach the intoxicated driver lessons in safety. Immediate action was required to avoid crashing into a passing train. "Either we grab the wheel from his hands and save ourselves, either we are sudden and extreme,—or else we meet that train and another war destroys us and our civilization. This is our only choice."[35]

In closing, he once again referred to the story of Abraham on Mt. Moriah, preparing to sacrifice his beloved son Isaac. When the call came to Abraham, he responded, "Here I am, ready, if need be, to lose that which I love most."[36] Soberly, Gittelsohn stated, "That was the answer of the first Abraham, and it must be the answer of the others, of ourselves, too."[37] His closing paragraph was identical to his sermon given in 1934, a year earlier.

• • •

Ten days after Gittelsohn's 1934 Rosh Hashanah sermon, he delivered another powerful sermon on the eve of Yom Kippur. He continued sharing his strong views, this time speaking on the concept of social justice. He called the sermon, "The Fast That We Have Chosen." He used the occasion of the holiest day of the Jewish year, the Day of Atonement, to frame his vision of what meaningful atonement should entail. He began by noting that the Day of Atonement had been referred to by many Jews and non–Jews as a convenient way to absolve the congregation of past sins. As such, people questioned the authenticity of Yom Kippur feeling that its existence led to a sort of moratorium on morals. As an example he recalled a non–Jew's comment on the observance of Yom Kippur: "You Jews can sin as you please all through the year confident that this one day will restore you in the good graces of God."[38] To Gittelsohn, these skeptics likened Yom Kippur to a little boy being caught misbehaving and then assuring his mother that it was all right, because he promised to be sorry the next day.

Even worse, he claimed, enemies of Judaism had often taken the Kol Nidre prayer, the traditional prayer recited in the synagogue on the eve of Yom Kippur, and tried to make of it something mean and contemptible. He explained that these enemies claimed the Jews came up with this as a scheme to cheat and deceive the non–Jewish world. To these enemies, Gittelsohn explained, "Yom Kippur is a cunning device which enables the Jew to escape all his vows and obligations of the year."[39] He pointed out that this thinking represented a total misunderstanding of the meaning of Yom Kippur to the Jew, and it certainly was not a recent development. The ancient rabbis had dealt with the same accusations as noted in the Mishnah, the written edition of the Judaism's oral traditions that had been first written nearly two thousand years ago. They decreed that one who sinned and then later vowed to repent would not be given a chance to repent. "He who says, 'I will sin and the Day of Atonement will wipe out my sin,'—in such a case, the Day of Atonement will not wipe out his sin."[40]

But in his next statement, Gittelsohn delivered the crux of his meaning of atonement as described in the Mishnah. "Yom Kippur wipes out the

sins between men and God: it does not wipe out the sin which men commit against men until they have first become reconciled with each other!"[41]
This was the basis of his Yom Kippur sermon that he passionately preached
to his congregation. "What a noble statement!" he exclaimed. "Man's sin
against his fellowman is more grievous than his sin against God. This is
not the easy way out charged by our critics."[42] Yom Kippur was a stimulant
and not a salve, one that demanded man's noblest conduct toward his fellow man. "This means in order to have a Day of Atonement, we must live a
year of atonement."[43]

He drove home this concept by relaying the prophet's description
from ancient times, when people wondered why their prayers had not been
answered, despite having fasted on Yom Kippur. True, Gittelsohn noted,
they had fasted, but "...even while they fasted to atone for the sin of yesterday, they were planning the sin of tomorrow."[44] Gittelsohn added, the
prophet then asked the people, "Is such the feast I've chosen?"[45] Does simply bowing one's head and praying make a person acceptable to God, he
asked. No, the prophet declared! Instead, he countered with a different
interpretation of atonement, alternatively asking:

> Is not this the fast that I have chosen? To loose the fetters of wickedness, to
> undo the bands of the yoke, and to let the oppressed go free, and that ye break
> every yoke? Is it not to deal thy bread to the hungry, and that thou bring the
> poor that are cast out to thy house? When though seest the naked, that thou
> cover him, and that thou hide not thyself from thine own flesh?[46]

Hence Gittelsohn rebutted the claim that Jews only need to pray on Yom
Kippur to atone for their sins of the past year. It wasn't simply one day to
pray and ask God for forgiveness as critics indicated. It was a yearlong commitment to deal with one's fellow man with dignity and respect, to live a
year of atonement between men and not simply one night to pray for God
to forgive one's sin. As he had pointed out, Yom Kippur wiped out sin
between man and God—it was up to man to reconcile their sins against
each other for true atonement to occur.

Looking out on his congregation, Gittelsohn asked them, which alternative have we chosen? "Do we use this day as a moral cathartic, or do we
answer the prophet's challenge? 'To loosen the fetters of wickedness, to
undo the bonds of the yoke, and to let the oppressed go free....'"[47] Having
described a framework for true atonement consistent with the writings of
the ancient prophets and rabbis, he proceeded on to describe current-day
examples of man's injustices to his fellowman, examples that would show-
case, possibly the first time in a public forum, his outspoken and often controversial views on social justice.

Gittelsohn chose to begin his discussion of social injustice with the story of Tom Mooney, a political activist and labor leader who was languishing in prison since 1916. Mooney had been convicted of the bombing of the San Francisco Preparedness Day march on July 22, 1916, that had killed a total of ten people. Many believed that Mooney, a known socialist, had been framed and there was a continuing campaign over the years to demand Mooney's release from prison.

Gittelsohn was a passionate believer in Mooney's innocence. To his congregation he stated that Tom Mooney loved peace but the powers that be were dependent on war, and for that reason Tom Mooney was thrown in jail. "Tom Mooney loved his fellowmen so much," Gittelsohn noted, "that he opposed a government which denied them freedom. Therefore, that government committed him to prison. That was in 1916."[48] Citing multiple examples of perjured testimony as well as suppression of evidence that would have exonerated Mooney, Gittelsohn noted with disgust that Mooney remained in jail in 1934 for a crime he didn't commit 18 years prior. (Mooney would eventually be pardoned and released from prison in 1939.)

The next paragraph from his sermon notes of 1934 is revealing. After erroneously stating that Mooney was a communist (he was, in fact, a socialist), he revealed to his congregation, "Not long ago when I mentioned his name from a pulpit, at least one woman left the Synagogue thoroughly convinced that since I defended him, I must be a communist too. It happens that I am not."[49] In the future he would be accused of being a communist on several occasions due to his leftist leanings, but he was never a member of the Communist Party. Significantly, the suspicion that Gittelsohn was a communist would again surface towards the end of World War II, after the battle of Iwo Jima. But his point in discussing Tom Mooney was that true freedom from oppression means freedom for those who choose to disagree with us. As he noted in his Yom Kippur sermon:

> This is the only freedom ever threatened; therefore it is the only freedom worth having. Why, to my mind, one of the noblest sentiments ever uttered by the human tongue was that spoken by Voltaire when he said: "I cannot agree with a thing you say, but I'd die for your right to say it."[50]

The precious freedom of speech, the right of dissent—these were critical American values that Rabbi Roland Gittelsohn cherished and believed were the right of every American. The case of the injustice suffered by Tom Mooney was illustrative of his example of the fast we have chosen; of wiping out the sin we commit toward our fellowmen before we can wipe out the sin between men and God. "But so long as Tom Mooney and others like him remain in jail," he declared, "we <u>haven't</u> loosened the fetter of wickedness, we <u>haven't</u> undone the bands of the yoke, and we <u>haven't</u> let the oppressed go free."[51]

In that Yom Kippur sermon Gittelsohn proceeded to discuss a second area of social justice that needed to be corrected for true atonement to be achieved: racial equality. This would also be a lifetime quest for him. He informed the congregation of a book that he had discovered entitled *The Negro a Beast; or In the Image of God*, written by an author named Charles Carroll at the turn of the century. With absolute disgust, he revealed to them that the publisher of the book was the American Book and Bible House. In addition to reviewing several examples of discrimination against Black Americans, he decried the economic and educational disparities between Black and White America. "Eight Southern states average $44 per year for education of each white child," he pointed out; "for each negro child they average $12.50. And the inhabitants of those very states dare to speak of the negro's low level of culture."[52]

The last area of social justice that he would discuss that day was poverty. He attacked the naïve assumption that before the stock market crash of 1929 leading to the Great Depression, there was no such thing as a hungry, unemployed person in America. Along with this assumption was another naïve belief of some that as a result of the New Deal, the country had returned to a state of prosperity. This was total nonsense, he declared. Before the stock market crash there were four million unemployed Americans. Now, after two years of the New Deal, there were close to ten million unemployed. Children were living in poverty on a daily basis. "How many of us, have," he asked, "burned deeply on our conscience and heart, the cry of a child without clothes for its naked body or food for its empty stomach?"[53] In contrast to this striking scenario, he pointed out that in 1931 the Electric Bond and Share Company made profits of 103 percent while millions of such children starved. The following year the Bank of Manhattan made record profits while many Americans were living in dire poverty. "What shall we say of our generation's method of dealing bread to the hungry?" he asked. "This is the challenge of Yom Kippur. How have we answered it?"[54]

To draw together the threads of his sermon into a defining statement, Gittelsohn went on to describe the short story written in 1866 by Leo Tolstoy entitled *How Much Land Does a Man Need?* In it, Tolstoy tells the story of an ignorant Russian peasant named Pahom. Although Pahom would toil every day in a backbreaking manner on his master's land, he was a happy individual. When his master died and left the little strip of land to Pahom, his days of contentedness were over. From that point on he wanted more and more land. After learning of the proposed giveaway of large tracts of land in Siberia, Pahom, craving more land, sold his home and everything in it, and he headed out to Siberia with his one faithful servant.

Once there, Pahom entered into an agreement whereby he would acquire all the land he could surround in one day by foot, provided he returned to the starting point by sunset. Readily agreeing to this, by mid-day he had acquired a large tract, but his craving for more and more land keep him going. Racing against time to return by sunset, he became totally exhausted. Returning to the starting point just as the sun's last rays were fading behind the hills, Pahom collapsed. His servant shouted out his congratulations that Pahom had won. But looking at his master, lying there with blood trickling from his mouth, the servant realized that Pahom was dead.

Gittelsohn then noted how Tolstoy's story ended: "Then the faithful servant of Pahom took his spade, and with it dug a space 7 feet long, and there laid his master to eternal rest. And that, said Leo Tolstoi [*sic*], answers the question, How much land does a man need?"[55]

It was at this point that Gittelsohn provided the answer to this question: Why haven't we been able to answer the challenge of Yom Kippur? According to him, "...we've become a generation of Pahoms, blindly killing ourselves as well as others, in a desperate effort to acquire land and wealth which we didn't need." In a controversial summary that sounds very much like the rhetoric of Karl Marx melded into his own socialist-leaning views, Gittelsohn announced what needed to be done. "The creed we must adopt is simple: First, the needs of all; second, the luxury of a few. Only after every man has what he needs can any man have what he wants!"[56]

Gittelsohn ended his sermon declaring:

> This is the fast that we must choose. It is the only way to change Yom Kippur from convenience to challenge. With it, our fasting and prayer on this day have meaning. Without it, every hour we fast and every prayer we utter is hypocrisy and sham. Let us, then, fill this day with meaning by consecrating ourselves to a year of ceaseless effort for those who are oppressed and hungry. We must defend the man who seeks to speak what he calls the truth, even if we think it false. We must protect the man whose skin is black even if our own is white. And we must feed the hungry and clothe the naked, even if it means less luxury for us.[57]

Thus, with two sermons delivered over the High Holidays in 1934, Roland Gittelsohn laid out his vision of America. The activist rabbi envisioned a world where the United States of America would refuse to ever be drawn again into a war; war driven by false propaganda that touted it was making the world safe for democracy when he believed it was to make the world safe for corporate profits. He envisioned a United States where justice would prevail to all, where freedom of dissent was tolerated and where racial equality was among the noble goals that our country could achieve. His views would remain consistent over the years, although his vision of pacifism at all costs would be greatly challenged within the decade, as it would for many committed pacifists of the 1930s.

FOUR

Discovery

The National Federation of Temple Sisterhoods (NFTS) was founded in January 1913 when 150 delegates representing 49 different temple sisterhoods met in Cincinnati. The purpose of their new organization, as stated in the preamble to the minutes of their first meeting, was "that the increased power which has come to the modern American Jewess ought to be exercised in congregational life and that the religious and moral development of Israel [the Jewish people] will be furthered by this co-operation."[1] The NFTS not only aimed to strengthen temple sisterhoods already in existence, but to translate women's roles in the home to a larger and more public sphere.[2]

For many years, the Nation Federation of Temple Sisterhoods walked a fine line between its commitment to Reform Judaism and its interest in general philanthropic work and contemporary political issues. The NFTS leaders always considered certain issues, notably peace work and separation of church and state in the public schools, at the center of the Sisterhood's religious mission.[3] It was in this peace effort that Roland Gittelsohn would play a vital role.

The NFTS' growing anti-war sentiment was expressed in a policy statement, "Resolution on Peace" passed at their 1931 annual meeting.[4] It cited the extensive military buildup taking place both in Europe and America, noting that these actions were "in direct opposition to the solemn pledge made by the fifty-eight nations who signed the Kellogg-Briand Pact never again 'to use war as an instrument of national policy....'" The NFTS's component committee, the National Committee on Peace, had a proactive, energetic chairman in the person of Jennie L. Kubie of New York City. With the exception of a two-year period, Kubie would chair the peace committee for the entire 1930s.

At the meeting of the NFTS held in New York City on March 1, 1933, Kubie delivered the Report of the National Committee on Peace, where she offered two key recommendations. She directed that every Sisterhood branch determine to further its peace work through establishment of a peace budget. Her next recommendation would have a lasting impact on the affiliated Sisterhood branches. She insisted that peace study groups be organized at each location with the special purpose of developing peace leaders.[5]

Involvement in peace work would become a much more sharply focused interest of the organization when Jane Evans, known as "the first lady of Reform Judaism," became the first full-time executive director in 1933. Together, Jane Evans as executive director and Jennie Kubie as chairman of the National Committee on Peace proved to be a very effective team in the movement for world peace.

In the Report of the National Committee on Peace that Jennie Kubie delivered in New York City on May 15, 1934, she discussed several of the committee's accomplishments.[6] Among these was the formation of Peace Study Groups. With pride, she pointed out that a study group created for the development of peace chairmen or leaders, had been organized. Kubie also reported about the creation of the "Peace News Flashes," periodicals intended to provide up-to-date information on worldwide peace developments for all peace chairmen. She advised that the Peace Study Groups closely follow the outlines that would be soon issued by the National Chairman in cooperation with the programs that were being formulated by the National Peace Conference.

Jane Evans' address, "Report of the Executive Director," was delivered in Cincinnati on March 8, 1935. It contained an interesting announcement by Evans. After apologizing for the delay in delivery of the new educational programs, she announced that the first two were now available: "But at this convention, we have on display for you in the Exhibit Room, the first two of our series, namely: *Dramatic Moments in Jewish History* by Dr. A.L. Sachar, and *The Jew Looks at War and Peace* by Roland Gittelsohn."[7]

It is unknown whether Jane Evans was actually in attendance that Rosh Hashanah in Cincinnati earlier that year when Gittelsohn delivered his sermon entitled "More Human Bondage." More likely, it was members of the local Sisterhood who were in Gittelsohn's congregation that day. So impressed were these women with the message they heard that they reported it to the national headquarters of the NFTS, which was how Evans first learned of it. Evans quickly realized that the views of this young rabbinical student and the passion with which he expressed them, were exactly what the NFTS needed to anchor its peace study groups organization-wide. And it was only the year before that the group had created the Sisterhood Publication Fund. In late 1934, Evans approached Gittelsohn with a request that he bring his message to various chapters of the NFTS. She also commissioned him to write a book that would become his first copyrighted work.

• • •

Published by the NFTS in 1935, "*The Jew Looks at War and Peace*" was a study guide that was intended to foster the message of peace and pacifism espoused by the organization. It was actually a series of five pamphlets, each about 20 pages long. Each pamphlet was organized into four sections: (a) a short lecture; (b) a series of questions to facilitate discussion (presented in pro and con format to stimulate debate); (c) suggestions for individual reports and activities; and (d) a bibliography.

Pamphlet I was entitled "Balancing our War Books." In his introduction, Gittelsohn revealed to all potential study group leaders his style of teaching and reasoning through issues that he learned from his debate teachers and his instructors at Hebrew Union College. He advised the group leaders to first give the group members every opportunity to think problems through for themselves and express themselves. "If some member of the group thinks her way through to an answer given here, the result is many times more profitable than if she simply hears it presented by someone else."[8] He ended the introduction by noting that, "My grateful thanks are due Miss Jane Evans, Executive Secretary of the N.F.T.S., who originally suggested this series, who consistently helped during its writing, and who waited patiently to have it completed."[9]

"Balancing our War Books" is essentially a repeat of his sermon "More Human Bondage," using virtually every part of the original sermon. He finished the lecture section with an even more passionate expression of the obligation that all pacifists must achieve, claiming there could be no more compromise. He once again pointed out that the adherents of Communism and Fascism each wanted one more war to further their causes, but all of these "isms" needed to be sacrificed on the altar of pacifism. He compared the volatile world situation, one where nations always appeared to be preparing for war, to a drunkard wanting just one more drink, something that would be disastrous for civilization that was already staggering in drunken delight. "Men must stop playing with the idea of peace as if with a hobby, and must make of it a life and a work."[10] Balancing our war books today, according to Gittelsohn, was impossible. But it was to the future that mankind must look. Balancing the war books would be a possibility for tomorrow, he reasoned, but it would only be possible if mankind made it possible.

Pamphlet II was entitled "Religion on Trial" and was a discussion about religion in general, not solely Judaism. He began the lecture with two examples of clergymen who displayed courage in their support of pacifism, much in the same way that Senator John F. Kennedy, nearly 20 years later, would describe the political courage of several members of the United States Senate in his book *Profiles in Courage*. Both Christian clergymen described by Gittelsohn suffered greatly for their opposition to the World War.

Gittelsohn described the one place where religion was needed the most during the war; it was the one place where men were taught to hate and to kill, namely the army. Here religion should have been able to teach the men to love and to heal. Yet it was here that the clergy failed greatly. He quoted the experience of Norman Thomas who noted that it was a common experience of conscientious objectors that their most bitter and intolerant enemies in the army were the chaplains and soldiers associated with Christian organizations such as the Y.M.C.A. Thomas observed "...they found that they were less understood and more contemptuously despised by these men than even by veteran soldiers who made no profession of allegiance to the principles of Jesus."[11] There was no doubt in Gittelsohn's mind—religion was on trial during the Great War and religion had failed miserably.

He feared that there was truly a danger of religion becoming a "pious irrelevancy" should war ever again come between nations. "If the peace religion preaches, is again to disappear when it is needed most, the danger is grave that with it religion too will disappear."[12] Having religious services dedicated to peace was not enough. "The houses of organized religion must declare now and forevermore that under no circumstances will they ever again support war."[13]

Gittelsohn ended the lecture in Book II with the story of Harry Emerson Fosdick. Although he erroneously stated that Fosdick was a pacifist long before 1917, his admiration for the man was obvious. He told the story of Fosdick's 1923 sermon, "Apology to the Unknown Soldier," spending an entire page quoting from the speech. Gittelsohn's passion built up to Fosdick's final words: "I renounce war and never again, directly or indirectly, will I sanction or support another! O Unknown Soldier, in penitent reparation I make you that pledge."[14]

Gittelsohn solemnly ended the lecture by saying, "May all religions make the same pledge."[15]

Pamphlet III was entitled, "Are Jews Pacifists?" In it, Gittelsohn attempted to answer the question with a definitive, "Yes." To support his position, he went back to the time of Alexander the Great and related the story of Alexander's dealings with Jerusalem. According to the Talmud, Alexander sent emissaries to Jerusalem to obtain food supplies for his massive armies. At the time, the city was under the rule of Persia and the residents feared offending the Persians if they complied with Alexander's request. Accordingly, they refused. Furious with their response, Alexander announced that his army would march on Jerusalem in three days and destroy it.

Panic began to set in among the residents of the city. No one seriously believed that they could defend their city against the mightiest army in the world. It was the High Priest, Jaddua, who came forward with the plan.

"It was a strange one," noted Gittelsohn. It entailed no armies or plans for battle. "My plan," said Jaddua, "is to meet the great Alexander with peace. Let us march out of the city to welcome him in friendship; that is our best defense."[16]

In spite of their fear and doubts, the residents of the city complied with the plan of Jaddua. Wearing their most festive clothing, they marched out of the city to meet the armies of Alexander with Jaddua leading the way. Alexander was astonished when he came upon the approaching throng. He had never experienced this—instead of weapons, they approached him with gifts and celebration. Alexander's soldiers looked on with amazement when he dismounted from his horse and then bowed before the Jewish Priest Jaddua. Alexander then turned to his soldiers and proclaimed that he could not raise a hand against Jaddua and his people. "This is the only people that has met me peacefully instead of with arms. The more glory to their leader, Jaddua, who was brave enough and wise enough to do this."[17]

To Gittelsohn, the story was typical of many in Jewish lore. For him it exemplified that all men are brothers, descended from one man who God had created. Why, wondered the ancient rabbis, did God, with all of His powers, create only one man? Gittelsohn pointed out that the dust out of which the first man, Adam, was formed was collected from every land in the world. Hence it was clear to Gittelsohn that God's plan to create one man from whom all others would descend reflected his intention that no group of men would ever fight against another group, being that they were all brothers.[18]

Gittelsohn explained why Jews hate war and want peace. The Jew could never rejoice over the plight of the vanquished. Noting that Jews have always been a hated minority, he stated, "Wars are not kind to strangers, and we are strangers in many lands. Therefore, we hate war and love peace."[19] He stated that "our experiences as a people have given us an all-consuming love of life." In spite of discrimination and the difficult lives they had often lived, Jews had learned to love life. It is war that destroys life, therefore the Jew hates war and wants peace.

He concluded by describing Jews as "an international people" who more than any other people should be lovers of peace and must pursue it. "We must continue to meet the force of Alexander with the peace of Jaddua, that our efforts may help bring about the day when nation shall not lift up sword against nation, Neither shall they learn war any more."[20]

In Pamphlet IV, Gittelsohn posed a crucially important question with his title: "Can Jews Afford to Be Pacifists?" Surely at no time, he began, has it ever been an easy thing to be a pacifist. But "to be a Jew and a pacifist is challenge enough for [requiring] the strength and skill of Hercules."[21] To graphically illustrate this dilemma, he related the story of President David

Israels, the fictitious American Jewish president, in Frank Copley's novel entitled "The Impeachment of President Israels."

In the novel, Israels was the first Jewish president in the United States, elected before the World War on a strong pacifist platform. After his election, tensions arose between the United States and Germany, and President Israels resisted all calls to increase American armaments and prepare for war. Shortly after, an American ship was sunk in German waters with the resultant loss of three American lives. The overwhelming majority of Americans demanded a declaration of war, which Israels refused to pursue. He instead counseled patience, believing that the German population was also being spun up in a patriotic fervor. Without restraint, Israels believed that a war was inevitable, but he let it be known both at home and overseas that he had confidence in the German government and would take no rash steps against it. Germany, he was sure, would realize that the sinking was a terrible accident and would apologize to the United States and end the war tensions.

Unfortunately, several months before, Israels had committed to send the American fleet to the Mediterranean to participate in an anniversary celebration for the Turkish republic. The President now faced a dilemma. The country was clamoring for him to send the fleet against Germany. To cancel the participation in the Turkish celebration would offend our Turkish ally. At the same time this would belie the confidence he had expressed toward Germany, and would further fan wartime passions in that country. President Israels decided to send the fleet to Turkey and was promptly impeached. In addition, anti–Jewish sentiment through the country was exacerbated by his actions. "People everywhere blamed not only him, but his people too," Gittelsohn explained. And he mockingly continued, "What else could one expect from lily-livered Jews? One grants them freedom and liberty only to be stabbed by them in the hour of need!"[22]

To Gittelsohn, David Israels served as a metaphor that represented the Jewish pacifist. The quandary that faced him was the dilemma that every Jew who loves peace must face. What would happen to the Jewish people, asked Gittelsohn, if another war were to start and every Jew in this country refused to fight? "The answer is frequently given that by such action we should be risking pogroms and massacres and death. How, then, can we afford to be pacifists?"[23]

Before an intelligent answer could be provided, Gittelsohn insisted that one must look at it from the Jewish point of view and ask, "What does war mean to the Jew?" Reflecting back on the Great War, it was easy for him to recall the horrible toll that that the Jewish community in Europe suffered. When the Germans entered Poland, they accused the Jews of being Russian agents and when the Russians took over the country, the Jews were accused of being German agents. All told, he recounted that 215 pogroms against Jews took place in Poland during the Great War. "Whatever the Jew did, he was wrong. And being wrong, he was persecuted and oppressed."[24] In Russia, many Jews served in the army, only to have their loyalty repaid with further discrimination and persecution.

Gittelsohn recounted a conversation that took place at the Paris Peace Conference in 1919 between President Woodrow Wilson and Polish Prime Minister Ignace Paderewski. Paderewski was urging Wilson and Prime Minister Clemenceau of France to grant certain concessions to Poland. "If these claims are not granted," said Paderewski, "the Polish people will be so furious that they would massacre all the Jews." Wilson naively asked what would happen if they agreed to grant the claims. "Ah," replied Paderewski with a smile, "that will different. In that case the Polish people will be so delighted that they will massacre all the Jews."[25] Sadly, Gittelsohn noted that "Klansmen and Nazis, Endeks and Cuzists,—all of them were revived, if not actually founded by the war to make the world safe for democracy!"[26]

All this led Gittelsohn to answer his question, "Can Jews afford to be pacifists?" with an unequivocal "Yes!" It wouldn't be easy, but the horrendous burden of war on mankind was even worse for Jews as they were often saddled with unmerited blame. He emphatically declared, "We must be pacifists … we Jews of today must work for peace, live for peace, and if need be die for peace, until the lips of all men echo the undying wish of the Jew: Shalom! Peace!"[27]

The last section of Gittelsohn's *The Jew Looks at War and Peace,* Pamphlet V, was directed at the target audience that the Nation Federation of Temple Sisterhoods intended to specifically reach. Entitled "If Women Wanted Peace," it spoke to the very essence of what Jane Evans and her newly discovered spokesman believed possible in the peace movement worldwide. Without mentioning it by name, Gittelsohn began by describing *Lysistrata*, the ancient Greek play by Aristophanes. In the play, the women of Greece, tired of war, threatened to withhold sex from their husbands until war had ended and peace had returned to Greece. "No sooner had the men discovered that their wives meant what they said than the war did end and peace did begin. Women succeeded where diplomacy and statecraft had failed."[28]

In primitive tribes, Gittelsohn noted, it was the men who made war, but it was the women who were the guardians of peace. It was the women who decided when the fighting had proven futile, and their word was law. This illustrated the potential role of women as makers of peace. However, many women had lost their way during the World War and supported it wholeheartedly. "They cheered the warrior and jeered the pacifist. They hated the 'enemy's' women, forgetting that they too had nursed sons, that they too suffered bereavement, and that their hearts too knew the ache of silent sorrow."[29] In Gittelsohn's view, it was women who largely urged that American citizenship be refused to Hungarian peace activist Rosika Schwimmer during the World War.

He did note that there were exceptions to female support for the war. He specifically noted the efforts of Schwimmer, Jane Addams, and Carrie Chapman in 1915, when they met at the Hague Congress of Women. There, women of twelve countries, including England and Germany, met in their quest for peace. What did they accomplish? "The very fact that it met at all was accomplishment enough. What international group of men met in the heat of hostilities? We rejoice that <u>some</u> women succeeded; we are grieved that <u>most</u> women failed."[30]

But Gittelsohn was emphatic that they cannot fail again, because if they do, civilization will fail with them. Men had failed in the quest for peace for eternity. It now rested in the hands of women. He quoted Albert Einstein when he said at the Disarmament Conference of 1933, "...since men have so utterly failed in what seems to be so simple to achieve, it is high time the women took a hand in the affairs of this world."[31] Women cannot fail, Gittelsohn reiterated, because men have failed.

Women would not fail, he explained, because their own happiness hung in the balance—the happiness that was taken from women when they became war widows. Failure would also destroy their own welfare, as war breeds a colossal contempt for women. Gittelsohn cynically pointed out that in times of war, women are needed to make munitions and keep industry running when men go off to war. And when the war is over, they are then sent to "breed more sons for the next war.... There is no room for women in the social scheme of Mussolini or Hitler, because there is no room for women in the social scheme of war."[32] His cynicism was accentuated by quoting the philosopher Oswald Spangler, who said, "Women are for breeding, and men for cannon fodder." Again, stressed Rabbi Gittelsohn, "Women must succeed."

And how could women succeed in their endeavor for peace in the world? Gittelsohn mentioned several steps for women to take to achieve the goals of pacifism. First, they must never condone war. There was nothing good, beautiful, or noble in war—there was only ugliness. "When once we have convinced ourselves of that, when once we have sworn never again to open our lips except to damn war, then we can first start to bring peace."[33]

And how might they bring peace about? Gittelsohn's next suggestion was the boycott. As an example, he suggested that if every woman in American vowed not to purchase any silk from Japan, the economic ramifications might well affect conditions in the Far East. While men held predictably worthless peace conferences, "women, who do most of the buying, could use [their] power to enforce peace."[34]

Gittelsohn urged women to use the power of the voting ballot to achieve peace. Toward that end women should learn the voting records of the candidates with regard to their views on war and peace. As an example, he mentioned what he considered the hypocrisy of Franklin D. Roosevelt in proclaiming, "The only way to disarm is to disarm," but then six months later signing one of the largest United States Navy funding bills in history. Women should hold candidates for office accountable, insisted Gittelsohn. Those candidates who speak for peace must also work for peace. Women should know the peace record of every candidate for every office. And in voting, they should let those records be their guide.[35]

Last, Gittelsohn stressed the importance of women educating their children about the concept of peace. He noted that women are responsible for about 90 percent of all of the training that children receive at home. In addition, it was the women who help shape the policies of temple schools. "We must teach our children that in the nursery and schoolroom, as well as in the larger areas of life, right is far stronger and nobler than might."[36]

Gittelsohn concluded this last book by quoting the horrific wartime experiences recorded by nurse Kathleen Norris. This was the hell, he claimed, that women must end. It would require courage and strength and he repeated an oath written by a Swedish female novelist. The oath ended with the quote, "I shall work for the sake of peace, though it cost me my life and happiness." He then concluded the five-pamphlet series by stating, "If we take this oath and meant it, tomorrow's world will be shaped by our hands."[37]

• • •

His affiliation with the NFTS established Roland Gittelsohn as a prominent spokesman for pacifism in the Jewish community. *The Jew Looks at War and Peace* quickly became a much-used teaching guide in temple sisterhoods around the country. New committee chairwoman Hortense L. Fox was concerned that the book would be used solely as material for programs on peace and expressed both her concern and advice in her Report of the National Committee on Peace that she delivered in Chicago on December 15, 1936. "The material provided by the National Office for study class material (I refer to 'The Jew Looks at War and Peace' by Roland Gittelsohn) seems to be used more as program material than as class material."[38] She suggested that the sisterhoods strongly consider using Gittelsohn's outlines for both study and for program material before discarding their use.

So influential was Gittelsohn's book that in 1937 one sisterhood member was inspired to write a play based on it. In the Report of the National

Committee on Programs delivered in Columbia, South Carolina, on December 15, 1937, committee chairwoman Helen Kohn Hennig reported, "Adding to this list of published material, the committee had this season presented *A Playlet based upon The Jew Looks at War and Peace*, written by Mrs. Arthur L. Reinhart."[39] The NFTS would publish an additional book by Roland Gittelsohn in the summer of 1937 entitled *The Jew Faces His Problems*.

Thus, with a fiery sermon entitled "More Human Bondage," written for Rosh Hashanah in 1934, Gittelsohn launched a career as a dedicated spokesman for world pacifism. He would deliver essentially the same sermon in November 1935, as well as for Rosh Hashanah in 1936, his first High Holidays sermon after his ordination as a rabbi.

In addition to his eloquence and his talmudic reasoning and logic, Rabbi Gittelsohn was also a member of the War Resisters League, had taken the Oxford Pledge, and would defiantly wear his 2 percent pin. Like many young Americans of the 1930s, he would have preferred to go to jail rather than go into the military and fight a war. Even though the events in Europe were first beginning to cause a sense of uneasiness for him and other Reform rabbis in particular, his mind was settled—he would never go to war under any circumstances.

FIVE

The New Rabbi

As his days as a rabbinical student at Hebrew Union College drew to a close, Roland Gittelsohn was becoming a rising authority in the anti-war movement. Pacifism was clearly his most passionate issue. To many, pacifism might appear to be a strictly secular concern and not within the realm of a rabbi's purview. But he had no problem reconciling this potential conflict with his religious outlook. His views were based on his concept of rabbinical duties, and how the roles of a rabbi had evolved throughout history. Gittelsohn observed that there were no rabbis until the time of Jesus—priests and prophets, but no rabbis.[1] He could have also added popular scholarly commentators known as Pharisees. The province of the priest was to implement the sacerdotal practices of the ancient Temple. The prophet was a moral guide and goad. The priest's purview, according to Gittelsohn, was easy to understand; the prophet's was far more difficult and complex. "I needed to appreciate both, for as a modern rabbi my responsibilities would encompass the boundaries of both."[2]

As his 26th birthday and his ordination were approaching, he was every bit the committed, outspoken activist, determined to reshape the world. Like most of his peers, he had a leftist view of societal issues that frequently called for exposure of the darker sides of a capitalist economy and the "few" villains, mainly bankers and armament manufacturers and dealers, who were no doubt working to embroil us into another war purely for profit. Like most of his peers, he had a black and white view of these issues and his mind appeared to be completely obsessed with the First World War and the "lessons" that had to be derived from it. It was almost as if radical pacifist proponents could not possibly envision a situation that could justify the United States' involvement in another worldwide conflict. Yet there was a looming conflagration which would engage Americans in combat against the pure evil inherent in certain societies at that time.

Pacifists of that era behaved as if all people were rational, pragmatic individuals like themselves. They further argued that the turmoil of the

World War and the "lessons" they derived from it, would make all nations realize that war was futile and that peace was the only answer. While they were espousing this approach, Japan had already invaded Manchuria and was murdering Chinese citizens by the tens of thousands. In Germany the Nazi regime had taken hold of the country and in 1933 Adolf Hitler had become its autocratic chancellor. Had many pacifists read his manifesto *Mein Kampf*, they could have easily seen that the "lessons" Adolf Hitler learned from the First World War were quite different from the ones they preached.

• • •

May 23, 1936, was a stiflingly hot day in Cincinnati. Graduating rabbinical candidates at Hebrew Union College stood in line, waiting for the cue to begin their processional into the chapel. Like his fellow ordinees, Gittelsohn could not wait to get inside and escape the oppressive heat that made him feel like his necktie was strangling him. Finally, at 2:30 p.m., the signal arrived and everyone solemnly marched into the chapel and took their seats. Standing on the synagogue platform (*bimah*), Dr. Julian Morgenstern, the college president, officiated at the ordination ceremony. Dr. Morgenstern would have a profound influence over the lives of virtually all the graduates.

Dr. Morgenstern held his hands solemnly over each student's heads as he pronounced the words of Jewish tradition that were already inscribed on their diplomas. "*Yoreh, yoreh, yadin, yadin*—he may surely teach, he may certainly judge." These were the succinct terms of a rabbi's responsibilities through the centuries, and they would now be carried out by the newly ordained students.[3] Like his grandfather, Gittelsohn was about to embark on a lifetime journey of teaching and adjudicating Jewish practice and tradition. In addition, his was to be a lifetime of study, social crusading and oftentimes one of intense controversy. After an hour, the newly ordained rabbis departed the chapel, each one of them headed for their first rabbinical postings or for further studies. For Rabbi Gittelsohn and his wife Ruth, it was time to pack their household goods as they departed from Ohio and started out to begin their new life on Long Island, New York.

• • •

On the evening of December 30, 1935, six months before Gittelsohn's rabbinical ordination, 58 Jewish families met at the Milburn Country Club in Baldwin, Long Island, New York. They shared a common vision, and that night they would enact a plan to transform their vision into a reality. The group considered a plan to establish a Reform Jewish congregation in their immediate region. The idea was enthusiastically approved by all, and

a provisional committee was established to organize the proposed synagogue. The committee members immediately and vigorously proceeded to
carry out their mission.

Their first objective was to acquire a temporary site where they could
hold both Friday night worship services as well as to conduct Sunday religious school instruction. They accomplished this by acquiring a building
with a decidedly non–Jewish sounding name: the McIntosh Studio. The
first Friday night worship service of the newly established Central Synagogue of Nassau County was held on February 13, 1936. This initial service
would be the true test for the visionary group of families that had met only
six weeks earlier: Would the Jewish community attend the initial worship
service and support the fledgling synagogue?

The turnout for the first service was described as "electrifying," more
than justifying the efforts of the founding families.[4] It clearly demonstrated
the need for the establishment of the synagogue. The Union of American Hebrew Congregations—the Reform Movement's umbrella organization, responded with great enthusiasm and encouragement, and provided
leading metropolitan rabbis for the pulpit through May of 1936.[5] Shortly
thereafter, the congregation moved to the Masonic Hall Lodge on nearby
Lincoln Avenue.

Earlier that year, in February, the first Synagogue School had been
established, enrolling 30 students. The enrollment would very soon rise to
62 students. Towards the end of the month, the Woman's Group of the Central Synagogue was founded with an initial membership of 30. Concurrent
with this rapid growth and organizational evolution, the synagogue's official incorporation took place in March. On April 21, 1936, the first regular
meeting of the Board of Trustees was held with William Godnick as president.[6] The new organization was up and running and was fully embraced by
the Reform Jewish community. Its rabbinical needs were being temporarily supported by the Union of American Hebrew Congregations. A permanent rabbi was needed to fully establish the synagogue and direct its future.
To fulfill this need, the board of trustees looked toward the largest Reform
rabbinical school in the nation, Hebrew Union College. Specifically, they
sought out and then selected an outspoken young rabbi with a reputation of
having a brilliant analytical mind: Rabbi Roland Gittelsohn.

In June of 1936, Gittelsohn began what would be a 17-year tenure as
rabbi to the Central Synagogue of Nassau County. During that time, membership in the synagogue would increase from the original 58 founding
families to over 900 families. A steady campaign of building and expansion would also take place during Gittelsohn's tenure. However, he would
acknowledge that despite all the apparent successes, there were some difficult times and issues that he had to face while he was at the temple.

When he took the job, he knew that very few of the families had ever belonged to a synagogue. From the start, the founders appeared to have mixed expectations of their new rabbi. "Many were not quite sure whether they wanted a rabbi who would lead or one who would cater to all their wants," he quickly learned.[7] Gittelsohn had already formed definite opinions of the role of the rabbi as both priest and prophet. Some members of the temple seemed to want a rabbi who would perform only "priestly" functions and would otherwise not involve himself with more operational and social issues that would fall under the "prophet" role. From the beginning, Gittelsohn made it clear that he would perform both the priestly and the prophetic roles as he carried out his rabbinical duties.

Early conflicts arose between the congregation and their new rabbi. Gittelsohn was never one to take criticism very well if he felt it was unjustified, and he was never one to back down in a conflict or difference of opinion. Perhaps the excellent debater within him made it more difficult at times to compromise. From time to time, when they questioned his judgment on matters he felt were clearly in his realm of expertise, he had to remind them that just as a physician must be presumed to possess more knowledge of medicine than a patient and an attorney more background in law than a client, so, too, he was the expert on Judaism.[8]

He would look back later in life at the early years at Central Synagogue and realize that he probably should have been more diplomatic on some issues and not have approached every disagreement as a debate competition to be won or lost. It was not simply principles that always drove his competitive arguments when he disagreed with policies or procedures, but he realized his own insecurities were a factor. "Like many young clergymen," he reflected, "I was in the beginning not yet secure enough within myself always to yield where I should."[9] He would look back with pride over his tenure at Central Synagogue, noting the impressive growth of the temple's membership, citing it as a "testament to a reasonably balanced relationship, though some tension persisted to the very end."[10]

The congregation would quickly see the passion of their new rabbi displayed in his High Holiday sermons, beginning on Rosh Hashanah Eve, September 17, 1936. Certainly there would be no doubt after the services that he intended to be both priest and prophet in fulfilling his rabbinical duties. As his congregants sat attentively in the Masonic Hall Lodge, Rabbi Roland Gittelsohn delivered the powerful sermons that he originally delivered in Ohio two years before: *More Human Bondage*, and *The Fast That We Have Chosen*.

For his initial High Holiday sermons as Central Synagogue's new rabbi, Gittelsohn chose to tone down some of the strident points he had annunciated two years earlier. Without diluting the power of his message, the subtle changes he made reflected both a growing degree of professional maturity as well as a sense of diplomacy appropriate to his new position. He wisely decided that his first High Holiday sermons were not a forum to potentially antagonize any of his congregation, nor to come across like an angry father berating his children. This was nicely demonstrated near the end of his 1936 Rosh Hashanah sermon. After once more, as in 1934, asking the congregation "What are we going to do about it?," he added a paragraph before launching into his two answers: We must disarm and we must sacrifice for peace.

In 1936, he diplomatically added, "First of all, let it be clearly understood by all of us that there is no simple answer to that question. There is neither a simple nor a single way of stopping human sacrifice. But there are certain things we _must_ do, certain steps we _must_ take even before we attempt anything else. These things are not panaceas, which will in themselves end war. But they are essential beginnings; they are conditions without which the other steps are fruitless."[11] Compared to the 1934 sermon, he came across to his audience as a teacher who was lecturing and educating, not scolding.

Even more revealing was the 1936 version of his Yom Kippur sermon. In it he once again told the story of Tom Mooney and how one of his congregants assumed that since he was talking about Mooney, he too must be a communist. This time he wrote, "It happens that I definitely am not!"[12] In addition, in this version he added more statistics about poverty and examples to illustrate his points. While remaining a powerful teaching experience in social justice, Gittelsohn's talk concluded with a key modification. He omitted the controversial line that stated, "The creed we must adopt is simple: First, the needs of all; second the luxury of a few. Only after _every man_ has what he _needs_ can _any man_ have what he _wants!_" As Central Synagogue's new Rabbi he never mentioned it again.

• • •

On November 18, 1936, Gittelsohn delivered the first of his peace group discussions since his ordination. Speaking at the local chapter of the National Conference of Jewish Women, he presented his talk, _If Women Wanted Peace_. In his presentation, he reiterated the main points from the fifth pamphlet of _The Jew Looks at War and Peace_. He would be a frequently invited guest speaker, covering the topics from his first book over the next two years. His notes indicate at least four more speaking engagements that included the Long Island Regional Sisterhood Boards in Jamaica, Queens on September 29, 1937, the United Order of True Sisters on November 22, 1937, and the Kew-Forest Welfare League on January 11, 1938.

SIX

Speaking Out for Peace
as the Temple Grows

Within the first year of Central Synagogue of Nassau County's existence, due to the rapid growth of its membership, the board of directors realized that they would need a larger capacity than the Masonic Hall Lodge offered for Friday night, holiday and other religious services, as well as the monthly meetings of the Women's Organization. Accordingly, they signed a long-term lease, assuring their access to the lodge while they formulated a long-range growth plan.[1] The first annual congregational meeting was held on October 5, a week after the temple's first High Holiday services. It was the first opportunity for congregants to hear reports from the temple's officers and committees, and elect officers and trustees.

On February 12, 1937, Rabbi Gittelsohn conducted the first anniversary service. He oversaw the Synagogue School classes that were conducted at the Cleveland Avenue School in Freeport, and during that time the school's enrollment steadily rose. On May 16, 1937, the first confirmation exercises for nine students were held, with Rabbi Gittelsohn conducting the service. Very quickly, adult study groups, Hebrew study groups and open forums to discuss national and international problems were initiated to meet the needs and interests of the membership.[2] All of these activities were well-suited for the energetic, activist young rabbi whose overriding interest in world affairs was dominated by his passion for pacifism.

The first year of Central Synagogue's existence proved to be successful, given its increasing enrollment and the initiation of many key programs. Fundraising went extremely well and, to a large degree, the increased growth and bright future potential that occurred was attributed to the enthusiastic efforts of their new rabbi. But synagogue membership was not the only thing that was growing in the life of Rabbi Gittelsohn that year. In early 1937, Roland and Ruth Gittelsohn learned that she was pregnant with their first child, due in the fall.

• • •

In a sermon entitled, *Is There a Road Back?* delivered later in 1937, Git-telsohn told the congregation of a panel discussion on peace that had been held six months earlier in a New York City church. Two panelists upheld a militaristic view, while another panelist argued the cause of peace. The first two panelists were newly-commissioned officers in the Army Reserve; the latter was an older man who also arrived in uniform, but it was an old faded uniform he had worn while fighting in the Great War. While the young offi-cers could speak glibly and theoretically about war, it was the older man, the veteran of the previous war who, Gittelsohn emphasized, was for peace because he knew war.

At this point, Gittelsohn acknowledged the presence of many mem-bers of the American Legion who were guests of the synagogue that night. He pointed out that these veterans also knew war because they had lived it, just as the older man in the A.E.F. uniform who supported peace had. Therefore, they should be better able to understand why war must be avoid-ed.[3] Noting that the audience contained Jews and Christians, veterans and non-veterans, and the variety of beliefs among them all, he declared that it was safe to say that there were two things that they all had in common that bound them together. First, Gittelsohn stated, all of them hated war and secondly, all of them wanted peace "…and especially at this moment all of us are asking the same question: 'Is there a road back? Is there a road that leads from war to peace?'"[4]

Wanting peace and hating war isn't enough, he argued. Using the examples of medical plagues, he pointed out that hating diseases wasn't enough. It took hard work to defeat a disease—man had to pay the cost in order to accomplish that goal. And that, according to Gittelsohn, was the problem—we haven't been willing to pay the cost of peace:

> We want someone to give us peace as a gift. We pray for peace, and then we confidently sit back as if we expected God to lean down out of heaven and pat us lovingly on the back and say to us: "Here my children, you've been good today. So I'm going to give you peace." But let's not fool ourselves, my friends. Peace isn't that easy to get. Peace isn't the product of a wish-bone. Peace is one of the hardest things humanity has ever sought! Peace has a price on it! Do you know when you and I will finally attain peace? Only when we're willing to meet that price![5]

Gittelsohn had stressed that peace would only become a reality when peo-ple proactively worked to achieve it. There could be no shortcuts and the costs would be steep. He proposed to the congregation that they look at the costs and if they would be willing to pay those costs to attain peace.

The first of those costs no doubt seemed radical to the congregation. He declared: "…each nation, in order to achieve harmony, must be will-ing to sacrifice some small part of its own sovereignty."[6] In all likelihood,

Gittelsohn was referring to the League of Nations, an organization that the United States never joined. He immediately took pains to assure the audience that he did not want to be misunderstood; that his love of the United States and patriotism in defense of America, the land that delivered freedom and opportunity to his family, was second to none. He went on to state that all nations, not just the United States, should consider sacrificing part of their sovereignty as needed. "Peace of any kind means a partnership, doesn't it?" he asked.[7] Just as each of the thirteen colonies had to yield a little of its sovereignty when forming our country, so too must all nations do the same in the quest for true peace. Only then will that goal be achievable.

The next cost to pay in the quest for world peace is the willingness to give up temporary profits of war. Once again, Gittelsohn railed against the armament industry and its influence that he perceived as pro-war. To illustrate the madness that he sensed, he pointed out that in 1932, both warring countries of China and Japan were buying their weapons from the same arms manufacturer in England. One day the representatives from each government happened to arrive at the British firm at the same time and spent the day comparing their munitions purchases and the prices that each were paying. The two "then issued to the company a joint ultimatum for lower prices. A fine business, isn't it?"[8] Gittelsohn asked with disgust.

Rabbi Gittelsohn then went on to the third cost to be paid to achieve peace in the world. This third cost was to once and for all, "...get rid of an old idea that most of us still have, the idea that any worth-while purpose can be accomplished through violence or through war ... today war is nothing but suicide,—senseless, shameless suicide!"[9] Appealing to the veterans of the World War in the audience, he pointed out that they all had clear aims when they went to war and that they fought the war to end all wars and to establish peace. Yet, the world was now closer to war than it ever was. "You wanted to save the world for democracy, didn't you? But look what's happened to that democracy!"[10] Dictatorship and fascism were now on the rise. "You won a war," he points out to the veterans, "but that victory didn't accomplish either of your purposes."[11]

Gittelsohn ended his sermon by asking: Is there a road back? Unequivocally he stated that there is, but that road wasn't simple or easy. We have to stop pretending or trying to bargain our way out of the dilemma, he declared. We have to stop trying to buy world peace on the cheap. "Let's face the facts and face them honestly without pretense. Are we willing to pay the price of peace?"[12] He, Gittelsohn, was willing to pay the price, no matter how high. He begged his audience to stand with him so that together they may be willing to pay the cost of peace.

SEVEN

Popular Front

On December 12, 1937, the American gunboat USS *Panay* was patrolling the Yangzte River in China when it, along with three Standard Oil tankers, was attacked and sunk by Japanese aircraft, resulting in 51 casualties from the *Panay* alone. The Japanese would apologize and pay the United States an indemnity of over two million dollars. However, even as world events such as the *Panay* incident were fanning Gittelsohn's pacifist passions, the anti-war movement, as a whole, was evolving and was beginning to fragment. By 1937, its emphasis was gradually ebbing away from pure pacifism and an endorsement of American isolationism to one of multinational collaboration against the threats posed by fascist regimes. Almost simultaneously occurring with the sinking of the *Panay*, the anti-war movement would alter its course dramatically.

As early as 1935 it was the activities of communist radicals that began to shift the movement's goals away from isolationism and towards one of a collective security arrangement on behalf of a "Popular Front" against fascism. Influenced by the Seventh World Congress of the Communist International in August of 1935, the efforts of communist students were now intended to shift the movement's foreign policy away from neutrality and focus on the endorsement of collective efforts among the United States, the Soviet Union, and other anti-fascist states to prevent military aggression by Germany, Italy, and Japan.[1]

By late 1935 there was a grassroots movement within the socialist League for Industrial Democracy (LID) to push for amalgamation with the National Student League (NSL). In October of 1935, the executive boards of both organizations recommended their merger into a new organization, the American Student Union (ASU), and this new organization's governing structure would be dominated by members who were former National Student Union activists.

The event that did the most to accelerate the emphasis of the anti-war coalitions as typified by radical student peace movement was the Spanish

Civil War. In July of 1936, military generals of the Spanish Republican Army, fearing the collapse of Spain into anarchy, staged a *coup d'état* in Spanish Morocco. The rebellion quickly spread throughout Spain, precipitating a civil war. The elected government, with its supporting factions of communists, anarchists, and various other left-wing groups, became known as the Loyalists or Republicans, whereas the rebelling military along with other elements became known as the Nationalists. The Nationalists, led by General Francisco Franco, soon had the support of the governments of Nazi Germany and fascist Italy. The Loyalists had strong support from the Soviet Union. International Brigades, consisting of volunteers from many countries, including the United States, traveled to Spain to fight for the Loyalists. It was in Spain that many historians note that a "dress rehearsal" for the Second World War took place between 1936 and 1939.

The Spanish Civil War served as the wakeup call for a generation of student activists who had been lost in isolationist slumber.[2] During the early 1930s, most students, Roland Gittelsohn included, assumed that the United States could be the vanguard in preserving peace by adhering to a policy of strict neutrality. In many ways, advocates of strict neutrality assumed that it was purely economic factors and profit motives that drove American entrance into world conflicts. Even as they uneasily read about the developing situations in Europe and the Far East, adherents of the anti-war Oxford Pledge and organizations such as the War Resisters League (which Gittelsohn was a member of) clung to the advocacy of strict isolationism and American neutrality.

The civil war in Spain would be the pivot point that would discredit United States neutrality in the eyes of many students, providing communist ASU members with many allies in their drive to convert the student movement from isolationism to collective security and anti-fascist interventionism.[3] Nearly 3,000 Americans volunteered to go to Spain and fight for the Loyalists as members of the Abraham Lincoln Battalion. Over five hundred were students and the majority of the volunteers were members of the American Communist Party. Over 700 Americans would die fighting for the Loyalists as part of the battalion.

The *Panay* incident of December 1937 was merely the last of a series of world events that year that worked to push the American anti-war movement away from isolationism and towards a Popular Front against fascism. In April of 1937, a thoroughly disgusted world observed the Nationalist forces, supported largely by the German *Luftwaffe*, destroy the Spanish city of Guernica, an event soon to be immortalized in Pablo Picasso's memorable painting. In July of 1937, Japanese military forces engaged in a battle with Chinese forces at the Marco Polo Bridge near Beijing that served as a pretext for a full-scale Japanese invasion of the Chinese mainland. On

October 5, 1937, President Franklin D. Roosevelt gave a speech indicating he would shift from American isolationism to interventionism on the world scene.

Speaking to a large crowd in Chicago and on broadcast radio, the President began by lamenting the current state of world events. He pointed out that in direct discord with the Kellogg-Briand Pact that outlawed war as a means of resolving disputes between nations, in so-called times of peace people were ruthlessly being murdered with bombs from the air and ships were being sunk without cause or warning. Roosevelt went on to issue a dire warning:

> Let no one imagine that America will escape, that America may expect mercy, that this Western hemisphere will not be attacked and will continue tranquilly and peacefully to carry on the ethics and arts of civilization.... The peace, freedom, and the security of ninety per cent of the world are being jeopardized by the remaining ten per cent who are threatening a breakdown of all international law.... The moral consciousness of the world ... must be aroused to the cardinal necessity of honoring the sanctity of treaties, of respecting the rights and liberties of others and of putting an end to acts of international aggression.[4]

The President was issuing a warning to his countrymen that the situations in Europe and the Pacific were spiraling out of control and that as much as he and all Americans would find it abhorrent, the United States might become entangled in the worldwide conflict.

Roosevelt next compared the actions that the world must take to the actions taken by the health community when combating the spread of disease to prevent epidemics. "When an epidemic of physical disease starts to spread, the community approves and joins in a quarantine of the patients in order to protect the health of the community against the spread of the disease."[5] War is a contagion, he stated, whether it was declared or undeclared. Like an epidemic, it could spread far from its place of origin. The United States was determined to stay out of war, but this might not be possible due to circumstances beyond the country's control. "We are adopting such measures as will minimize our risk of involvement, but we cannot have complete protection in a world of disorder in which confidence and security have broken down."[6]

With his Quarantine Speech, Roosevelt's remarks signaled an abandonment of isolationism, the need for collective security, and a preparedness to face down aggressors, peacefully if possible but by force if necessary.[7] While angering isolationists like Gittelsohn, FDR's speech provided strong support to leaders in the American Student Union. At the time ASU leaders hoped to transform the ASU officially into a pro-collective security organization. That was a move which would alienate the student movement's Trotskyist, Young People's Socialist League (YPSL), and pacifist minorities, while retaining the support from liberals, who constituted a majority of the national student body.[8] They made their move two months after FDR's speech.

At their national convention held at Vassar College in December 1937, both opposing factions—interventionists versus pacifists—came prepared to do battle over whether the pro- or the anti-collective security stance should become the ASU's official position. The key issue emerging for the fight to come was the Oxford Pledge which advocated total pacifism. The topic was a tremendous source of friction in both the pre-convention preparatory meetings as well as the convention itself, which was held over the Christmas school break.

Although seemingly allowing equal debate on the subject, in fact, the pro-collective security advocates (who were largely members of the communist faction) had used manipulative tactics to achieve their goal. One pro-collective female security activist later gloated over the disingenuous behavior of the communist students to achieve their goal. She boasted that, "The story is that the YCL (Young Communists League) pulled in a lot of delegates who never even registered to vote on it. Anyway, the whole thing is very sweet."[9]

Before the final vote for or against collective security, the Young People's Socialist League (YPSL) was privileged to have the Socialist Party's most eloquent spokesman, Norman Thomas, address the convention. "Any involvement by Washington in these conflicts would only serve the interests of American imperialism and militarism," he warned. "...We are not anxious to join the collective suicide club as proponents of collective action by governments would have us do."[10] Despite Thomas' impassioned arguments, most of the delegates were unimpressed. By a lopsided vote, the convention voted 282 to 108 to drop the isolationist Oxford Pledge from the ASU platform, and endorse collective security instead.

The ASU proceeded to pass resolutions naming aggressors on the international scene, like Japan, as well seeking to boycott them. To reinforce their new position, the ASU embraced the principles outlined by President Roosevelt's Quarantine Speech, although Roosevelt would not yet follow up his speech with any concrete action. The ASU president, Joseph Lash, requested and received from Roosevelt a letter of welcome to the delegates of the convention, which the ASU highly publicized. While now promoting a national policy of collective security, the ASU still clung to policies that opposed United States preparations for war, including the "skyrocketing military budget," and mandatory ROTC—positions the organization had avowed since its founding.[11]

In 1938 the ASU's sizable dissenting factions continued supporting the Oxford Pledge. This included the YSPLs, the Trotskyists, and other pacifists like Gittelsohn, and they broke away from the ASU. They formed their own organization, the Youth Committee for the Oxford Pledge (YCOP), soon to be renamed the Youth Committee Against War (YCAW). This new organization attempted to compete with the ASU for the hearts and minds of the American student population as well as the youth of America. They did so by organizing a separate student strike for 1938 in competition to the annual strike called by the ASU. But in the end, the ASU was able to draw the lion's share of student interest. They out-organized the YCAW and effectively invoked FDR and his Quarantine Speech to appeal to the majority of liberal students who were admirers of the President.

The final defeat of the YCAW anti-war faction occurred in August 1938 at the second World Youth Congress (WYC) held in New York City and Poughkeepsie. The American Student Union's goal was to translate the success of its student strike against war into an international demonstration of student solidarity. Attracting more than 500 delegates from 53 nations, the World Youth Congress meeting concluded by adopting a strong collective security statement, the Vassar Peace Pact. This enraged the Youth Committee Against War and proved to be a fatal blow to it and its isolationist allies. The pact codified the delegates' pledge to take the necessary concerted action to prevent aggression and to give effective assistance to the victims of "…aggression and to refrain from participating in any aggression whether in the form of essential war material or other financial assistance."[12]

The collective security stance of the World Youth Congress added greatly to the sense of progress and momentum among student activists. Ulterior motives of the ASU's communist leadership were no less important as a driving force away from isolationism and towards collective security. Demonstrating their dogmatic loyalty, as well as their spectacular naiveté, ASU's communist student leaders regarded the USSR as a leftist utopia, a worker's paradise. A Popular Front security, they believed, was essential for the protection of the Soviet Union against its fascist enemies.[13]

But the ASU's importance and dominance would come to a crashing halt a year later when Adolf Hitler, widely known to be a rabid anti-communist, signed a non-aggression pact with the Soviet Union. The West was stunned by the hypocrisy of Joseph Stalin and the Molotov-Ribbentrop Pact, signed on August 23, 1939. Here, American peace advocates were in many instances working for a Popular Front solely for the protection of the Soviet Union from fascist Nazi Germany, and now Stalin signed a non-aggression pact with the devil incarnate. The non-communist members of the ASU abruptly abandoned the organization. The ASU, which would meet for the last time in 1941, would be exposed for the communist front organization that it largely was.

Roland Gittelsohn had never been an ASU member, but instead was a pacifist and a member of the War Resisters League. As such he opposed the precepts espoused by President Roosevelt in his Quarantine Speech. Gittelsohn frequently commented on what he considered the hypocrisy of the president, saying he seemed to talk out of both sides of his mouth when it came to armaments and national defense. Gittelsohn would continue to speak out against war, promote isolationism, and argue against the economic incentives that he believed threatened to entangle us in another overseas war.

Rabbi Gittelsohn would continue to restate the lessons of the First World War in many fiery sermons. War, he believed, must be avoided at all costs. But by May 1940, given Hitler's numerous conquests, Gittelsohn would begin to have his doubts about the appropriateness of absolute pacifism.

Eight

"The Next War
for Democracy
Will Kill Democracy"

In 1938 Europe continued to fall under the domination of Nazi Germany. That year, on March 12, the *Anschluss*, or annexation of Austria into Germany took place. For years, Germany had been pressuring the Austrian government to submit to annexation, and there was a sizable part of the Austrian population that favored the action. Austrian Chancellor Kurt Schushnigg attempted to resist Germany, but bowing to pressure from both German and Austrian Nazis, he scheduled a national referendum to vote on the issue. In spite of the chancellor's intentions and hopes that Austria would remain independent, the Nazi Party in Austria engineered a *coup d'état* on March 11 and the following day, Hitler annexed Austria.

The actions of Nazi Germany against Austria infuriated many Americans, especially those, who like Gittelsohn, loathed fascism. He would address his congregation less than three weeks later on April 1 and deliver a stinging denunciation of fascism and war. His ardent opposition to war would not be a surprise, but his emphasis on the dangers of fascism would not be directed toward Germany, but rather to the threat of fascism that he perceived arising in the United States. The bulk of his wrath would be directed towards legislation pending in the United States Congress.

In a sermon he called, "Should We Fight for Democracy?," Gittelsohn began by admitting that he, as a pacifist, was going through a period of discouragement. To him, mankind's short memory was frustrating, as he noted that it had only been nineteen years since the end of the World War, when the country had vowed never again to fall into the abyss of war. Yet, he exclaimed, had we kept that vow, the congregation would have no need for a sermon with a title that asks if we should fight for democracy.

He told of conversations he had with two members of the congregation

70

after the announcement of the Nazi annexation of Austria. Knowing that their rabbi was a pacifist, one congregant asked him whether the actions of Germany had changed his opinions. He said that he, too, hated war; he too loved peace and wanted peace. But then he explained to Gittelsohn his conclusion that force must be met with force. "The only way to stop Hitler is to smash him. Much as I love peace, … I wouldn't hesitate to enlist tomorrow in a war against fascism."[1] Less than a day later, a woman from the congregation who had a son nearly of draft age told her rabbi, "I would gladly sacrifice my son in a war against Hitler and for democracy."[2]

Gittelsohn explained that he wanted these conversations to be the background for the evening's sermon as, in a sense, he would be speaking to these two people through the entire audience as they pondered the dilemma posed by the sermon's title. It seemed to him that there were certain things these two people had forgotten—as most of the audience likely had forgotten also—and it would be his role to remind them of these things. He would be speaking plainly and bluntly, especially to those who would be ready to take up arms.

Reminding the audience that it wasn't the first time that many were ready to take up arms in a fight for democracy, he quoted an eloquent statement that claimed, among other things, that right is more precious than peace. Were these the words of the two previously mentioned congregants? No, Gittelsohn informed them. They were "…not the words of 1938; they come from 1917; and they're the words of President Woodrow Wilson, spoken 21 years ago tomorrow, when he asked Congress to declare war."[3] Read these words over and over, he advised those who would willingly go to war for democracy, and remember what these words resulted in for Americans in 1917 and 1918.

In the next part of his sermon, Gittelsohn vented his frustrations, passions and absolute hatred of fascism. In preparing for this address, he had often asked himself, "What's the use? If history hasn't taught people anything how can I?" With bitter cynicism, he exclaimed, "We fought to save the world, to make the world safe for democracy, didn't we? What we did in the name of democracy sounds like a funeral dirge."[4] After listing the horrendous cost of blood and treasure, he demanded to know, "Well, where is the democracy that these 10 million boys died for? Answer me, where is it?"[5] How could he make them see and how could he impress these things on them, he asked the congregation. "If I thought it would do any good, believe me, I'd get down on my knees this very moment and plead with you…. Let's at least be willing to learn that we can't defend democracy by war!"[6]

Democracy, he informed them, could no more be created by war than love could be created by war. After all, democracy is the opposite of war.

To illustrate the preposterous idea that war will result in democracy, he used the following example: a doctor believes he can prevent the spread of scarlet fever by infecting the population with typhoid. True that the scarlet fever would be wiped out, but the Pyrrhic victory would of course result in the death of the population, not preserve it. "That's the only way war will wipe out fascism;—if it destroys the last living remnant of humanity and civilization, then perhaps the monkeys who remain will have more sense than to be fascists."[7] Gittelsohn continued his analysis:

> We've forgotten that fascism was itself created by war and thrives on war. After all, what is fascism if it isn't an extension of the psychology of war? … You can't teach men for 4 years how best to kill and then suddenly to think human life is sacred. You can't tell men for 4 years that everyone must obey an absolute leader and then suddenly expect them to recognize individual freedom…. We must understand that war and fascism are like the two sides of a coin; you can't have one without the other…. The last war created fascism, and the next war isn't going to end it … the next war for democracy will make fascism supreme. The next war for democracy will kill democracy. Remember that! It will stifle it and strangle it and choke it! After the next war, democracy will be something to read about in books.[8]

Like most pacifists at that time, Gittelsohn was haunted by the memories and the "lessons" of the Great War and couldn't envision any circumstance that would justify going to war or serving in the military. His view of the military as a fascist "undemocratic" culture was naïve, uninformed, and largely ironic given that he would serve honorably and effectively as a member of the United States armed forces not long after.

At that point in his sermon, Gittelsohn stated that on the day the United States entered its next war for democracy, America would automatically become fascist. What was the basis for such a seemingly outrageous assertion? The answer lay in legislation then being proposed in Congress. The Sheppard-May Bill, a wartime industrial mobilization bill introduced in both houses on January 6, 1937, represented to Gittelsohn as big a threat domestically as Nazi aggression did overseas. The House's version, the May Bill (HR 9604), sponsored by Military Affairs Committee chairman Andrew J. May, was then under debate in the House. To Gittelsohn and others, it represented nothing less than an executive branch power grab by President Roosevelt, one that would make him a dictator.

The expressed purpose of the May Bill was to take the profits out of war, and the bill had many supporters such as the American Legion, the Secretaries of War and the Navy, and influential presidential advisor Bernard Baruch. Gittelsohn insisted that the bill did not remove the profits from war, and he was actually correct. The flawed legislation was described by critic Senator Gerald Nye of North Dakota as a "…very peculiar kind of bargain. It offers something for every shade of believer in what ought to be done in time of war,"[9] but actually offered pious hopes of eliminating excessive war profits, while offering no concrete means of achieving such elimination.[10]

To Gittelsohn and others this was bad enough, but it was other provisions of the bill that outraged him even further. Referring to the expanded powers of the president under this proposed law, he noted that, "He could draft every man in America within the age limit for fighting."[11] In addition, he pointed out to the congregation that the president would be allowed to freeze wages and fix prices. Senator Nye described the legislation thusly: "In general, the bill provides for an undisguised dictatorship to be set up under the executive."[12]

In the Minority Report of the Military Affairs Committee, dissent to the bill was expressed by Texas Representative Maury Maverick who denounced the bill as taking absolutely no profits out of war and giving to the president "gigantic, impartial, dictatorial power of the most extreme kind."[13]

"Well, how do you like that?" Gittelsohn asked his audience. "Is that fascism or isn't it? Of course it is! You know it is!" he thundered. "Then remember that when the next war for democracy begins, that's what you and I are apt to have in this land."[14] Did this all mean that he was an isolationist, he rhetorically asked. No, he explained, not at all. "I am an isolationist only in this sense: isolation from everything that leads to war; cooperation with everything that makes for peace." He believed in the need to defend democracy, but not through war. "I don't propose to defend democracy by killing it. We can defend democracy by preserving it and protecting it at home, not by passing the May Bill."[15] Gittelsohn's solutions to defend democracy included economic cooperation with other nations, boycotts of all belligerent nations, and other means of non-violent defense.

Before ending his sermon with an illustrative story from ancient history, Gittelsohn looked down at his congregation and explained that time constraints prohibited him from going into more details on his theories for the preservation of democracy. He did, however, issue a dire warning: "And that is that we should not, we cannot, we dare not, we must not fight a war for democracy. War will be the end of democracy."[16]

The United States Congress never did pass the Sheppard-May Bill. Instead, it passed the Act of May 17, 1938. This Act amended the Vinson-Trammel Act of 1934, legislation that dealt with navy shipbuilding, in an effort to regulate shipbuilder's excess profits.

NINE

"On Three Things Does the Whole World Depend"

As the United States continued its struggle to recover from the Depression, factions with strong isolationist sentiments clashed with others who warned of the dangers of Nazi aggression. Meantime the Popular Front, which advocated unified resistance to fascist aggression, continued to gain influence over the anti-war movement. As the Popular Front's conflict with advocates of unconditional peace raged on, Hitler began to escalate his aggressive advances on the world stage.

First Hitler set his sights on Czechoslovakia. He used the three million ethnic Germans living in the Czech portion of the country known as Sudetenland as a basis for Nazi Germany's claims on Czechoslovakia, when addressing its president Edvard Beneš. Though he agitated for Sudetenland's autonomy, Hitler used the "Sudeten Crisis" as a pretext to launch the first phase of his intended wars.[1]

As the crisis deepened, Great Britain and France made it clear they did not intend to go to war over Sudetenland. Hitler planned to stage "atrocities" against ethnic Germans in Sudetenland as his excuse for ordering his armies into the country. It was the active efforts of Prime Minister Neville Chamberlain of Great Britain that ultimately ended the crisis. However, he did so in a very poor and cowardly manner.

Chamberlain had proactively agitated for a peace conference and had agreed to meet Hitler and negotiate without Czechoslovakian President Beneš even attending the sessions. Stepping back from his initial demand that Czechoslovakia be overrun by the German war machine and incorporated into Nazi Germany, Hitler at the last minute changed his demand and insisted on annexing the Sudetenland. On behalf of England and France, Chamberlain agreed to give in to Hitler, feeling that it would be Hitler's last

territorial request. The Munich Agreement, a classic example of appeasement of an aggressor country, was signed on September 29, 1938. The next
day, Neville Chamberlain returned to England and announced to ecstatic
crowds that the agreement had attained "peace for our time."

Less than five months later, Hitler would overrun the rest of Czechoslovakia and less than five months after that the Second World War would
begin in Europe with Hitler invading Poland.

• • •

On October 1, 1938, Rabbi Roland Gittelsohn would deliver one of the
most significant sermons of his career. On first glance it would appear to be
another in a series of stinging rebukes on the world situation and the continual slide into a state of war. However, it touched on several issues affecting war and peace around the world, not just concerning Nazi Germany,
whose policies and leadership he totally despised. For the first time, his
notes for the sermon reveal his thoughts on the worsening plight of Jews in
Palestine and the deteriorating relations between Jews and Arabs.

Gittelsohn's speech also conveyed three key concepts on which the
world depends, based on the first-century writings of Rabbi Simeon ben
Gamliel. "*Al sh'loshaw d'vawrim haw-olawn ka-yawm,* he said; on three
things does the whole world depend; on truth, on justice, and on peace."[2]
For Gittelsohn, the significance and relevance of these three points would
only grow over the years. Ultimately, at the end of World War II, he would
come back to these three concepts in his analysis of why pacifism was
doomed to fail.

Gittelsohn's notes indicate the title for the sermon simply as "Shabbos
Shuvah, 5699–1938." Shabbos Shuvah is the Sabbath that falls in between
Rosh Hashanah and Yom Kippur. Apart from Yom Kippur it is the holiest
Sabbath of the whole Jewish year. As Gittelsohn explained to his congregation, Shabbos Shuvah is correctly translated into "the Sabbath of Returning." "I don't think there ever was a time before in human history when the
real, literal meaning of this day was needed so desperately," he declared.[3]
And that, he explained, was because Americans like to move forward and
not return or look back. Why look back when mankind has accomplished
so much? Perhaps it was because of this feeling, he suggested, that Shabbos
Shuvah had diminished in importance in the lives of modern Jews. "And
yet," he stated, "the sad thing is that it is precisely and exactly the Jews of
this century, those who want it least, who need it most."[4]

In spite of mankind's accomplishments, Gittelsohn assured the congregation that they indeed had lost something from the past. He pointed
out that we "most definitely and assuredly do need to return…. And on
this Shabbos Shuvah, this Sabbath of Returning, we need to return to that

something."[5] That something was the teachings of Rabbi Simeon ben Gamliel, who had lived before the Jewish Temple in Jerusalem was destroyed by the Romans (CE 70), nearly 2,000 years earlier.

Rabbi Simeon ben Gamliel's simple but eloquent emphasis on truth, justice, and peace would remain with Gittelsohn his entire lifetime.[6] Gittelsohn told his congregation that there doesn't seem to be anything profound or spectacular about this simple statement. That is, he pointed out, unless you mean the eternal eloquence of great and abiding and permanent truth. Once again, he repeated Rabbi ben Gamliel's mandate to humanity.

Gittelsohn's sermon evaluated the volatile world situation with this aphorism in mind. First, he considered truth. His cynicism of international politics came to the forefront in his discussion of truth. Nations, he said, do not believe in the truth—they have perverted, twisted and rejected truth and in its place have substituted expediency. For his prime example he cited the ongoing war in Spain. It is a ridiculous myth that there is a civil war going on in Spain, he maintained. He then pointed out several examples to make his point. He noted that there were close to 100,000 German and Italian troops in Spain as well as more than 800 military planes, flown by the forces of Franco but manufactured in Germany or Italy. Gittelsohn next pointed out that months before the war started there were as many as 36 newspapers published in Spain but paid for by the Nazis. After stating that Mussolini was also financing the war efforts of General Franco, he explained in exasperation that "...these facts are not secrets! You know them, I know them, all the governments and nations know them. And yet they insist on denying truth."[7]

To further elaborate how the truth was distorted in regard to Spain's ongoing war, Gittelsohn turned his audience's attention to the Non-Intervention Agreement. This agreement had been signed in August of 1936, followed by the establishment of the Non-Intervention Committee that first met the following month. While originating with the British and the French, this committee also included representatives from Fascist Italy and Nazi Germany. In all, 24 nations were represented on the committee. Its expressed purpose was to keep the rest of the world neutral in regard to the Spanish Civil War and to prevent the flow of war materials into Spain. Consistently, Germany, Italy, and the Soviet Union violated the agreement and sent war materials to the opposing sides, as the Fascists and the Communists used the war in Spain as their proxy war.

When addressing his congregation, Gittelsohn vociferously protested the hypocrisy of the committee's actions. To the passionate young rabbi, the committee's very existence was the ultimate lie. It was enough to make the very corpse of truth turn over in its grave, he lectured. "Non-intervention! We might just as well call Germany the land of the free and the home of the brave; it would be just as close to the truth."[8] He angrily declared if anything in the world had caused intervention it was the Non-Intervention Committee, the very committee that was formed to prevent it.

As his congregation was digesting this fact, Gittelsohn then added more fuel to the fire by pointing to the brutal distortion of truth in light of its German Nazi participants' and others' vicious designs. The Non-Intervention Committee had announced a few weeks earlier that it needed to suspend its operations due to the lack of funding. "And do you know who came to its financial rescue to the tune of 36,000 [English] pounds in valuable and precious foreign exchange?," Gittelsohn thundered. "Our newspapers didn't tell us of about that. The government of Germany. Just imagine that! The government of Germany rescuing the committee on non-intervention!"[9] Anticipating many surprised expressions on his congregant's faces, he explained that the Nazis were smart enough all along to know that the whole thing was a big smoke screen, a convenient bluff to help the very thing it presumed to prevent.[10]

England and France were also complicit, he charged. They too, were smart enough to see through the smoke screen, but they willfully turned a blind eye to real workings of the committee. With disgust, he added: "That's how much they're concerned with the truth." To summarize his analysis of the first of Rabbi Simeon ben Gamliel's three concepts, Gittelsohn concluded by saying, "If, then, the first pillar on which the world stands is truth, it shouldn't surprise us in the least that today that world seems to be a bit wobbly and unsteady and weak."[11]

Gittelsohn next moved on to justice—the second of the pillars elucidated by Rabbi Simeon ben Gamliel. He noted that this second pillar was not much sturdier than the first one he had just finished discussing. For his analysis of the true meaning of justice in the world, he chose to make his primary teaching point by using the Arab-Jewish conflict that was ongoing in Palestine. It is the first time that the subject appears in the notes of his early sermons and serves to emphasize his passionate belief in Zionism, a conviction strongly influenced by the teachings of his father, Reuben.

Gittelsohn was well aware that before the Great War ended, British Foreign Minister Arthur Balfour issued a policy statement in a letter to Lord Rothschild that came to be known as the Balfour Declaration. This short letter, dated November 2, 1917, expressed "sympathy with Jewish Zionist aspirations," proclaiming "His Majesty's Government views with favour the establishment in Palestine of a national home for the Jewish people...."[12] In turn, the Balfour Declaration was formally approved at the San Remo Conference on April 24, 1920. Formally known as the San Remo Resolution on Palestine, it also incorporated the requirement stated in the Balfour Declaration that in establishing the Jewish homeland, "nothing should be done which may prejudice the civil and religious rights of existing non-Jewish communities in Palestine."[13] Palestine was to become a Mandate, administered by Great Britain.

However, the presence of the industrious Jews who were buying the land, improving and modernizing areas of the region, was greatly resented by the native Arab population. Stormy relations between the Jews and the Arabs became a way of life in the British Mandate of Palestine. A series of anti-Jewish riots broke out, the first major one in August of 1929. In April of 1936, violence again flared, precipitating the Arab Revolt that would flare up over the next few years.

The British response to the Arab Revolt was initially tepid. The British were hesitant to further erode any potential goodwill between themselves and the Arabs. That is because the British sensed that an international conflict was looming in the near future and they realized they would depend on Arab oil for their war aims.

In July 1936, the British government established the Peel Commission to investigate the Jewish-Arab conflict. A year later the commission concluded there were irreconcilable differences between the Jews and the Arabs in that region. They specifically noted that "Their cultural and social life, their ways of thought and conduct, are as incompatible as their national aspirations."[14] The Arab desire for independence, coupled with their hatred and fear of a Jewish national homeland were the underlying causes of the riots and the strike. The solution recommended by the Peel commission was to partition Palestine into separate Jewish and Arab states. The Arab leaders rejected the partition plan outright. The Zionist Congress accepted it with qualifications—against the wishes of a substantial minority.[15]

It was in this context that Gittelsohn addressed his congregation on October 1, 1938, and used his disgust with the ongoing Arab riots as his teaching point concerning the second of Rabbi Simeon ben Gamliel's pillars on which the world depended—that of justice.

There hadn't been any justice in international politics for a long time, Gittelsohn declared. So long, in fact, that he doubted that any of them could remember what it looked like. Look only to Palestine, he offered, for the prime example of the twisted form of justice that exists in the world today. With pride he pointed out that Jews went to Palestine and in 20 years created a garden out of a desert, and built cities, schools, universities, and hospitals. They created a society that was a shining example of social justice in action. They also lifted the Arab in peace from his miserable existence, cleaned him, cured him, and served him. This was accomplished in two decades and then what happened? "The world watches while two gangsters light up a fire of terrorism against us, and the world pretends to be blind, and the world does nothing. That's justice!" he raged. It wasn't the kind of justice Simeon ben Gamliel meant, but to Gittelsohn, it seemed to be the only kind that other nations seemed to know.[16] While it is not entirely clear who the two gangsters are who he referred to, one was almost certainly the Grand Mufti Haj Amin al-Husseini, a notorious pro–Nazi antisemite.

Gittelsohn mentioned two other examples of the sad state of modern justice to emphasize his point. He asked his audience, what kind of justice did the Spanish Republic receive? The justice of Francisco Franco! It was the same kind of justice that Czechoslovakia had just received at Munich. "Perhaps it's a good thing that Simeon ben Gamliel isn't here to see what a mockery the nations have made of the truth and the justice he loved," he somberly reflected.[17]

Rabbi Simeon ben Gamliel and generations of Jews after him, loved peace—the third pillar on which the world depends. The point that Gittelsohn wanted to drive home to his audience was that it wasn't an accident that Simeon ben Gamliel placed peace immediately after justice and truth. It was intended to be the last of the three pillars. In modern times, he noted, man has tried every possible method of achieving peace. There is only one method they haven't tried:

> …that's the method of righteousness; that's the method of ethics and morals. It's the only method that we haven't tried and it's the only method that will work.… It's strange that … we haven't learned that yet when Simeon ben Gamliel knew it 1,900 years ago. That's why he spoke of truth and of justice and then of peace. Once we enthrone truth and once we establish justice, we won't have to worry about peace.[18]

Promote the truth, establish justice, and only then will there be peace. This is what Rabbi Gittelsohn called for on this Shabbos Shuvah, this Sabbath of Returning: a real return to ancient truths as exemplified by the world's necessary pillars described nearly two thousand years before by Simeon ben Gamliel. It was the three pillars described by that venerated first-century rabbi that Roland Gittelsohn would once again turn to in 1945 at the end of World War II, when he would reflect on the failure of pacifism in preventing the most horrendous war that mankind has ever known.

TEN

Munich

On September 30, 1938, Prime Minister Neville Chamberlain returned to England with the Munich Agreement in his hand to the deafening cheers of adoring citizens. Invited to come immediately to Buckingham Palace to personally report to King George VI, it took him an hour and a half to make the nine-mile journey due to the massive crowds. Afterward, he returned to 10 Downing Street where he addressed the large throng of people in the street from a window upstairs on the first floor. Recalling the words that Benjamin Disraeli spoke on his return from the Congress of Berlin in 1878, he told the crowd, "My good friends, this is the second time there has come back from Germany to Downing Street peace with honor. I believe it is peace for our time. Now I recommend you go home and sleep quietly in your beds."[1] Chamberlain received overwhelming support from the British press and had great support in the House of Commons during the October 3 debates on the Agreement. One notable exception to the tide of support was Winston Churchill, who proclaimed, "England has been offered a choice between war and shame. She has chosen shame, and will get war."[2]

On October 1, 1938, German troops marched into the Sudetenland. Four days later, Edvard Beneš resigned as president of Czechoslovakia and would go into exile in Great Britain. In the United States, public opinion was largely supportive of the Munich Agreement, with 59 percent of those polled expressing the opinion that England and France did the right thing in giving in to Germany instead of going to war.[3]

Among the sizable minority of Americans who opposed the Chamberlain agreement was Roland Gittelsohn. It would take him several weeks before he could speak in public about Munich, and he broke his silence on Friday, October 21. Being so opinionated about the evil he believed the agreement represented, it would take him two sermons to thoroughly express his thoughts.

He called his sermon, "Peace with Honor or Dishonor without Peace: Which is It?" He began by explaining his view that the outcome of the

80

Munich conference was self-evident. At first, he did not see any point in discussing it. But then he realized that there was likely much confusion over Munich; that people looked at the result and didn't know whether to laugh or cry. And that was his purpose that evening, to clear up any confusion. The suddenness of the agreement that seemed to prevent war was an intoxicant, but now, "it's the morning after," and "the drunk is ended."[4] It was time to forget about laughing and crying and it was time to sober up and look at what really happened at Munich and what the likely results would be.

The first question that the congregation all should consider was this: How much did Hitler actually accomplish at Munich? Was there really a genuine negotiation? "Was it a case of legitimate bargaining, or was it one of barbaric, brutal brow-beating? This is the first question we've got to ask."[5] With disgust, he informed the congregation that the answer to this question was easy because the sad, shameful truth was that Hitler was handed everything free of charge. The only difference was instead of gobbling down his dinner in one gulp, "...the vulture was persuaded to eat a little slower and finish his prey on October 10th instead of October 1st. That was the phenomenal diplomatic success for which the world has been applauding Chamberlain!"[6] Hitler had been handed 21 percent of the territory and 23 percent of the population of Czechoslovakia without any strings or reciprocal obligations. "That's Chamberlain's idea of compromise! ... That's what Hitler got at Munich and that's why the answer to our first question tonight is unfortunately so easy."[7]

The second question posed by Gittelsohn was not so easy, but was even more important—just how much was compromised by this unprecedented sacrifice of land, materials, and population? To answer this question, he started down a course that suggested his thoughts were not that different than the British prime minister's, but he was merely setting his congregation up to jolt them with his main point. "All of us are agreed, I think," he began, "that the betrayal of Czechoslovakia was one of the most colossal pieces of injustice in all human history. But we're also agreed that modern warfare is even worse, that it's tragic and senseless and shameless and useless."[8]

In his very next sentence, Gittelsohn likely stunned his audience when he proceeded to sound identical to Neville Chamberlain, a man he detested, when he declared: "And I think most of us would be willing, if necessary, in spite of ourselves and in spite of our ideals, to give up the Czechs and forget about justice if at least that would mean the prospect of a lasting peace."[9] If the congregation was initially confused by what seemed to be an agreement in principle between the minds of Gittelsohn and Neville Chamberlain, he quickly disabused them of that idea:

> But let me assure you, my friends, … that the results of Munich do <u>not</u> mean a prospect of peace. We aren't closer to peace today than we were 4 weeks ago; we're farther from peace. We've rejected peace; we've sabotaged peace; we killed and crushed and murdered peace. Or I should say, Mr. Chamberlain and those whom he leads and those who lead him,—I should say that they have killed and murdered and crushed peace.[10]

Gittelsohn's angry statement was spoken with assurance and confidence in its accuracy. What was the source of Gittelsohn's certainty that Munich represented a betrayal of Czechoslovakia and just the latest in a series of lies propagated by Hitler? How could he have been so certain that war hadn't been averted by the Munich Agreement and instead just the opposite had been achieved by it? The answer is simple: he had read Hitler's book, *Mein Kampf*. "Over 10 years ago," Gittelsohn informed the audience, "in his self-written Bible, *Mein Kampf*, Hitler announced to the whole world that he would use any kind of chicanery or deceit to achieve his ends…. So far that's the only promise he <u>has</u> kept."[11]

He went on to note that the blueprint for Hitler's actions in Europe— the rearming of the Rhineland, the annexation of Austria, the probable expansion into Czechoslovakia—were all clearly laid out in *Mein Kampf*. All laid out for the world to see, without any secrecy or subtlety. Noting that most diplomats were hesitant to announce their plans even so much as 24 hours in advance, Gittelsohn angrily pointed out that Hitler had announced his 10 years in advance, providing the whole world a blueprint of exactly what he intended to do if he ever attained power. "And since he has come to power, he hasn't departed from that blueprint one single iota. He's done everything he intended, and he's done it the way he intended, and he's done it exactly when he intended."[12]

In an ominous tone, Gittelsohn went on to explain that for Hitler, Czechoslovakia was not his only goal; rather it was a necessary means to German control over Europe:

> As a matter of cold, hard fact, Hitler couldn't stop with Czechoslovakia even if he wanted to. Hitler's trouble to begin with is the fact that he has too many mouths to feed and not enough food to fill them. Austria and Czechoslovakia won't help him. Austria and Czechoslovakia gave him more mouths to feed. He took them for one reason only. Because they weren't an end. Because after them come the oil fields of Rumania [*sic*]. And after that comes the rich grain fields of the Ukraine. And after that comes an about-face and the absolute, resolute crushing of France. This isn't idle prediction or prophecy. This is a plain, honest, literal reading of *Mein Kampf*, by which Hitler has been guided in the past and from which he hasn't any intention of departing in the future.[13]

Tying together the situation developing in Europe with the intentions elucidated by Hitler in *Mein Kampf*, the analysis that he provided was precise, to the point, and highly accurate. It is almost striking that a clergyman—a dedicated and committed pacifist—would come up with an analysis that was so prescient one would almost conclude it had been written by planners at either the State Department or the War Department.

Gittelsohn mocked Neville Chamberlain by bemoaning that if only he had read Hitler's book (or had the intelligence to believe it), he too would know that the only place where Germany could acquire both the resources and the *Lebensraum*, or living space, that it needed "—and I quote the book [*Mein Kampf*] literally now—is 'from Russia and her border-states.'"[14] Apparently Joseph Stalin was too busy purging his own military to also note that part of *Mein Kampf*, an omission that Russia would pay dearly for when Germany invaded Russia in 1941, despite the fact that the two nations had a non-aggression treaty between them.

Next Gittelsohn outlined the events that had occurred in the three weeks since the Munich Agreement had been signed. Not only had England immediately launched "the biggest race for armaments in all British history," but Mussolini had begun openly expressing threats against Hungary. Japan, in its campaign against China had imposed a naval blockade that threatened to starve out the population of Hong Kong, despite its previous promises to England that it wouldn't touch the British Crown colony. If Munich meant peace, he asked, why had Germany and Poland just launched a massive publicity campaign against Lithuania that strongly suggested another aggressive move, similar to the actions against Austria and Czechoslovakia? That, Gittelsohn caustically stated, indicated how much Czechoslovakia appeased him. "Only 3 short weeks have passed, and so far are we from peace that already Herr Hitler has begun the next step in his uncanny and rotten progress," declared Gittelsohn with disgust.[15]

Before closing his remarks, Gittelsohn informed his audience that he would continue this discussion at a future date, when they must also examine whether Neville Chamberlain was really as stupid and naïve as he thus far seemed or whether he was perhaps strangely not so naïve. And then they must also to examine what possible alternatives there were, and whether a different stand on the part of England and France would have drawn Europe and the world into war.[16]

In closing, he promised his congregation that he would conclude his discussion of Munich at a future date. If the congregation thought they had witnessed their rabbi at his angriest that evening, they were dead wrong.

• • •

Two weeks later on Friday, November 4, Gittelsohn resumed his highly charged analysis of Munich with the second part of his sermon entitled, "Peace with Honor or Dishonor without Peace: Which is It?" He began by relating to the congregation that after he finished the first part of his analysis of Munich, one of the members of the synagogue came up to him and thanked him, as he was delighted that he was not the only one who was bitter and angry over the actions of Neville Chamberlain. Although he was tempted to assure that member that he hadn't seen anything close to real anger from his rabbi, Gittelsohn now admitted to the audience that he felt like reassuring him that his feelings and emotions expressed two weeks ago, "…bitter as they may have sounded and excited as they may have been—were like the peaceful cooing of a dove compared to the things I have left unsaid for tonight."[17] He explained the reason for his fury in advance, claiming that in the last sermon on Munich he was simply reporting facts. This night he intended to discover the hidden motives behind those facts, "…and needless to say, there's much more about which to be bitter and angry in a discussion of motives than there is in a simple and straightforward reporting of facts."[18]

Briefly reviewing his points from his previous sermon, he recalled to the audience that the Munich Agreement was as ineffective as the Treaty of Versailles. Hitler completely dominated the proceedings in Munich, gave nothing, and took everything. Using the analogy of throwing oil on a fire, feeding victims to dictators like Hitler could not, in the wildest stretch of the imagination, lead to peace. Using this summary of his previous lecture and asserting that it was factual and accurate, he now moved on to the next logical question—why did Chamberlain do what he did?

Was Chamberlain simply a stupid old fool or just a weary old man betrayed by his colleagues? After putting those choices out on the table, Gittelsohn quickly asserted that Chamberlain was in fact neither. Rather, he was something more dangerous. Before proceeding with his line of thought, he gave a word of caution to the audience. He warned them that he would be saying some extremely harsh things about the Prime Minister of England. He would do so intentionally with malice aforethought. "I do so because I'm firmly and profoundly convinced that some extremely harsh things about the prime minister need to be said."[19] After explaining that he was not only critiquing Chamberlain's action at Munich but also his entire record since assuming the office of prime minister, Gittelsohn then proceeded to answer the question that he posed about the man. "My answer," he told the congregation, "is that Neville Chamberlain was neither an innocent fool nor a helpless victim. He was a deliberate and scheming deceiver. He was a malicious and conscious betrayer. He was a cunning and conniving and vicious pretender!"[20] The whole business at Munich was a deceitful subterfuge, a cleverly manipulated smokescreen according to Gittelsohn.

Then he railed against Chamberlain's motivations for compromising with Hitler, while providing an analysis of how Hitler could have been stopped at Munich without having to go to war. Gittelsohn's explanations for this were highly biased by his largely anti-capitalist sentiments concerning the causes of war and are questionable, as was his description of the political nature of Chamberlain which appeared to be highly influenced by his hatred of the man. His analysis of the British leader and his compromising stance was simplistic and largely inaccurate, in contrast to his earlier sermon's excellent analysis of Hitler's war plans.

The primary reason why Chamberlain betrayed Edvard Beneš and the Czechoslovakian people was, according to Gittelsohn, "because Beneš didn't mean enough in dollars and cents to the financial overlords of England for whom Chamberlain is both a representative and a puppet."[21] It was a question of practical economics—Czechoslovakia simply wasn't worth it. "I submit to you that as a true explanation of what happened at Munich this simple mathematical fact which most of you haven't heard is worth more than all the cheap eloquence that you have heard."[22] But this wasn't the only motive of the controlling financial overlords of England, explained Gittelsohn. Chamberlain was willing to sacrifice Beneš because the controlling financial oligarchy of England wasn't afraid of fascism. According to Gittelsohn, the oligarchy deliberately and consciously wanted fascism. Explaining that the controlling industrialists of England were witnessing their control of the welfare and happiness of the masses beginning to diminish and a new society dawning, he assured his audience that these industrialists didn't like the trends that they saw. According to Gittelsohn, they were quite ready to set up some form of fascism to protect their selfish rights.

The above explanations are highly exaggerated, largely untrue, but actually quite representative of leftist ideology in interpreting the results of Munich. Gittelsohn's sermon that evening actually pre-dated several prominent anti–Chamberlain interpretations that also delved into the "financial oligarchy" explanations of Chamberlain's actions. Written in 1939 by British lawyer Arthur Wynn using the pseudonym Simon Haxey, the book *England's Money Lords* almost looks like it was largely based on Gittelsohn's earlier assessment of the Munich compromise. Like Gittelsohn, Haxey bitterly excoriated the Conservatives, stating that while they are in power "… the class of the major employers of this country direct the nation's destinies. This class uses Parliament as a weapon to facilitate the pursuit of profit and as a means to fortify its power and authority."[23] What are we to think of the promises of Conservative leaders to defend against fascism when they can't even exclude fascists from among their members of Parliament? he asked.

Haxey assessed the virulent anti–Communist sentiments in the Chamberlain government as the reason behind Britain's rejection of the Soviet Union as a potential ally, deducing that they preferred the rise of Nazi power to that of the specter of Moscow.[24] Mirroring a strong sentiment expressed by Gittelsohn in his sermon, Haxey concluded that the reason for the Conservative sympathy for fascism was that they believed "...that unless fascism succeeds in Europe, the privileged position of Britain's wealthy governing class may be irretrievably lost. Their policy of retreat before fascism is the instinctive act of self-preservation of a wealthy oligarchy:..."[25]

It is accurate to state that the upper class of Great Britain was more accepting of Hitler and fascism and some were outright admirers of Hitler. This was exemplified by the so-called "Cliveden Set," an aristocratic social group anchored around Cliveden, Lady Astor's Buckinghamshire estate, who supported the appeasement of Hitler and friendly relations with Nazi Germany. From 1932 through 1940, the British Fascist Union, led by Sir Oswald Moseley, gained some notoriety on the British political scene but was never a major force in British political life.

However, it was not economic protectionism that guided Neville Chamberlain at Munich. He can be faulted for not being proactive early on by promoting a robust alliance with France and other European states against Hitler, and for his overly simplistic assessment of Hitler's ambitions. But his actions at Munich had little to do with protecting the pockets of England's industrialists. The memories of the carnage of the past World War were still vivid in the minds of many Englishmen and Chamberlain was no exception. They would do virtually anything to avoid another war, and Chamberlain chose appeasement of Hitler in his sincere attempt to prevent war. It is highly dubious that the "industrial overlords" had anything to do with his actions at Munich. Gittelsohn was much more accurate when he noted the British aristocracy's greater loathing of Russia and communism than its distaste for fascism.

Gittelsohn next went on to accuse Chamberlain of being a fascist himself. To support his accusation, he referenced the German novelist and social critic Thomas Mann who said he was firmly convinced that Mr. Chamberlain was a fascist and that he knew the true state of affairs. "There is no use in sparing words," Mann wrote. "There is a growing party in England which leans strongly toward fascism not perhaps because it believes in it, but because it fears Russia."[26] Mann was wise enough to accuse Chamberlain of being a fascist, Gittelsohn claimed, because he knew Munich wasn't just an isolated event. Closing the frontier of France to Spain, the whole policy of non-intervention, and the "Anglo-Italian conspiracy" against Spain, were all aspects of Chamberlain's true fascist ideology.

Gittelsohn cited the two semi-official visits made by Chamberlain's sister-in-law, Ivy Chamberlain, "...one to that great democrat, Mussolini, and the other to his humanitarian colleague, Franco,"[27] as more proof of

Chamberlain's political leanings. As a further indication of the treachery of the prime minister, he noted Chamberlain's manipulation of the press in England, claiming that in the 50 weeks since November 19, 1937, the day that Lord Halifax, representing Prime Minister Chamberlain, arrived in Berlin to begin negotiations with Hitler, not one single cartoon offensive to either Hitler or Mussolini had been printed in any English newspaper.[28] Another example of the media control exercised by Chamberlain was the inability of British novelist Phyllis Bottome to get her scathing criticism of the Chamberlain government printed in any British paper, even when she offered to do it at her own expense.[29]

Gittelsohn's assertions concerning Chamberlain's manipulation of the press are entirely accurate. Only on rare occasions would the thoroughly compliant media fail to parrot the party line in support of the prime minister and his agenda. As Chamberlain's premiership progressed, he became increasing aggressive towards journalists and openly manipulative, refusing, for example, to answer off-the-cuff questions and insisting that any questions should be submitted four hours in advance if the journalist was to expect a reply.[30] Richard Cockett best described the relationship of Neville Chamberlain and the press when he wrote in 1989: "If a democracy can be defined as a healthy, continuing clash of opinion, then the Chamberlain government, through its close control of the press, certainly succeeded in subverting democracy during the years 1937 to 1940."[31]

Chamberlain's name will be forever linked in history with appeasement and while he displayed many flaws in his foreign policy dealings with Hitler, Gittelsohn's assertion that Chamberlain, too, was a fascist in league with Hitler, is patently absurd. He took over a government that was paralyzed with the memories of the World War and had tremendously cut back its military. The Spanish Civil War was raging and the fear of Bolshevism was great in the minds of many in Europe. It was his fear of another war and his naïve belief that he could trust Hitler to be satisfied with the acquisition of the Sudetenland that was the driving motive behind Chamberlain's actions. While it is true that Chamberlain's policies also served some of the goals and desires of fascist sympathizers in Great Britain, this no more proves he was a fascist than Gittelsohn's own leftist sympathies prove that he was a communist. Chamberlain can be accused of being a mediocre prime minister at a time when his country truly needed greatness. He can and should be accused of being an appeaser who clearly did not understand Hitler.

To begin the second part of his sermon, Gittelsohn told his audience that many of them have already asked him the question he was going to answer next. "You want to know how I, a confirmed and extreme and radical pacifist, can condemn the Conference at Munich if the only alternative

was war. My answer to that is that I still condemn it and I am still a pacifist, because the only alternative wasn't war."[32] He immediately followed
with his explanation in a discussion that was largely wrong and stunning
for its misguided analysis, especially when one considers his superb analysis of Hitler's vision in *Mein Kampf* that he delivered only two weeks before.
Claiming that Hitler was bluffing, he explained thusly: "Hitler could have
been stopped and he could have been stopped with peace. I for one am
more convinced that if England and France had refused to betray Czechoslovakia, Adolf Hitler would not have gone to war."[33]

After announcing that stunning conclusion, one that would be proven
wrong within nine months, Gittelsohn provided three basic reasons to
explain why Hitler would have not gone to war over Czechoslovakia. The
first involved an analysis done by Dr. Edward Sampson of Princeton, who
concluded that "Germany is by no means ready to undertake a protracted
war, and indeed has probably not gathered sufficient supplies to support
her full manpower in a short war against a major power." So, according to
Gittelsohn, there wouldn't have been a war, "because Hitler couldn't fight
one."[34] Sampson's analysis was written at a time when concepts such as
Blitzkrieg were unknown, as were the even greater depths of perfidy that
Hitler would sink to in order to achieve his goals, such as attacking the
Soviet Union after negotiating a non-aggression pact with them.

The second reason that Gittelsohn offered as to why Hitler would not
have gone to war was that he would be very reluctant if not actually afraid
to do so. To support this argument, he claimed that Hitler wasn't "as big
a dumbbell as the world sometimes pretends he is,"[35] and he had to have
noted how none of the rulers who got their countries into the World War
were still in power at the war's end. The rabbi also cited the revolt of the
coal miners in Upper Silesia the previous July; when rumors surfaced that
war had broken out, a melee erupted that required thousands of secret
police to put down. Gittelsohn was sure that these types of incidents would
make Hitler think twice about initiating a war. Yet as he explained this, he
also noted that it took the importation of over 5,000 secret police to put
down the rebellion. Hitler was not reluctant at all to brutally crush dissent as he amply displayed in 1934 on the Night of the Long Knives, when
he liquidated all potential opposition within his own Nazi party. It is highly
unlikely that Hitler was in the least bit worried about dissent or about using
ruthless force to crush it.

The third reason given by Gittelsohn was that everything Hitler had
achieved, was done through bluster and bluff. "And yet they know that
every time someone had the courage and the gumption to say stop, immediately and unhesitatingly Hitler stopped! And that happened not just once,
but at least three different times."[36]

The examples he proceeded to give are not only weak, but they are not accurate. The logic of his first example is difficult to accept as indicating anything other than Hitler's duplicitous and manipulative nature, discounting any theories that he may display weakness and a tendency to back down when confronted. Referring to Hitler's abortive *coup d'état* in Munich in 1923 known as the Beer Hall Putsch, Gittelsohn pointed out that Hitler had proclaimed that if the putsch failed, he would kill himself. Hitler, of course, did not kill himself after the putsch was put down. He was tried, convicted, and sentenced to five years imprisonment in Landsberg prison, where he served only nine months. Gittelsohn used the fact that he didn't commit suicide as indicating that he was bluffing and would back down when confronted, as if dishonesty and lies were something new in Hitler's repertoire. One must logically weigh the adversity produced by Hitler's theoretical "promised" suicide against the reality of his decision to live, and while in prison, write the manifesto for his world plan—*Mein Kampf*—and then go on to wreak havoc on the world. In this example, Hitler's "bluffing" and backing down led to the bloodiest war in world history.

For his next example, Gittelsohn listed Hitler's actions when dealing with the dictator of Poland, Marshal Pilsudski. The nation of Poland had been established by the Treaty of Versailles in 1919, which also created a "Polish Corridor" extending northward to prevent Poland from being landlocked. The free city of Danzig at the northern end of the corridor was to provide a port for Poland. This corridor separated Germany from East Prussia and was a constant source of friction between Poland and Germany. When the Nazis rose to power, reuniting Germans in the Polish Corridor with Germany became one of their bellicose aims, as they threatened to take the corridor from Poland. Gittelsohn told his congregation that a prime example of Hitler's bluffing was a few years prior when Hitler decided to march in and reclaim the Polish Corridor. But according to Gittelsohn, Hitler wasn't dealing then with a toy dictator like Chamberlain. He was dealing with a real dictator. Marshal Pilsudski offered Hitler his choice of signing a ten-year pact of non-aggression and renouncing the Corridor, or else they would go to war. "Hitler didn't fight," stressed Gittelsohn. "He signed and he renounced. His bluff had been called and he quit!"[37]

Gittelsohn's interpretation of the situation is questionable. It is undeniable that there was no love lost between Hitler and Pilsudski. However, most historians report that driven by his fear and distrust of the Nazis, Pilsudski approached France with a proposal that their two nations invade Germany with the purpose of overthrowing Hitler and the Nazis. The French rejected the plan out of hand. Scholars have cited France's refusal of Pilsudski's proposal as one of the reasons for Poland signing the German-Polish Non-Aggression Pact in January 1934. There is no evidence that Pilsudski threatened Hitler as Gittelsohn suggested, or that he was eager to go to war with Germany. Hitler's plan of rapprochement with Poland bought him time to rearm Germany, which was a much stronger nation militarily at the time of the Munich conference than it was in January 1934. Hitler's word on a treaty, even if it had been forced as Gittelsohn suggested, was as worthless in 1934 as it was less than a year after Gittelsohn's sermon when Germany invaded the Polish Corridor, precipitating the Second World War.

For his third example of illustrating the tendency of Hitler to bluff and back down when confronted, Gittelsohn chose a more convincing example to argue his point. He described the assassination of Austrian dictator Engelbert Dollfuss in July of 1934 by Austrian Nazis and noted that it was supposed to be a signal for Hitler to march into Austria just as he actually did three and a half years later. But this went against the wish of Benito Mussolini who then mobilized his Italian troops at the Brenner Pass on the border between Italy and Austria. He threatened Hitler that when the first German soldier set foot on Austrian soil, Mussolini would march. "Needless to say," explained Gittelsohn, "the first German soldier didn't set foot on Austrian soil, and Mussolini didn't have to march."[38] In this example, Gittelsohn was accurate. Hitler was surprised by Mussolini's reaction and despite many Nazi-provoked riots in Austria following Dollfuss' murder, Hitler did not want to risk intervention at that time.

Again, the power of Nazi Germany in 1934 was not nearly what it was at the time of the Munich conference. Mussolini would soon embroil Italy with a war in Ethiopia as well as providing support for Franco in the Spanish Civil War. By 1937, Mussolini would come under the spell of Hitler and ally with him. The following year, by annexing Austria without consulting Mussolini, the increasingly powerful Hitler had relegated him to junior partner status. While Gittelsohn's third example did actually show Hitler backing down, this 1934 incident was largely irrelevant to the realities of 1938.

Gittelsohn ended his sermon by decrying Chamberlain's actions at Munich, stating, "...whenever Hitler's bluff has been called in the past, without a single exception he has surrendered. That bluff could have been called again."[39] He provided a somberly accurate prediction when he stated that what happened at Munich was simply a prologue for a more tragic drama the end of which was nowhere in sight. Quoting Edvard Beneš, he cautioned, "I do not wish to criticize, nor must you expect from me a single word of recrimination. History will be our judge."[40]

In summary, Gittelsohn provided an excellent analysis of the long-range plan that Hitler outlined in *Mein Kampf*. However, he also revealed a total misunderstanding of Hitler's evil nature that drove Nazi expansionism. His incorrect belief that Hitler was all bluff and no action when confronted was even further compounded by his almost bizarre belief that Hitler could have been stopped with peace. Hitler could not have been stopped by peace at Munich. He had decided in early May 1938 to attack Czechoslovakia to both strengthen Germany's strategic position in central Europe, as well as to use ethnic Germans in that country to expand his armies for the next war.[41] It was to be the first in a planned series of wars he intended to fight. However, at the last moment, Hitler changed his mind and decided to settle for the Sudetenland portion of Czechoslovakia at Munich. Much of the world saw this as a German triumph. Hitler, though, came to consider the Munich Agreement as the worst mistake of his career.[42] He would come to feel that he had been cheated out of his war at Munich and he had no intention of being cheated again.

Hitler would clearly outline his plans for phased wars in his unpublished sequel to *Mein Kampf*, written in 1928.[43] As noted above, a war to destroy Czechoslovakia and secure the German position in central Europe would be the first war. Next, he would attack the western powers—England and France. After the conquering of these countries, he would next turn his sights on the Soviet Union. Conquering the Soviet Union would provide the food and the "living space" that expansionist Germany would need. Lastly, he would ultimately have to destroy the United States of America. When Chamberlain appeased Hitler at Munich, "cheating" him out of the war he desired, Hitler turned his sights on Poland in order to secure his eastern border as a reason to initiate his first war. Manufactured incidents against ethnic Germans in the Polish Corridor would provide Hitler the pretext to invade.

Hitler was not bluffing. He could not have been stopped with peace. The only thing that could have stopped Hitler was the very thing that ultimately did stop him six years later: the total destruction of Nazi Germany. After 1938, Hitler managed to avoid being cheated out of the wars he planned and wanted so badly. He sowed the seeds he planted and ultimately reaped a world war. As a result, after 12 years, Hitler's "Reich to last a thousand years" would come to an end.

Eleven

A World on the Brink

Events in the troubled British Mandate of Palestine, in late 1938 and early 1939, led to Gittelsohn's increasing hatred of Neville Chamberlain and further fueled his distaste for England in general. In November 1938 the British government issued a "Policy Statement Against Partition." This new policy effectively reversed the 1937 Peel Commission's position on partition, that recommended Palestine should be divided between its Arab and Jewish populations. Arabs and Jews alike were vehemently opposed to partitioning Palestine into two separate states. Given this conflict, the British government called on representatives from both Palestinian Arabs and the Jewish Agency to meet in London and attempt to work out their differences. Should the meetings not produce any agreement within a reasonable time frame, it was the British government's intention to examine the problem and to propose a policy that they intended to pursue.[1]

The London conferences met in February and March with the Arab delegates attending only on the condition that they would have no direct negotiation with the Jews. This forced the British government representatives to hold separate meetings with the two groups. After two months, the meetings ended without the Palestinian Jews and Arabs resolving any differences. On May 17, 1939, the British government issued its new policy statement known as the White Paper. The paper formally dismissed the idea of partition and called for an independent Palestinian State, stating that, "It should be a state in which the two peoples in Palestine, Arabs and Jews, share authority in government in such a way that the essential interests of each are secured."[2] Starting with this highly unrealistic goal, given the history of the region since the formation of Palestine, the White Paper went on to basically provide support for the Arab position.

The White Paper represented nothing less than the betrayal of the San Remo Resolution of 1920, as well as the spirit and stated intentions of the Mandate for Palestine. It called for a limitation on Jewish immigration to Palestine, limiting it to a maximum rate of 15,000 Jews a year for the next five years, to cease completely after that, unless the Arabs would be willing to accept more Jewish immigrants. The White Paper also put restrictions and certain outright prohibitions on Jews purchasing any additional land.[3] The Jews of Palestine, as well as Jews and Zionists worldwide, were outraged by the new policy. Interestingly, the Arabs also rejected the White Paper, demanding that Palestine become an Arab state immediately and that Jewish immigration to Palestine be abruptly ended. In addition, they demanded that the status of every Jew who immigrated since 1918 be reviewed.[4]

On May 18, a Jewish general strike was called to protest the new policies. On July 13, the Mandate authorities announced the suspension of all Jewish immigration to Palestine until March 1940, citing an alleged increase in illegal immigrants arriving there.[5]

Shortly after the White Paper of 17 May 1939 went into effect, Gittelsohn erupted in anger over both the new policy and England itself in an undated sermon from that time frame. As usual, he was preaching against the United States' getting involved with the deepening morass overseas. The sermon, entitled "America and the Next War," contained the usual elements of his sermons. It was heavily laced with economic motives that promoted war as well as the hypocrisy of going to war to preserve democracy when history had indicated that if anything, these idealistic wars ruined democracy. He strongly warned his congregants to be wary of the barrage of propaganda that they were all being subject to about fighting for democracy. It was in this context that he brought up recent developments in the Middle East.

Harking back to the propaganda that helped fuel the Great War, Gittelsohn warned that they should not fall for that kind of "tommyrot" again. Let's not kid ourselves, he cautioned, about what they would be fighting for and stop mouthing a lot of cheap clichés about defending a noble cause with the great democracies of England and France. Claiming that England betrayed every sacred promise it ever made and was at that very moment crushing the hopes of the Jewish people in Palestine, he venomously declared, "I do not love England! I hate England! I will not fight for England!"[6]

Further showing his contempt for the British, Gittelsohn made a comparison of England to Germany, claiming that at least Hitler's Germany never pretended to be a friend or a friend of democracy, writing, "Germany never embraced us so that it could knife us ... never made us a sacred promise in the highest tribunal of mankind, and then, when we needed the fulfillment of that promise most, held it to be meaningless and cheap."[7]

• • •

On the morning of March 15, 1939, Hitler had already summoned elderly and frail Czechoslovakian President Emil Hacha to Berlin and warned him that Germany was about to invade his country. Suffering a heart attack during the meeting, Hacha capitulated to Hitler's demands and German troops entered the country encountering minimal resistance. The betrayal of Czechoslovakia that began at Munich only six months earlier was now complete. The reaction to Germany's latest aggression was swift. The British were especially infuriated by Hitler's actions. Lord Halifax warned the German Ambassador to Great Britain thusly: "I can understand Herr Hitler's taste for bloodless victories, but one of these days he will find himself up against something that will not be bloodless."[8]

Neville Chamberlain's initial public statement regarding Hitler's subjugation of Czechoslovakia was tepid at best in claiming that England was not bound to protect Czechoslovakia. The resultant outrage from the press, which he had controlled only months earlier, caused him to have an apparent change of heart when he spoke in Birmingham two days later on March 17. Explaining that he had never denied that the terms which he secured at Munich were not those that he would have desired, he proceeded to ask rhetorically, what was the alternative? He told his audience that they must ask: "Is this the last attack upon a small State, or is it to be followed by others? Is this, in fact, a step in the direction of an attempt to dominate the world by force?"[9] Stating that there was hardly anything that he wouldn't sacrifice for peace, he noted, "There is one thing that I must except, and that is the liberty that we have enjoyed for hundreds of years and which we will never surrender."[10]

Closing his speech, Chamberlain made his position clear and sent a message to Adolf Hitler, claiming it would be a mistake to assume because England believes war to be senseless and cruel, that it would not take part to the utmost of its power in resisting such a challenge. He claimed to have not only the support, the sympathy, and the confidence of his fellow countrymen and countrywomen, but "…the approval of the whole British Empire and of all other nations who value peace, indeed, but who value freedom even more."[11]

On March 31, both England and France gave military guarantees to Poland, Romania, Greece, and Turkey and also inaugurated political and military talks with the Soviets.[12] England was now committed to the protection of Poland, the object of Hitler's next planned war. On May 22, Germany and Italy signed a military alliance, the Pact of Steel, pledging to fight alongside each other in the event of war. Europe was on a collision course, headed for a war planned and desired by Hitler.

• • •

Hitler next set his sights on Poland. But first, he had business he needed to conduct with the Soviet Union. Hitler needed to keep the Soviets out of any potential war with Germany. His master plan called for him to wage war against England and France after destroying Poland. He needed his eastern front quiet to accomplish this and sought a non-aggression pact with Stalin, despite his known hatred of communism and all things associated with it. In secret, he sent his foreign minister Joachim von Ribbentrop to Moscow to negotiate with his Soviet counterpart, Vyacheslav Molotov. In early August they negotiated an economic deal and commenced to negotiate a political alliance. They set aside their foreign policy differences and found common ground in the anti-capitalism of both countries.[13]

While German-Soviet negotiations continued, Stalin also negotiated with representatives from England and France over a possible military alliance against Germany. Stalin then cut off these negotiations and proceeded to sign a non-aggression pact with Nazi Germany. Included in the pact was a secret protocol carving up Europe into spheres of influence for both Germany and the Soviet Union. Poland was to be immediately cut roughly in half, the western part going to Germany, the eastern part to the Soviet Union. The entire Ribbentrop-Molotov pact was signed on August 23, 1939. The following day a stunned and upset world awoke to the news of the new alliance between these seemingly incompatible partners. The citizens of Poland were dismayed, knowing that Hitler planned to attack them in the near future since they knew that the new treaty cleared his eastern front. President Roosevelt wrote to Hitler, urging him to "refrain from any positive act of hostility for a reasonable and stipulated period."[14] Hitler ignored the request.

As previously mentioned, the news of an alliance between Nazi Germany and the Soviet Union spelled the death knell for the largely communist-dominated student anti-war movement in the United States. Many lost faith in the Communist Party, viewing the Molotov-Ribbentrop Pact as a sellout of communist principles to Hitler, and many wanted no part of this apparent abandonment of anti-fascism.[15] Their naïve, idealized picture of the Soviet Union as a "worker's paradise" was forever destroyed as Stalin partnered with Hitler, the very embodiment of the fascist evil that they opposed so vehemently.

For pacifists such as Gittelsohn, the Nazi-Soviet pact was another indication of the world descending into chaos. While many felt war was inevitable now, they felt it was still their duty to push for American non-involvement in war developing in Europe. Unlike 1917, they were determined to keep America out of the conflict.

TWELVE

The War Begins

Hitler had already made his decision in regard to Poland months before the Molotov-Ribbentrop Pact. On April 3, 1939, he had issued a war directive marked "Most Secret" and had it hand-delivered to his most senior commanders. Outlining the upcoming attack on Poland, named "Case White," Hitler instructed his military leaders: "Since the situation on Germany's eastern front has become intolerable, and all political possibilities of a peaceful settlement have been exhausted, I have decided upon a solution by force."[1] The attack would begin on September 1.

The pretext for the German invasion of Poland would be a series of staged provocations conducted by the SS depicting atrocities allegedly committed by Poles against ethnic Germans in Poland. The staged campaign, named "Operation Himmler," culminated on August 31, when members of the SS wearing Polish army uniforms attacked various border villages, committed acts of terrorism, and left behind dead bodies in Polish military uniforms. The bodies were actually those of concentration camp victims who were killed in order to add to the ruse. The week before, Hitler had informed his generals of the plan, stating "I will provide a propagandistic *casus belli*. Its credibility doesn't matter. The victor will not be asked if he told the truth."[2] The following day Hitler invaded Poland.

The day of the invasion, Neville Chamberlain contacted both the Germans and the Poles attempting to get both parties to cease any hostilities and come to the negotiating table. The Poles immediately replied in agreement with England's proposal. Germany never responded to Chamberlain's request. On September 2, the British government consulted with France in order to consolidate their response to Hitler's aggression. Accordingly, on September 3, 1939, Prime Minister Chamberlain addressed the House of Commons. He informed them that he had sent their ambassador in Berlin instructions that he was to deliver to Hitler that morning. The instructions included the vow that the United Kingdom would not hesitate to fulfill its obligation to Poland. Noting the lack of response to Chamberlain's prior request, the ambassador informed Hitler that unless England received satisfactory assurances from Germany in that regard by 11 a.m. that morning, a state of war would exist between the two countries. Not having heard a reply by the deadline, Chamberlain informed Germany that a state of war did exist between their two countries and that the French government would be pursuing an identical course in alliance with Great Britain.[3] In a little under 21 years since the Great War, the world was at war again.

For the next several months, although war had been declared in Europe, there was no combat on the ground. The seemingly "peaceful" version of war between Germany and the British-French allies led to a phase of the Second World War that would be referred to as the "Phony War." While the antagonists postured on the ground, real warfare broke out in Finland on November 30, 1939, when the Soviet Union invaded the country. The West roundly condemned the Soviet Union for this action, which led to its expulsion from the League of Nations. Although the Soviet Union prevailed in the conflict, they did not accomplish their goal of total conquest of Finland due to the rousingly strong defense by the Finns of their homeland. As a result of the Moscow Peace Treaty, signed in March of 1940, Finland ceded 11 percent of its territory and 30 percent of its economic assets to the Soviet Union.[4] The Soviet losses were high and, accordingly, its international reputation suffered.[5]

The Phony War ended on April 9, 1940, when the Germans, using *Blitzkrieg* tactics, attacked Denmark and Norway. Less than two months later, the Nazis occupied both countries. The Low Countries—the Netherlands, Belgium and Luxembourg—desired to remain neutral in the war, and resisted efforts by the British and French to entice them to ally with them. On May 10, the Germans occupied Luxembourg and attacked Belgium and Holland. As the British and French fought their way north attempting to assist the Belgians, a massive armor attack by the XIX German Army Corps, assisted by the *Luftwaffe*, fought its way to the English Channel. By May 20, they had cut off the British Expeditionary Force (BEF) along with a large number of French and Belgian troops. Isolated in an ever-tightening noose, the BEF fell back to the port of Dunkirk.

In what was referred to as the "Miracle of Dunkirk," nearly 340,000 British, French, and Belgian troops were then rescued by a makeshift flotilla and transported across the English Channel to England between May 27 and June 4. The German high command had halted the German ground offensive and instead relied on the *Luftwaffe* to destroy the BEF. In spite of this strategy that allowed a large number of allied soldiers to escape, it was a devastating defeat for the Allies, regardless of the spin put on the evacuation. Using *Blitzkrieg* tactics, the Germans had mauled their armies with speed and precision. Later that month France surrendered to the Nazis. Europe was effectively under Nazi control.

Back in the United States, Gittelsohn was closely watching the developments from the war in Europe. Dunkirk would prove to be a watershed moment for him. For the first time, he began to feel doubts about his absolute pacifism. In his memoirs, he would later confirm that it was the Dunkirk evacuation that first led him to realize there was something worse than war itself—that perhaps there really was something worth fighting for.

•   •   •

As war broke out in Europe, things were going well for both Rabbi Gittelsohn and his new congregation in Rockville Center, New York. By fall 1939, temple membership continued to grow steadily and Gittelsohn had established several adult study groups, Hebrew classes, and open forums to discuss national and international problems. He proved to be a lively and exceedingly knowledgeable facilitator of these various discussions. He was highly regarded by the congregation, who became accustomed to the detailed sermons on social responsibility and pacifism that he would frequently deliver. In spite of the deteriorating situation in Europe that distressed him, coupled with his fear that the United States would once again be dragged into a European conflict, his professional life and his personal life were sources of great pride and satisfaction.

In fall 1939 the Synagogue School with 160 pupils began Saturday classes in the Wilson School. A Kol Nidre appeal was made to raise a sufficient sum for the purchase of property for a permanent home. Later, in 1940, a suitable site was found on DeMott Avenue, and the synagogue's purchase contract was consummated on November 7, 1940.[6]

THIRTEEN

Private Life

After Pearl Harbor was attacked by the Japanese on December 7, 1941, Congress declared war on Japan and days after that Hitler declared war on the United States. By the end of summer 1942, the United States had launched its first offensive against Japan in the Pacific theater of war. After the Americans thwarted the Japanese in the Coral Sea and at Midway, Japan aimed its sights on the Solomon Islands. After Japanese forces occupied Tulagi, they began construction of an airfield on nearby Guadalcanal. Realizing that a Japanese bomber base there could interrupt vital lines of communication between the United States and Australia, the American military command chose to attack and acquire the airfield, landing the First Marine Division at Guadalcanal on August 7, 1942. It was the beginning of a series of battles that comprised the campaign for Guadalcanal, culminating with the Japanese defeat and withdrawal by February 1943.

On Long Island, Gittelsohn followed the events of the war in Europe and the Pacific with increasing interest while the Central Synagogue of Nassau Country continued to grow and flourish. In addition, he was very contented with his home life. On October 8, 1937, Ruth Gittelsohn had given birth to the young couple's first child, a healthy baby boy they named David Benjamin. Roland and Ruth added a sister for David when their daughter Judith was born on November 24, 1940. A couple of years later, Roland and Ruth had two growing, healthy children at their home at 88 Lewis Place in Hempstead, Long Island. By 1942, David was now nearly five years old and Judy nearly two. However, Roland experienced a growing restlessness accompanied by a new sense of mission and calling that he could not ignore. That new perceived mission would become public less than two months later.

Based on Gittelsohn's own words and other accounts at that time, he was an extremely intelligent, stern, and serious young man who appeared to relish debate and was often confrontational and uncompromising in his views. In his most passionate sermons, he almost comes across as an angry,

99

bitter individual. One is tempted to consider if this is really an accurate description of Gittelsohn. What was the man really like? Was he that way at home with his family? What type of a husband and father was he?

According to his son David and his daughter Judy, their father was not an angry man in his daily life. They put a human face on Gittelsohn that paints quite a different picture of him. Looking back to their earliest memories of him, both of them remember their father as a strong, bright, and opinionated man. However, they also described him as being a completely different personality at home. Judy would refer to his "multifaceted" personality in this regard.[1] He displayed a great sense of humor and even as young children, David and Judy felt that he was a fun person to be around. Judy recalled how he enjoyed going to his rabbinical conferences every year because, among other things, he would always arrive home with a fresh supply of jokes to share.

In the Gittelsohn household, he was the disciplinarian; their mother Ruth was more of the quiet, artistic soul. Both Roland and Ruth were very sociable and were wonderful hosts who loved to entertain. Judy would describe how her parents would go out to a party every New Year's Eve; but before they did, their dad would always bring home Chinese food and the four of them would have this "traditional" New Year's Eve dinner before both parents left for their party. At least once a year, the family would travel to New York City to go to a Broadway show and dine in the city.

Although he was not athletic, Roland would regularly take his children roller skating in nearby Jones Beach. One of the rituals Gittelsohn began after World War II was an annual deep sea fishing trip for members of the synagogue. This was strictly a "dads and kids affair," no moms were allowed. All of the participants from the temple looked forward to this yearly treat, especially Gittelsohn. With laughter, both David and Ruth recalled that on all the fishing trips they went on with their father, they never saw him touch a rod or a reel. Instead, he would always bring a book and read, while constantly taking part in the discussions and thoroughly enjoying himself.

Their home life was always centered around their father's schedule. He would be home promptly every night for a 6 p.m. dinner and at times have a cocktail before dinner. Afterwards, it was very common for him to return to the temple for congregational business or to meet with members of his congregation. He did not have a lot of time to be with the family during the school year.

The summers were different. Gittelsohn would take a large part of the summer off and, starting when Judy was seven or eight years old, the Gittelsohns would rent a cottage in New Hampshire and spend the summers there. The family of four had their daily routine in the summer: Mornings were reserved as quiet time for Roland to write and also read. (Judy described her father as a meticulous student and also a voracious reader.) The rest of the day was family time. These were very happy days for the Gittelsohns.

When asked about his father's skill as a public speaker, David's answer was unequivocal. He described him as a spellbinding speaker, a "golden-tongued" orator.[2] David's views are consistent with many other people's descriptions of Gittelsohn's oratorical skills. Clearly his sermons were quite striking because of his style of delivery as a dynamic public speaker. David described his father as a natural debater and proudly recounted the many awards he attained as a high school and college debate team member at Western Reserve University. David also described how his father would rehearse his sermons at home to get the timing perfect. At the outset of each sermon, it was his ritual, when approaching his temple pulpit, to begin by removing his wristwatch and placing it next to his notes, so he could stay precisely on schedule.

Both children recalled that despite his superb debating skills and his vast knowledge, Roland was perfectly capable of admitting when he was wrong. His daughter-in-law, Donna Gittelsohn, related a humorous anecdote to illustrate this very point, involving a "debate" between her father-in-law and herself over correct grammar. During a visit to her dentist, Donna mentioned that she was nauseous; her dentist corrected her grammar, saying that the correct term was "nauseated." When she mentioned the grammar debate to Roland, he informed her, "You were wrong. The correct term is 'nauseated.'" Then she cited *Webster's Dictionary* to bolster her case, but he replied, "*Webster's*! What do they know?"

Several days later Donna contacted a friend who worked in the English Department at Harvard University and mentioned the disagreement. A few days later, her friend called her back and announced, "It's the consensus of the English Department that you were correct." A very pleased Donna Gittelsohn could not wait to inform her father-in-law later that week, when she and David joined Roland and Ruth for dinner at a Boston restaurant. She knew that the Rabbi relished debate and also admired people who stood up for their beliefs. Proudly, she informed him that it was the opinion of the Harvard University English department that she was right and he was wrong. Gittelsohn smiled at her and said, "You have to tell me this, when I'm paying the bill?"[3]

Toward the end of World War II after what would be a long separation from his family, Roland sent his family a letter that included a photograph of him with a mustache. Never having had a mustache before, and always the true believer in democracy, he asked his family to vote if he should keep it. Judy voted "yes," but both Ruth and David voted "no." Democracy prevailed in the Gittelsohn family and he dutifully shaved his mustache off. He did, however, mail the clippings to Judy, the one member of the family who appreciated his brief hirsute appearance.

From the accounts of his children, Gittelsohn was an attentive, loving husband and father. His home persona did indeed differ from the stern, sometimes strident lecturer that he may have appeared to be from the pulpit.

In his 1988 autobiography, Gittelsohn conveyed his paternal concerns and the effect that being the community's rabbi may have had on his children as they grew up. Noting that a rabbi's children must often pay a price for his success, he observed, "In this respect they are like the children of any person in public life. The community expects them to be perfect; other parents demanded more of them than from their own sons and daughters."[4] Looking back on his own busy life, he commented on the effect that his long hours away may have had on David and Judy. "They suffer too—as do the sons and daughters of all busy professionals and executives—from their parents' busyness."[5]

FOURTEEN

A Vision
of the Common Man
at War and a Surprise

Throughout the 1930s some of the harshest criticisms of President Roosevelt's New Deal appeared in the pages of the *Saturday Evening Post*. A staunchly conservative magazine that espoused an isolationist point of view over the developing conflicts in Europe and Asia, it attracted old guard journalists and editorialists such as Garet Garrett who regularly attacked FDR and his policies. The October 10, 1942, issue contained an editorial entitled "Neo-liberal Illusion: That Collectivism Is Liberty." While the actual author of the editorial was unknown, for the purposes of his sermon, Gittelsohn would attribute the editorial to the magazine's recently hired editor, Ben Hibbs.

Although the *Post* had been expressing similar views for years, the United States was now engaged in a two-front war. Its message, as well as its timing, especially enraged Gittelsohn. After reading it several times, he decided to devote a sermon addressing the editorial and its message. He had so much to say on the matter that he delivered his sermon in two parts, on October 23 and on October 30, 1942. The title of his sermon was "Saturday Evening Post Americanism."

He began by stating his position on the article up front and unequivocally. The editorial with the "quasi-scholarly title ... contained just as much outrageous and impossible nonsense as anything we've seen on page one in a long time."[1] Hibbs proposed a vision of Americanism which Gittelsohn and many other similarly-minded individuals had hoped was dead long ago, "...but which apparently is still very much alive and with which we'll have to reckon with in this war to end in anything other than the ghastliest and costliest joke in history."[2]

This opinion should not be surprising to any of them, he noted, as the

Saturday Evening Post had always embraced a strange concept of Americanism and had remained rabidly isolationist right up to the attack on Pearl Harbor, almost to the point of appearing to be "Nazi sympathizers." The magazine had fired their previous editor after a series of controversial articles that expressed a view of Americanism that appeared to be both fascist and antisemitic and for which the magazine also issued a public apology; after the incident, they had hired Ben Hibbs, who seemed to adopt a less strident approach. With the publication of the October 10 editorial, the "paint wore off and the leopards' spots became visible again," with Gittelsohn calling the editorial unblushingly fascist.[3]

Uncertain if many in the congregation had read the editorial, Gittelsohn continued by reviewing the key points made by Hibbs. According to the editor, the United States was considering abandoning individual responsibility and going back to earning its living in packs, in what he referred to as the "total state." This avoidance of individual responsibility led to an economic imbalance that swept through Europe and eventually reached the shores of our country in the form of the Great Depression. The results, Hibbs claimed, was "a horde of economic cure-alls, each one of which marked a step backward toward the old, old situation of the strong state and the weak citizen."[4] Natural forces were not allowed to cure the economic body; instead the patient was loaded with artificial "stimulants" and "sedatives" in the form of debt, subsidy, and federal handouts.

According to Hibbs, the progress of civilization, "...had been measured by the people able to leave the pack and care for themselves without the leader doing their thinking for them."[5] In general, history evolved from the social group or "pack" to the individual. However, the war had accelerated the reversal of this process by putting in place military controls on individuals, for the sake of promoting socialized industry for the common good.

With this, Hibbs noted with dismay that our national character had changed. To him, this was largely due to the wave of immigration coming to the United States since the turn of the century. Too many of the 19 million immigrants who came to America since 1900 did not come seeking freedom, he astonishingly deduced. "They came," according to Hibbs, "to share a ready-made prosperity. Ignorant of basic American ideals, they are easy prey for demagogues, and no one knows exactly what changes this new blood has made in America."[6]

In Hibbs' analysis, there were two types of people in the country: the talented people who have economic genius, and semi-talented or untalented people who were the parasites of society. There appears to be no other group of people between these two extremes. The relationship between the two was cyclic in nature. It was the talented, capable individuals who exercised their creative talents that created work and opportunities for the untalented who are unable to create their own. Hibbs claimed, "The result is a rich reward to the talented and a very substantial reward to the semi-talented or untalented individuals clinging to the kite tail of genius."[7]

Hibbs explained that technological advancement made the individual less and less capable of directing his own work. Hence, someone else must direct it. According to the editor, there were only two agencies capable of doing this: private enterprisers using free labor, and the government using Hitler's type of labor. "We must choose between freedom and state control. Those who say that the people can collectively direct their own industrial efforts are either liars or fools."[8] Allowing the gifted minority to use their own money and allowing them to compete with one another for public patronage provided a benefit to society that it should not take for granted.

Displaying his elitist version of charitable thought, Hibbs turned to the plight of the "untalented." Stating that there is no way, in the long run, of rewarding an individual beyond his fair value to society, he noted that the "brutal truth" was that there will always be those whose contribution to society was so meager as to warrant little more than a minimum living standard. While generously acknowledging that they cannot be allowed to starve, Hibbs noted that the only way to make up the deficit between what the untalented need and what they earn was to take it away from those able to produce more than they need. And herein lies the crux of the problem as envisioned by Ben Hibbs. Although it was human nature to help the unfortunate, it was also human nature to restrict charity to bare living standards. If the state persists in subsidizing and pampering the relatively useless citizen at the expense of the useful citizen, one of two things will happen: Either the useful citizen will rise up in his anger and attempt to overthrow the state, or if unable to, "...he will lose his initiative and sink toward the level of the group which he is being made to support."[9]

Having set the stage by summarizing the editorial's content, Gittelsohn launched into his scathing analysis of Hibbs' views. Belittling Hibbs' "two-class" American society, he described the editor's view of Americanism as "Let the rich get richer—then they'll have all the more money with which to give charity to the poor, out of whose sweat and labor they got rich in the first place."[10] But remember, Gittelsohn sarcastically cautioned his audience, not to give too generously to the poor—this may be bad for them. "Just give them enough to keep them alive."[11]

Although Hibbs never outright said it, his total rejection of government involvement in any aspect of business clearly indicated his preference that the New Deal be rescinded before it destroyed the American way of life. Gittelsohn indicated his strong support of FDR's New Deal, an interesting endorsement from a man who was a frequent critic of the president's policies. Beyond this, Hibbs clearly claimed that state-owned enterprises were never efficient, a statement that Gittelsohn called "obvious rubbish."

Having indicated to the congregation that he believed that he had just presented an accurate summary and portrayal of Ben Hibbs' view of Americanism, Gittelsohn declared that he violently objected to this interpretation of Americanism for half a dozen reasons. He would like to express and explain only the first two of them that night and then necessarily leave the others for the following week.[12]

His first objection was succinct—he believed that the editorial's explanation of Americanism was an inaccurate distortion of human history. According to Ben Hibbs, the course of human history had been to minimize the importance of the group and to increase the absolute economic independence of the individual. "I'm curious to know in what school or from what books did Mr. Hibbs study his history," countered Gittelsohn. "Oddly enough, every scholar from whom I've ever studied history interpreted the course of human events the very opposite way."[13] He was taught, as he presumed most of his congregation was taught, that human beings began as individualists and that only gradually they at last begin to learn the meaning of cooperation in groups. Hibbs was trying to reverse the whole meaning of human affairs.

There were no two ways to look at this, Gittelsohn stressed. History was a one-way street; it doesn't move in two directions at once. Either history was moving from the group to the individual, or vice versa. "If Hibbs is right, then both Isaiah and Amos were wrong. They envisioned a human society of growing justice and righteousness in which men would more and more cooperate with each other rather than compete versus each other."[14] If Hibbs was correct, declared Gittelsohn, then both Judaism and Christianity were dead wrong. In an elegant explanation, Gittelsohn informed his congregation both Judaism and Christianity insist that the wealth of this world was a loan made by God to humans, to be managed by humans. "So take your pick—Ben Hibbs or religion—we can't have both because they are mutually exclusive."[15]

To further underscore his point, Gittelsohn turned to America's founders. He declared, if Ben Hibbs was correct, our American pioneer fathers were wrong. They were not "rugged individualists," he informed his audience. They were rugged all right, but they were rugged cooperatively, not individualists. Helping their fellow pioneers was the American way, he explained. Together they developed the land and built their cities and their homes. Gittelsohn concluded this first reason for his violent disagreement with Hibbs by telling the congregation to read, as he had, the accounts of the founding of any one of the new settlements in pioneer America, "…and you'll see how true it is that this nation more than any other in history was founded on the cooperative efforts of men and women acting together in groups for the good of all."[16]

Gittelsohn next turned to his second objection to the vision of Americanism presented by the *Saturday Evening Post*. It was Hibbs' "outrageous libel against one-fifth of the American population."[17] His comments on the immigrants coming to America and their motives, seeking "ready-made" prosperity, infuriated Gittelsohn. His fury was fanned by the memories of his father's and grandfather's experiences in tsarist Russia and their arrival in America, where they proceeded to become hard working and respected figures in the community. Gittelsohn considered the 27 million immigrants to the United States over the prior 60 years when he then declared that as a son of one of those immigrants, he deeply and bitterly resented Hibbs' claiming that those people came here for ulterior motives or that they were ignorant of basic American ideals. He was infuriated by the insinuation that these immigrants were less loyal to American democracy than the *Saturday Evening Post*. Citing well-known immigrants such as Albert Einstein, Thomas Mann, Arturo Toscanini, and Robert Wagner, he stated unequivocally that "I'll take their understanding of American democracy and ideals 1,000 times over before Ben Hibbs' misunderstanding."[18]

After relating an anecdote about immigrants in his home state of Ohio, Gittelsohn felt no further need to belabor his point:

> You and I are entitled to whatever interpretation of American democracy we want. For my part, I'll pass up the mud and silt of the *Saturday Evening Post*, if you don't mind; I'd rather trust our twenty-seven million immigrants and their children than I would Ben Hibbs to cherish and preserve Americanism, and his gratuitous insult to twenty percent of our population is my second reason for rejecting his specious ersatz Americanism.[19]

As one can ascertain, Gittelsohn saw the welcoming of the flood of immigrants to America as a very American ideal, and he believed these immigrants embraced democracy and freedom wholeheartedly. In many respects, accepting immigrants such as Gittelsohn's family, who had come from primarily Eastern European lands without freedom and where persecution was rampant, created an "ultra-American" who truly appreciated what this country offered.

When finishing with his analysis, Gittelsohn was out of time and he asked his congregation for permission to continue his examination of the *Saturday Evening Post* the following week.

On October 30, Gittelsohn resumed his critical analysis of Ben Hibbs' editorial. After a brief summary of the previous week's discussion, he continued on with the third reason that he so violently objected to the *Saturday Evening Post*'s vision of Americanism. It must have startled his congregation to hear him exclaim, "I resent the *Saturday Evening Post*'s Americanism because it's a libelous and unfounded insult to American businessmen and industrialists." He no doubt smiled when he told them, "I suppose that some of you think it is strange that I of all people should be defending businessmen and industrialists. Don't let it floor you—stranger things than that will happen before this war is over," he assured them.[20] His congregation had no idea how prophetic and close to home his statement would prove to be.

To drive home his point, he repeated Hibbs' statement concerning the two courses of action for the "useful citizens" if the state persisted in subsidizing the "useless citizens": either the overthrow of the state or the loss of his incentive to work toward profit generation and hence loss of benefit to the state. Gittelsohn was totally appalled by the brazen statement of Hibbs, comparing it to both the situation in fascist Spain and also to a little child who can't get his way and will not play anymore. If he himself was a businessman or an industrialist with a conscience, declared Gittelsohn, the absurd, petulant accusation by Hibbs would make him livid. There was a myriad of ways of proving that Hibbs' cheap, dishonest statement wasn't true. "As a matter of fact, every American industrial leader who recognizes that even from its own selfish point of view our capitalism needs rather drastic overhauling, is himself an effective answer to Ben Hibbs."[21]

Gittelsohn surprised his audience further by stating that Wendell Willkie provided a pretty good answer to rebut Hibbs' slander of American business. Claiming that Willkie had the right to speak for large segments of the American business community if anyone had, he reminded the congregation that he had opposed Willkie in the past election of 1940 and remained delighted that he was defeated by FDR (who then began a third term). Still, he was nonetheless pleased that Willkie had learned more in defeat than he possibly could have in victory. He jokingly asked the audience not to construe his upcoming compliment as an endorsement for the man in the next election of 1944.

Gittelsohn's praise of Willkie was due to Willkie's radio broadcast on October 26, four days earlier. He had recently returned from a trip abroad where he visited the Middle East, Russia and China, traveling as a free citizen and not as a representative of the government. In his speech entitled, "Deliver the Materials of War—Define Our Peace Aims," Willkie noted that "The people of every land, whether industrialized or not, admire the aspirations and accomplishments of American labor, which they have heard about, and which they long to emulate. Also, they are impressed by American business and industry."[22]

With great pride, Gittelsohn noted that Willkie had observed that people all over the world admired the accomplishments of American labor, not only because they improved the quality of life, but also because it revealed that American business enterprise, unlike that of most other industrial nations, did not necessarily lead to political control or imperialism.[23] He looked out on his congregation and asked, "Does this sound like Ben Hibbs and the *Saturday Evening Post*? Does it sound like American businessmen closing up shop or overthrowing the state because they can't have their way?"[24]

Gittelsohn then proceeded with an even more striking example to counter Hibbs' slander of American business: a statement provided by a witness called to testify to the Senate Military Affairs Committee, Colonel Lewis Sanders. Sanders, the chief of the re-employment Division of the Selective Service System, had been an industrial engineer between the wars and had been employed by some of the largest corporations in the United States. Gittelsohn pointed out that he had never belonged to a labor union and would hardly have been expected to be very sympathetic to the concerns of labor.

The week before, in testimony before Congress, Sanders stated, "I believe that eighty percent of our labor trouble has its basic origin in management, and I speak as one whose background is primarily of management."[25] Gittelsohn was adamant that his point in presenting Sanders' testimony not be misunderstood. He was merely pointing out that there were large numbers of American businesses and industries where managers like Colonel Sanders, "...have accepted labor, have learned to live with the regulations and restrictions of the New Deal, and who don't intend to revolt or stop production!"[26] Hence, according to Gittelsohn, the *Saturday Evening Post* has no right to speak for the business community of America; nonetheless, they did have the perfect right to speak for the extreme fringe—the "Fritz Thysssens of America" he called them, referring to Nazi industrialist Fritz Thyssen. These were the types who would rather beat Roosevelt than Hitler, he claimed. Thank God, he explained that our "Thyssens" were neither representative of American business nor all-powerful, as they had been pretty much repudiated by their fellow businessmen.

Having concluded his defense of the American businessman, Gittelsohn went on to the next reason for his opposition to Hibbs' editorial. Here his passion was obvious as he claimed that in attacking the common man, the *Saturday Evening Post*'s Americanism in fact attacks both religion and democracy. To those members of the congregation who hadn't yet read the editorial, he assured them that they would be stunned by Hibbs' "... naked, disgusting contempt for the common man.... Compared to Ben Hibbs, Marie Antoinette was a lover of the masses and Czar Nicholas II was a union leader."[27]

Gittelsohn claimed he had to read the article four or five times as he could not believe Hibbs' vile descriptions and choice of language in describing most Americans. Hibbs referred to the wealthy members of society as "those talented members of society," "those talented, capable individuals," "the gifted citizen," and "the useful citizen." In contrast, Gittelsohn pointed out, Hibbs used the following insulting descriptions for the poor, the unemployed, and the unhealthy: "'the untalented,' 'the relatively useless citizen,' who Hibbs later refers to as simply 'the useless citizen,' and finally 'the semi-talented or untalented individual, clinging to the kite tail of genius.'"[28]

To put these descriptions into perspective, Gittelsohn offered a biting interpretation of Hibbs' logic. He mentioned the name of Charles Steinmetz, the immigrant from Germany who discovered alternating current and thus started the harnessing of electricity in America. He then pointed out that according to Hibbs' logic Steinmetz, who "...died with [only] $300 to his name, was a semi-talented individual clinging to the kite tail of Tommy Manville." Here Gittelsohn referred to the multimillionaire playboy whose main lifetime accomplishment would be to get married thirteen times, and, "whose chief distinction in life is that his father was born before him. That's really rich."[29]

The other example that Gittelsohn used to repudiate Hibbs was that of Lillian Wald, a woman born into wealth, who became a nurse and then dedicated herself to helping the poor and founding the Henry Street Settlement. Obviously, she had then become a "relatively useless citizen," Gittelsohn noted sarcastically.

It was at this point that Gittelsohn drove straight to the heart of his argument, the crux of his violent disagreement with Hibbs' version of Americanism. His next words would serve not only to clarify and drive home his point, but would also define who Rabbi Roland Gittelsohn truly was, what he believed, and why he loved America. It wasn't just a matter of quibbling or debate, he explained. It went to the very essence and heart of democracy, because according to Gittelsohn democracy was a much simpler thing than most political theorists made of it. "Democracy," he stated, "is nothing more nor less than love of, and abiding faith in, the common man. That's all—it's as simple as all that."[30]

He then defined the simplicity of his definition with everyday examples. "If you believe in treating your maid (assuming you have one) and your gardener and the waitress who serves you in the restaurant as human beings equal in dignity and rights to yours, then you believe in democracy."[31] Gittelsohn cited Thomas Jefferson and Theodore Roosevelt in affirming his love of the common man and his vision of Americanism. He then asked his congregation to compare and contrast this with the Americanism espoused by the *Saturday Evening Post*. Compare the words of Jefferson and Roosevelt with those of Hibbs, he urged, and you'll easily reach your own conclusions.

Realizing that the end of his allotted time was drawing near, Gittelsohn quickly got to the heart of his third objection to the editorial. He claimed that the editorial was a thinly disguised effort to sabotage the American war effort. He noted he had heard a speech two weeks earlier by Senate Majority Leader Alben Barkley, who claimed that there were "three groups of Americans today who wanted us to win the war, but (a) without Russia, (b) without England, and (c) without Roosevelt. I wish it were funny."[32] *The Saturday Evening Post* wanted to win the war, explained Gittelsohn, but they didn't want Roosevelt or the New Deal to win it. And the publication, he said, is "willing, if necessary, to keep Roosevelt from winning it by risking the nation's losing it."[33]

If any of the congregation doubted his analysis of the *Post's* intentions, he invited them to look back with him over each of the four major points made by Ben Hibbs and evaluate what their only possible effects on the war effort could be. First, he argued, if the direction of history was away from the cooperative group and toward the wealthy and successful individual as Hibbs stated, why would groups of people fight as a team under those circumstances?

Next, he asked, if the 30 million immigrants and their sons were no good, why are they fighting as many of them were, and why were they willing to die in defense of their country? If American industrialists would only produce to their maximal capability if they received unlimited profits, then why would labor sacrifice any of its rights? Under this scenario, how could America possibly obtain the equipment without which it would be impossible to win the war?

Last, and most strikingly, Gittelsohn asked that if the common man was so useless and deserving of scorn, then why on earth would he be fighting for our country? Did the *Post* really believe that the common man would be fighting for the right of Tommy Manville and other millionaires to get richer? Or perhaps the *Saturday Evening Post* was hoping that this kind of talk would discourage the common man from fighting altogether and thereby lose the war "...and put an end to the New Deal; and thereby bring in Hitler with whom the *Saturday Evening Post* perhaps stupidly believes it could do business better than it can with Roosevelt?"[34]

In light of all this evidence, Gittelsohn pronounced that whatever Hibbs and his backers were, they were not infantile and naïve. "Their words as published here," he claimed, "are calculated to hinder, not to help out striving for military victory."[35] In closing, he told the congregation that they probably had wondered why he had dedicated two sermons to the "ridiculous editorial." He hoped that by now they understood the reasons for his objections to the *Post*'s editorial.

Gittelsohn ended his second sermon with a final salvo against the distorted Americanism envisioned by the *Saturday Evening Post*, stating, he opposed it "Because this is the last disgusting lunge of those who are determined not to permit this war to be the people's war, nor to let it usher in the century of the common man."[36]

• • •

Gittelsohn's battle with the *Saturday Evening Post*'s vision of Americanism is both interesting and instructive on many accounts. It revealed his taking the first step in his evolution from total pacifist to supporting a "just war" fought by the common man in the United States.

As a historical aside, Gittelsohn made Hibbs the object of his wrath. However, in all likelihood, the editorial was written by Garet Garrett, the editorial writer-in-chief at the *Post* from 1940 until 1942. The tone and arguments presented in the piece were clearly reflective of the ideology of Garrett. The iconic Garrett, who so strongly opposed American entry into the war, then volunteered for military service at the age of 64. Hibbs on the other hand, served as editor of the periodical from 1942 until 1962, when he left to become the editor of *Reader's Digest*. Ironically, Hibbs was described by the Kansas Historical Society as an unassuming, humble man who consciously kept in touch with the common man.[37]

Historically, the elitist business community described in the editorial never really existed. In January 1942, by executive order, FDR established the War Production Board to regulate the production of materials and consumption of fuels during the war. Industry in the United States worked hand in hand with the government to develop unprecedented industrial power in the war-time economy. Labor and business worked cooperatively to support the American war effort. The American public in general dutifully submitted to price controls and gasoline rationing to support the war effort. Business titans such as Henry Kaiser and Andrew Higgins responded not with the resentment that the editorial had predicted, but with drive, innovation and genius to contribute greatly to the American war goals. The self-centered "my way or the highway" reaction foreseen by the *Post*'s Americanism never materialized.

Gittelsohn's definition and description of democracy say much about the man. His lifelong focus on "democracy" would continue to define him. And there was one fact in his analysis that stands out: that the war would, in fact, become a war of the common man. When World War II broke out in September of 1939, the United States had a small military force, smaller than such countries as Belgium and Portugal. After Pearl Harbor, thousands of Americans would flood enlistment centers on a regular basis. By the war's end, there would be 12 million Americans in uniform. It was a military made up of ordinary Americans, not professionals. They were citizen soldiers. According to Stephen Ambrose, "They wanted to be throwing baseballs, not hand grenades, shooting .22s at rabbits, not M-1s at other young men. But when the test came, when freedom had to be fought for or abandoned, they fought."[38] These were the common men who Gittelsohn empathized with and admired so much.

The *Post*'s use of the term "useless citizens" was most offensive to Gittelsohn and for good reason. It was disturbingly close to the Nazi description of mentally handicapped citizens under the authority of the Third Reich. They were referred to as "useless eaters" whose very existence was a burden to the German *Volk* and hence they needed to be sterilized and ultimately destroyed, lest they propagate more burdens for the German citizenry to support.

Gittelsohn's use of examples such as Albert Einstein and Charles Steinmetz to counter the Post's anti-immigrant stance was brilliant. His sense of outrage over the slanderous statement implying that immigrants weren't seeking freedom but were instead coming to America as part of a virtual "get rich quick" scheme, was well justified. Gittelsohn correctly pointed out the high percentage of the immigrant population currently serving in the military. He needed only to reflect upon the contributions of his immigrant father and grandfather to find powerful ammunition to counter the ridiculous claims of the *Post*.

After reading his sermons that refuted the *Saturday Evening Post*, one can discern a transition in Gittelsohn's thinking about participating in war when necessary. True, he would always remain a civil libertarian devoted to the rights of the common man and to justice and fairness for all. His basic support of labor in issues where labor and management conflicted would also remain unchanged. Now, however, his focus on Franklin D. Roosevelt had shifted away from what he had perceived and had highly criticized as FDR's efforts to entangle us into war; instead, Gittelsohn had come to support the president's New Deal policies. The rabbi appeared to no longer view Hitler and his European hegemony as something that the United States could or necessarily should avoid, as evidenced by his support of Russia in their war against the Nazis. And most interestingly, he now could speak in positive terms about American businessmen and industrialists while still retaining a distaste for certain forms of capitalism when they stressed excessive profits over the good of the working man. His core principles were immutable and would remain unchanged until the day he died, but some of his perceptions were changing and evolving.

• • •

As mentioned above, in his October 30 sermon, Gittelsohn jokingly warned his congregation after he told them he was about to come to the defense of American businesses, "Don't let it floor you; stranger things than that will happen before this war is over." That month, he indicated just how strange things had gotten. He announced that he was taking a leave of absence as rabbi to the Central Synagogue of Nassau County. Then he dropped a real bombshell by stating his reason for the leave of absence. *He was joining the United States Navy.*

PART II

WARRIOR

O Lord! Thou knowest how busy I must be this day:
If I forget Thee, do not Thou forget me.
—Sir Jacob Ashley at the Battle of Edge Hill, 1642

Praise the Lord and pass the ammunition.
—Inspired by the actions of Chaplain William Maguire
at Pearl Harbor on December 7, 1941.

FIFTEEN

Becoming a Chaplain

Like virtually all Americans, Roland Gittelsohn's life was forever changed that first Sunday in December 1941. On the afternoon of December 7, the Gittelsohn family was driving on the Long Island Expressway, not far from Hempstead where they lived. Gittelsohn was absorbed in the sounds of the New York Philharmonic Orchestra when suddenly the music stopped. Annoyed at the interruption, he began fiddling with the volume and station knobs, suspecting that the radio station transmitting equipment had died. Hearing the voices of announcers from the station reassured him that this was not the case. For a brief moment, his annoyance began to build when suddenly the announcer on the radio urgently spoke: "Ladies and gentlemen, we interrupt this program to bring you a late news bulletin. Japanese planes have attacked the United States Naval Base at Pearl Harbor...."

Rabbi Gittelsohn was now at the threshold of confronting the greatest challenge to his convictions that he would ever face. The main thought that went through his mind over and over that day was, "I don't believe it!"[1] As details of the attack on our naval base in Hawaii emerged throughout the day, Gittelsohn could only protest to himself, "I don't believe it!" Here was a man who was an ardent pacifist his entire life, a rabbi who had delivered a sermon in the recent past where he insisted that the United States must stay out of the war in Europe. Despite reminding his congregation of his hatred of Hitler and his wishes for the defeat of Nazi Germany, he displayed his total opposition to war thusly: "You will know how I want America to stay out of this war if I tell you from the bottom of my heart that, much as I want Hitler to lose, I want us to stay out of the war even if he seems to be winning."[2]

Here was a man who in the 1930s had been a member of the War Resisters League and had signed the Oxford Pledge. Here was a man to whom the concept of total pacifism was uncompromising and crystal clear. Now, with Japan's bombing of Pearl Harbor, his lifelong belief in avoiding war at all costs came to a sudden halt. He agonized over the collision between classroom theory and cruel reality; one where his long-held views on pacifism, when weighed against the Japan's outright aggression against his country, suddenly didn't seem quite as clear cut. The choices suddenly were no longer as simple as war is bad, peace is good. Evil, in the form of the Japanese attack on our soil, had made his conceptual argument less focused and at the same time, it had now crystalized into a more basic black and white issue; that of good versus evil and the struggle of the United States and her allies versus the destructive threats of the Axis powers' fascism and fanaticism. The next day, December 8, 1941, the United States declared war on Japan. Gittelsohn knew that now he and his fellow Americans would now have to commit themselves to war.

At the end of the war, Gittelsohn would reflect on the three basic reasons for his initial astonishment and disbelief about Japan's attack on Pearl Harbor.[3] The first reason was overconfidence. Since his high school debating days, he had opposed every naval appropriation bill and was convinced that the United States—and especially the United States Navy—had built an impregnable military force due to excessive spending. No one nation would be mad enough to attack so great a military force that America could deploy.

As a pragmatic man, Gittelsohn had a second reason for his astonished reaction to the Pearl Harbor attack. Until then he had refused to believe that the Japanese were any more warlike than Americans. It used to infuriate him when people would insist otherwise. Leave the Japanese alone, he had reasoned, and they will leave us alone.

Last, and most important, Gittelsohn was a pacifist, or as he described himself, "a complete, convinced, literal, unreasonable, dogmatic, unchangeable pacifist!"[4] He had even told friends that he was prepared to spend the next war in prison. He had argued with his father that submission to the worst evil was better than resisting it by force.[5]

In reality, Gittelsohn's previously unshakable belief in pacifism had already begun to waver over a year before the Japanese attack on American soil. By his own admission, he began to question his own views in the spring of 1940 as he was following the events of the war in Europe. In May of that year, the British Expeditionary Forces were driven back to the coast by the forces of Nazi Germany. From May 27 through June 4, more than 338,000 British soldiers were evacuated from the French port of Dunkirk, along with nearly 140,000 French, Polish and Belgian troops. An armada of 861 vessels (including 243 sunk by the Germans) was involved in the evacuation.[6] On June 22, 1940, France surrendered to Germany. The world was stunned. Nazi Germany now controlled all of Europe.

Reading about the evacuation at Dunkirk, Gittelsohn was shaken. The four months following Dunkirk proved to be very difficult for him as he kept weighing the choices that now seemed to be facing him.[7] For the first time, he began to have his doubts about his rock-solid, uncompromising views on war and peace. The lines began to blur for him between the theory of pacifism at all costs versus the reality that evil was on the march in Europe and the Far East.

World War II would have similar effects on the belief systems of other longtime committed pacifist Reform rabbis.

Approximately two miles away in nearby Lynbrook, Long Island, Rabbi Harold Saperstein of Temple Emanuel was undergoing a crisis of conscience similar to Gittelsohn. Born in the same year as Gittelsohn, he too had been a lifelong and staunch pacifist. He admired Gittelsohn for the strength and clarity of his sermons, and his own sermons were as passionate about the cause of pacifism as were his neighbor's. By October of 1940, Saperstein's doubts became evident in his Rosh Hashanah sermon, when he acknowledged that he had come to realize that some things are worse than war, and some things more important than peace. "And so as I pray for peace," he told his congregation, "I find myself fearing a peace on Hitler's terms, a peace of submission to the forces of barbarism."[8]

Three days after the attack on Pearl Harbor, December 10, 1941, Saperstein received a letter from the influential Rabbi Stephen Wise. In it, Wise asked Saperstein if he was willing to take a leave of absence from his congregation and to serve as a chaplain in the U.S. Army for the duration of the war. Wise acknowledged, "…that this might entail a great sacrifice on your part, but nothing short of the greatest sacrifice on the part of us all will carry us through to victory."[9] On June 23, 1943, Saperstein said farewell to his congregation and left for the Army Chaplain School at Harvard University.

Even more representative of the crisis of conscience experienced by many Reform rabbis was that of Rabbi Judah Magnes. After the entry of the United States into the First World War in 1917, Magnes, already an outspoken pacifist, became one of the country's most vociferous critics of the war. Joining with other prominent pacifists such as Norman Thomas, he became the first chairman of the pacifist political organization, the People's Council of America for Democracy and Peace.

After emigrating to Palestine in 1922, Rabbi Magnes became chancellor, then president of the Hebrew University in Jerusalem. In a speech he delivered to the student body to begin the academic year on October 29, 1939, the lifelong committed pacifist revealed that he reluctantly supported the war against Germany. He asked his audience to bear with him if he discussed "the problem of those radical pacifists and conscientious objectors, of whom I was one during the last war, and who now regard it as their duty to give their support to this war."[10] Comparing Hitler to the devil who used the power of persecution against Jews and other minorities, Magnes ruefully posed a question to his students: "Peace at almost any price is better than war. But what is that price? For myself, I would answer in a word: that the devil be bereft of the power of persecuting."[11] He reluctantly concluded that the only way to deal with the devil was to support the war that the western powers would wage to destroy Hitler and his allies.

Gittelsohn would look back at the end of World War II in an unpublished book and recall his feelings on the military before the war. In a surprisingly candid admission, he revealed the somewhat naïve thinking that was more suitable to a debating society than to confronting the realities of a world moving almost inevitably toward another world war. "In the old days we pacifists used to base part of our unalterable opposition to war on the fact that it and democracy were incompatible ... we insisted that a military machine had to be a dictatorship, could not be democratic."[12] His views on the military would undergo a sobering revision after the onset of the Second World War.

Gittelsohn's evolving thoughts on war and peace were strongly influenced by the views of his closest friend, Rabbi Jacob P. Rudin of Great Neck, New York. Rudin shaped Gittelsohn's soul searching and his search for answers on his journey from anti-war rabbi to military chaplain. Like Gittelsohn himself, Rudin had been an ardent and outspoken pacifist while the chaos in Europe evolved in the 1930s. He and Gittelsohn had many discussions about the direction they should take. Rudin struggled in his mind over what course to follow, and by the beginning of the summer of 1942, he had made his decision. He sought a commission as a chaplain in the United States Naval Reserve. Ever since the attack on Pearl Harbor, the two men met frequently to discuss what paths they should take and what God intended for them.

Despite being the best of friends, the two rabbis took fundamentally different approaches to their dilemma. By Gittelsohn's own admission, Rudin had a much keener insight into the issue than he did.[13] In the month following the attack on Pearl Harbor, Rudin felt the issue was both immediate and intensely personal. It was a decision that he felt he needed to make at once and without equivocation. Immediate personal action was called for and Rudin intended to respond in that manner. On the other hand, Gittelsohn approached the whole situation as a matter of theory, one to be analyzed in a detached, impersonal manner. The situation had to be studied from all angles and all facets needed to be examined and evaluated. In his theoretical approach a decision would have to be made, although not necessarily in the immediate future.

Gittelsohn struggled for several months with the pros and cons of following his best friend's decision to volunteer for military service. Rudin had undoubtedly influenced him, and by the fall of 1942, Gittelsohn came to the conclusion that he, too, must join the military and that, "this was where I come in."[14] Certainly one of the key factors influencing his decision to join the military came from his studies of Jewish scripture and thought. He knew that Jewish tradition describes two kinds of war, *milchemet chovah*, compulsory or obligatory war, and *milchemet r'shut*, optional war.[15] Every Jew is obligated to participate in the first.

Unlike denominations such as Quakers and Mennonites, Jewish tradition did not force absolute pacifism upon its adherents. Tradition had franchised each Jew to decide whether for him a given military conflict is a compulsory war or an optional war. Clearly, the war against Hitler and the Axis powers where nothing less than the survival of the Jewish people was at stake, was a *milchemet chovah*. This was a "just war" that Gittelsohn could reconcile with his previously strident views on pacifism.

It was this common thread that ran through the thinking of all these rabbis who had been avowed pacifists. The rise of Nazism and violent antisemitic persecution made it crystal clear: It was a fight for the survival of the Jewish people. This understanding imbued Jewish religious military personnel with a determination to serve in the armed forces not generally expressed by their Christian counterparts.[16]

During those difficult times of reflection and introspection after the Pearl Harbor attack, Gittelsohn's decision-making was also influenced by several lines of thought that would lead him away from pacifism and towards military service. His Jewish religious roots and values inspired his various lines of reasoning.

As a Jew, and especially as a rabbi, he was immensely proud of the part that his people played not only in this war, but in every struggle in American history.[17] Reflecting on these previous conflicts, he proudly noted that while American Jews during World War I represented about 3 percent of the nation's population, they accounted for close to 5 percent of the men in the armed forces. He also reflected on how much gratitude his family owed to America, the nation that received his father and grandfather with open arms when they fled from the oppression and vicious antisemitism of Tsarist Russia. Didn't he, Rabbi Roland Gittelsohn, owe a debt to the United States? What better way to pay that debt than with military service in support of American troops?

A second major reason influencing Gittelsohn's ultimate decision was the rise of Hitler and Nazism. Although the total nature of Hitler's "Final Solution" for the Jewish people was not completely known at that time, certainly enough was known of the actions of the Nazi regime by the United States and its allies to realize that Jews in Europe, and ultimately Jewry worldwide, were in true peril. Every day, as Gittelsohn would read in the Jewish Telegraphic Agency of a new bloodbath or similar atrocity, he would ask himself the question, "And what are you doing about all this? … Would I play a part that is immediate and direct, or be a good cheerleader on the sidelines? Which will it be?"[18]

His next line of reasoning was a common motivation for clergymen of all faiths when deciding to join the military. He knew that young men and women who were previously indifferent to religion, would for the first time feel the need for religious support and comfort in wartime. This fact was borne out by virtually every chaplain already serving in the military. The effects on servicemen's lives, their spouses, children, and parents, were overwhelming, and many turned to the synagogue or church in their time of need for succor and guidance. There simply weren't enough chaplains on active duty to deal with the ever-increasing numbers of military men and their families. To Gittelsohn, religion was "on the spot," and he stated unequivocally that, "If religion has nothing to offer our soldiers and sailors now in their moment of greatest need, they will have nothing to offer religion, indeed, no use at all for religion when the war is over."[19]

His last line of thought was intensely personal. To him, his decision would be a test of his own faith, of whether he was willing to live what he preached. He had preached that it wasn't material comfort or ease that mattered most in life; it was the moral and spiritual values that were most important. That it was better to die for a good purpose than to live for no purpose. That sacrifice for the common good was often necessary. Did he truly believe in these concepts or was he really saying, "Do as I say, not as I do?"[20]

He went on to answer his own question, citing Jewish sages centuries earlier, when they said, *"Lo ha-midrash iker, elo ha-ma-aseh"*: "Not study (or theory) is the essential thing, but action!" He, Roland Gittelsohn, had to practice what he preached, or he would never be able to say these things again.[21]

His country was in peril, and now he realized it was his duty to take an active role in helping save the very country that had given refuge to his earlier generations of his family, including his immigrant father and grandparents. After all, America had given him and others many freedoms, including the freedom to dissent with policies that he disagreed with. He would now seek to join the "undemocratic" military that he had, for years, looked on with disdain. By this very action, he was providing answers to the timeless questions posed two thousand years earlier by the Jewish sage Hillel who asked: "If I am not for myself, who will be for me? If I am only for myself, what am I? And if not now, when?"[22]

Years later, in his late seventies, Rabbi Gittelsohn would write:

What made me, after the most excruciating moral dilemma of my life, renounce my pacifism and apply for a military commission? Several things. Hitler's nefarious ambition to exterminate the entire Jewish people had become transparent. I couldn't possibly accede to so ugly and evil a price for my pacifism. Young men whom I had taught and confirmed were being drafted. I had no right to hide behind my rabbinic exemption or to leave them away from home and in combat bereft of religious leadership. Finally, I felt a heavy sense of responsibility to my colleagues.[23]

By the fall of 1942, after six years as a congregational rabbi, and with the total support of his wife Ruth, he made his decision. His journey that began with the evacuation of Dunkirk was complete. He was no longer the total pacifist who would prefer to go to prison rather than serve in the military. He would seek a commission to become a chaplain in the United States Naval Reserve, just as his good friend Jack Rudin had. His path was now clear as was his conscience.

And so, in October of 1942, Rabbi Gittelsohn announced to his congregation his plan to enter military service the following spring. The radio broadcast of December 7, 1941, had crystalized the seeds of doubt that had been planted the previous year by the evacuation of Dunkirk. "Dunkirk had found me a pacifist,—disturbed but still convinced. Pearl Harbor had jolted the last of my uncomfortable pacifism. By the beginning of 1943 my conscience had completed the cycle, had compelled me to apply for the right to wear the uniform of a chaplain in the navy."[24]

• • •

Gittelsohn embarked on a path that few rabbis had ever tread. The records of the Navy Chaplain Corps reveal that only two rabbis had served in the United States Navy prior to December 7, 1941.[25] He certainly met the newly formulated entry qualifications developed by the Navy Chaplain Corps. The criteria required that all applicant clergymen be male United States citizens between the ages of 21 and 45 years old. They must be regularly ordained and be duly accredited by and in good standing, with a religious denomination or organization which held an apportionment of chaplain appointments in accordance with the needs of the service. Applicants must be graduates of both a four-year college and a three-year theological seminary. Although the United States Army also required that applicants have an additional three years experience post-seminary studies as an active clergyman, the Navy had no such requirement.[26] As a rabbinical candidate for a Navy commission, Gittelsohn also had to obtain an endorsement from the National Jewish Welfare Board.

After he received his endorsement, he had to successfully complete written examinations administered by the Chaplain Corps. He accomplished this task and was next found to be within physical fitness standards for commissioning. Having successfully jumped through all of the hurdles required of him, Gittelsohn was ready to answer Hillel's question, "If not now, when?"

He had come full circle. The fire-breathing pacifist of the pre–Dunkirk days was now accepted for entry into the United States Naval Reserve. He was commissioned as a lieutenant (junior grade) in the Chaplain Corps on May 12, 1943, the day before his 33rd birthday. That summer, Lieutenant (j.g.) Roland B. Gittelsohn, Chaplain Corps, United States Naval Reserve, reported for his initial military training in Williamsburg, Virginia.

• • •

Prior to World War II, clergymen joining the military received no formal military training. They were apprenticed to experienced military chaplains and learned by shadowing them and watching them perform their religious duties in the military environment. After the onset of the war, both the Army and the Navy acknowledged not only the need for a much greater number of chaplains on active duty to minister to the soldiers, sailors, and airmen, but

Front and side photographs of Roland Gittelsohn from his commissioning application for the Unites States Navy, 1943 (courtesy St. Louis Personnel Records Center).

also the need for a more formalized training curriculum for their incoming clergymen if they were going to be an effective asset to the troops. The Army re-established a Chaplain School in Indiana in January of 1942. Later that year, the school was moved to Harvard University. In February of 1942, the United States Navy established the Naval Chaplains School (NCS—now known as the Naval Chaplaincy School and Center, or NCSC) at Naval Station, Norfolk, Virginia. The purpose of the new school's mission was succinctly described in its mission statement:

> Crowd[ing] into two months the indoctrination that a chaplain would ordinarily acquire through long service. It will include lectures and reading courses on Navy Regulations and Procedure, Customs and Traditions, Etiquette, Naval History, Marine Corps History, Applied Psychology, Counselling [*sic*], a course in physical fitness, and actual practice among men of the area. Students will be made thoroughly acquainted with sociological program of the Naval Service, particularly as it concerns the work of the Navy Relief Society and the American Red Cross.[27]

It was an ambitious but critical curriculum that would familiarize the civilian volunteer clergymen with all aspects of the Navy and the Marine Corps. It would teach them what they needed to know and understand in order to effectively minister to their troops.

In an effort to provide better and more spacious facilities, the school was moved about an hour's drive north of Norfolk to the campus of the College of William and Mary, in Williamsburg, Virginia. On February 22, 1943, the school was reopened in its new location and renamed the Naval Training School for Chaplains. The College of William and Mary, the second oldest college in the country, was then and remains now a beautiful collection of colonial-style buildings, located about an hour north of the home of the United States Atlantic Fleet in Norfolk, Virginia. Adjacent to the campus was the recently restored Colonial Williamsburg, an effort that had been spearheaded by the Rockefeller family. The school held classes in Marshall-Wythe Hall, then located near the center of the campus, as well as Old Dominion Hall. Religious services were held in the Christopher Wren Chapel at the south end of the campus.

The new school was the inspiration of Captain Clinton A. Neyman, a Baptist minister and a career Navy chaplain. Neyman has conceived of the school, designed the curriculum, and served as the Officer in Charge until the summer of 1944. He staffed the school with about a dozen faculty members. Every faculty member that served under him had key background experience that made them eminently qualified for their roles as mentors to their students. In addition to being Navy chaplains themselves, they all had prior shipboard experience or overseas experience with the Navy. Most of them had combat experience.

The curriculum that Neyman designed was eight weeks long and had three main goals. The first and foremost was to train all of the students, who were already ordained clergymen and "hopelessly unmilitary civilians," and to transform them into naval officers. Next was to prepare them physically and get them into excellent physical shape. These chaplains would be going overseas with their men, going to sea with them, and ultimately living "in the field" with them. They had to be physically ready for the challenge. Lastly, the school would give them the tools of their future trade, the ones that they would require to attend to the special needs of military servicemen.

The course was unlike any course of instruction its students had ever attended. The experiences of Neyman and his fellow instructors would assure that this was not just a collection of courses in theology. They would translate their naval experiences into a teaching program that would make it crystal clear to all the students what it meant to be a chaplain in America's fighting Navy. Given what these instructors had lived through, there could be no other way. Two of the instructor chaplains had each served aboard aircraft carriers that had been sunk by the Japanese in combat in the Pacific theater. Two of the first chaplains ever to serve with the United States Marines were also faculty members.

The training curriculum was divided into three phases. The first three weeks consisted of classroom lectures and training, as did the last three weeks. In between these two blocks of classroom work was a two-week field exercise at one of the naval installations in the region. During this time, they would be working with Navy chaplains, acting in the capacity of an apprentice. There was two hours of field drills and physical exercises a day, as well as weekly swimming sessions.

A common theme was woven throughout the training that the chaplains received. It was a concept new to them and crucial to their future success as Navy chaplains. For the first time in their lives, they would be ministering to men of other religions in addition to their own. They had to learn about all religions and their customs and rituals in order to serve the entire naval force. At Williamsburg, they were constantly told: "You are Navy chaplains first, denominational chaplains only secondly! Your job is to provide for the needs of all men of every faith!"[28]

Gittelsohn reported to the school on June 21, a sweltering June day that was typical for Tidewater, Virginia, summers. He was a member of Class 12-43, a class that consisted of 50 newly commissioned Navy chaplains. He was one of two rabbis in the class.

Gittelsohn and his 49 classmates were immediately thrown into a new world that was both exciting and a bit bewildering to adjust to. Many graduates of the Naval Training School for Chaplains would later note that one of the first immersion techniques used by Neyman and his faculty was to teach them the new Navy language they would use to communicate when they entered the fleet.[29] They quickly learned that floors were "decks," walls were "bulkheads," stairs were "ladders," and beds were "racks." Sailors didn't eat meals prepared in the kitchen, they ate "chow cooked in the galley." As Gittelsohn accurately observed, "Sailors are very apt to lack the time or the inclination to translate a sermon as they listen."[30]

An anecdote serving to emphasize the importance of the new "language" that they were learning was mentioned in a *Time* magazine article about the Chaplain School, written while Gittelsohn was in attendance there. In the June 21, 1943, issue, an article about the Williamsburg school entitled "Religion: Seagoing Men of God," noted that a typical remark by an instructor in class had been to point out that the last Sunday they preached from their home pulpit, some nice lady probably came up and said, "That was a wonderful message, Doctor." Conversely, the first Sunday that they would preach after they finished this school, "…some bluejacket may come up and say, 'Damn good sermon, padre.' You must realize that there is as much sincerity in one as in the other."[31]

The next orientation sessions taught the newly commissioned chaplains naval customs and courtesies. All of the students learned how to properly wear their new uniforms, how to identify the various ranks and corps of the Navy as well as the Marine Corps. They were taught how to salute and whom to salute. Naval protocol was drilled into them. Among these skills were the proper way to board and disembark a Navy ship. Gittelsohn would recall at the end of the war his first clumsy attempt at boarding a ship. To make the experience even more humiliating to him, it was a British aircraft carrier. After very self-consciously walking up the gangplank, he tripped at the top, falling into the arms of the bewildered British officer of the deck.[32] He and his fellow students would come to appreciate very quickly the skills that they were learning at Williamsburg. They all realized that unless they knew how to comport themselves like naval officers, unless they knew how to be "one of them" among their troops, their usefulness to the men who they would be serving would be considerably diminished.

"Tools of the trade" was a critically important concept for the students to master. To completely minister to their men, the new military chaplains would have to attend to more than only spiritual needs. Chaplains would have to be familiar with real-world issues affecting sailors, issues that would inspire them to turn to their chaplain for guidance when there was no one else to whom they could turn. The chaplains would be taught about insurance, allotments, and family allowances. They would learn how to prepare a will or a power of attorney. They would be taught in detail about the policies and procedures of both the Navy Relief Society as well as the American Red Cross. The official handling of weddings and funeral services in the Navy, as well the proper procedures for burial at sea were thoroughly taught. Often it was the chaplain who would be in charge of the ship's library, so library science was also included in the curriculum, as was the ships' newspaper. For Class 12–43, there was one lecture on the United States Marine Corps and its relationship to the United States Navy. Although Gittelsohn couldn't possibly have known it at the time, it was a subject that would soon have a profound impact on his life.

One aspect of their training that had a surprisingly beneficial effect on many of the students was the physical fitness program. By the end of the first week, all of the chaplains were suffering from aching muscles that seemed to be worsened by even the slightest movement. There was much complaining and moaning by the majority of men who were not used to a vigorous exercise program, although many admitted that they really enjoyed being forced to exercise and getting into better physical condition. In addition to abandon ship drills and survival swimming, there were the frequent long-distance runs over the two-and-a-half mile running trail near the campus. It was with much pride that Gittelsohn noted that by actual testing, in his class there was a 35 percent improvement in strength and endurance by the week of their graduation.[33]

One of the most important aspects of the training curriculum was to teach the students about different religions. This was crucial if a Navy chaplain was to be able to minister to the needs of all Sailors and Marines, many of whom would be members of different religious denominations. They needed to learn how to comfort and sustain a dying Sailor or Marine of a faith different from their own, which was something they had never done before in their lives. In this particular aspect, the Naval Training School for Chaplains was highly successful. Every student who went through the course was unanimous in their appreciation of the interfaith training that they received in Williamsburg. As Gittelsohn wryly noted, "Nothing but a war could bring three hundred clergymen—Protestants, Catholics, and Jews—to live together intimately for a period of two months."[34] He estimated that in his seven years as a rabbi before joining the Navy, 90-plus percent of his contacts with clergymen had been with clergymen of his own faith, namely rabbis. No doubt, he surmised, it had been a similar situation with his Christian classmates. He thought it not improbable that the majority of his fifty classmates had never spoken to a Jew for more than a fleeting second, face to face, before they had come to know him and his fellow rabbi in their class.

Gittelsohn's appreciation of the unique comparative religion "learning laboratory" offered by the experience in Williamsburg was shared by virtually all its graduates. The Rev. Ross Trower offered an opinion of the program in a 2003 interview for the University of North Carolina at Wilmington that was common to all the graduates. There were two or three things that meant a great deal to many of them, he recalled, but most important, they suddenly became involved with ministers, priests and rabbis of many persuasions, and many traditions, "…a consequence that hardly any of us in those days and few of us even in these days experience in rubbing shoulders with other religious leaders of other faith groups. It was wonderful."[35]

Time magazine, writing at the time when Gittelsohn was in attendance, also noted the beneficial impact of clergymen of different faiths living together and learning together. An article described a Protestant minister who at first wanted to quit the school because, "there were Papists there." By the end of the course, his best friend was a Catholic priest. Also quoted was a Navy student they interviewed who "wondered out loud how he can go back to strictly denominational ministering after the war."[36]

A facet of the Chaplain Training School that proved to be universally popular and highly successful was the assignment of roommates. This policy, adopted by the Navy when the school opened in Williamsburg, was the same as that espoused by the Army in February of 1942. Student chaplains would live with other students of different denominations. Gittelsohn noted that he had three roommates during his two 3-week stays in residence at the school. They were a Presbyterian, a Southern Baptist and a Roman Catholic. Enthusiastically, he would state, "If they learned half as much about my faith as I learned of theirs, they will never regret an experience which to me is priceless."[37] Every night before securing, his Christian colleagues would kneel and recite their bed-time prayers while at the same moment Gittelsohn laid in his rack, "…reciting to myself the watchword of Judaism, '*Shema Yisroel, Adonoy Elohaynu, Adonoy Echod*; Hear O Israel, the Lord or God, the Lord is One!' In what other land could that happen? Under what other circumstance *would* it happen?"[38]

All the students heard lectures about faiths other than their own, given by the respective clergymen of that faith. For the first time in his life, Gittelsohn attended both Catholic and Protestant masses in the form of a "dry mass" to learn about Christian doctrine, necessary for him to minister to Christians. In turn, his Christian colleagues saw a Torah and an Ark for the first time in their lives. He and his fellow rabbi classmate, in addition to holding Sabbath Services each week at the Christopher Wren Chapel library, would attend the daily Protestant devotions at 6:40 each morning. With pride, he noted that during his entire stay at Williamsburg, one of the twelve members of each class who were invited to conduct these daily Protestant devotions was always a rabbi.

Gittelsohn wrote that words would be insufficient to capture the living thrill of what he and his classmates experienced together at Williamsburg.

Describing it as just an honest effort to understand each other in an honest determination to help each other, he pondered, "Did we succeed?" To answer his own question, he turned with pride to the words of one of his roommates on the day they dispersed to their assigned units: "I wouldn't hesitate to entrust the religious training of my Christian child to a rabbi like either of you in the class."[39]

By the end of their eight-week course, Roland Gittelsohn and his classmates were ready. They were now trained in the various aspects of the Navy and Marine Corps that they would need in order to be successful chaplains. They were in the best physical conditions of their lives. It was August of 1943 and their assignments were announced. A stunned Lieutenant (j.g.) Roland Gittelsohn learned that he was the first rabbi ever to be assigned to the United States Marine Corps.

Sixteen

The First Marine Rabbi

As Nazi aggression expanded in Europe and the Japanese broadened its military targets in the Pacific, the United States slowly woke up from its doldrums. President Franklin D. Roosevelt had declared a limited national emergency on September 8, 1939. Nearly two years later he declared an unlimited national emergency on May 27, 1941. In July 1941, there were 53,886 Marines on active duty. A year later, after FDR declared war, there was a national rush to volunteer for military service. The Marine Corps strength had nearly tripled to 143,388.[1] To accommodate the training of these new Marine recruits, major training centers had to be enlarged on both coasts.

The Marine Corps looked to train troops at Camp Kearny, an old U.S. Army base established in World War I in the Kearny Mesa section of northeast San Diego. Earlier, in 1934, the Marine Corps had acquired a portion of that base and on June 14, 1940, they renamed it Camp Elliott in honor of Major General George F. Elliott, the 10th Commandant of the Marine Corps. Through a series of rapidly acquiring adjacent lands, the base grew in size, ultimately reaching 26,034 acres.

The 2nd Marine Division, commanded by Major General C.F.B. Price, was activated on February 1, 1941, at Camp Elliott. Its mission was to train individual replacements for combat duty, and in January 1942, the division assumed responsibility for all of the training on the base. In September 1942, Camp Elliott became the home of the Fleet Marine Force Training Center, West Coast, at which time there were more than 10,000 Marines in the San Diego area.

Looking back in 1988, Gittelsohn would humorously recall that he applied for a commission in the Navy by explaining facetiously that his wife preferred him in blue, that he wanted to eat off a white tablecloth, and that he didn't want to carry a knapsack or dig foxholes. "So I became a Marine Corps chaplain, wearing only khaki and green, never blue; there were no tablecloths of any color; I carried a knapsack and dug foxholes."[2]

As the United States Marine Corps is part of the Department of the Navy, all medical and religious personnel assigned to the Corps are from the U.S. Navy.

After a cross-country drive, the Gittelsohn family arrived in San Diego in August of 1943. Gittelsohn formally reported for duty at Marine Barracks, Camp Elliott on August 30, 1943. Before reporting for duty, Gittelsohn had already looked into the physical requirements for serving in the Marine Corps. During his commissioning physical for the Navy his height was measured as 65 and ¾ inches, ¼ inch below the minimum standard of 66. Accordingly, the Navy granted him a waiver. He didn't want to have to possibly go through another waiver process with the Marines so on his intake paperwork for the Marine Corps, he listed his height as 67 inches. The Marines never actually measured his height.[3]

Gittelsohn reported in as an assistant chaplain to the Fleet Marine Force, Pacific Fleet Chaplain, Captain William A. Maguire. Maguire was already a legend in the United States Navy. A Roman Catholic priest, he had joined the Navy in July 1917. He had received the Navy Cross for heroism in April of 1918 as a result of his efforts to rescue men from another ship that was on fire and laden with explosives. Maguire was present at the Japanese attack on Pearl Harbor, in a motorboat en route to the battleship USS *California* (BB-44) to conduct morning mass when the attack commenced. He made multiple efforts to rescue men in the water and also commandeered a Navy ferry to help transport more wounded Sailors to the hospital. The expression "Praise the Lord and pass the ammunition" was widely attributed to him, although he insisted that he had never said it.

Maguire had served as Fleet Chaplain, U.S. Pacific Fleet, from October of 1941 until May of 1942. He was appointed as Chaplain for the Naval Training School at San Diego on June 13, 1942, and on July 22, 1943, he was appointed to the staff of the Commanding General, Fleet Marine Force (FMF), Pacific Fleet. A little more than a month later, LT (j.g.) Gittelsohn reported to Maguire's staff as an assistant chaplain.

As the only Jewish chaplain on staff, Gittelsohn covered all of the half-dozen or so Marine installations in the San Diego region. He quickly learned that being a military chaplain entailed more than just administering to the spiritual needs of his Marines. To him it meant boosting the morale of his men, which he defined in his writings as "the measure of determination to succeed in the purpose for which the individual is trained or for which the organization exists."[4]

He considered the key to bolstering the morale of his men very basic: just be available to them. The young men, many of whom were teenagers and away from home for the first time in their lives, needed someone to talk to, a friend away from home. On many occasions, young Marines would seek him out without an obvious reason. Gittelsohn quickly realized that often these young men just needed a quiet place to feel at home with someone they could talk to and vent, who would understand this need for companionship and council. There were very few people in their Marine Corps hierarchy to whom they could turn for this comfort, and their chaplain filled this needed role for them.

Gittelsohn loved having these young men come into his office just to shoot the breeze. Young Marines would turn to him and his fellow chaplains to discuss anything from marital problems, or girlfriend problems, to financial problems. He often provided this morale booster by just listening and letting them unburden themselves to a chaplain whom they may have only met minutes before. Many came from broken or troubled homes and he would become a surrogate big brother or even father to them. Whom else could these men turn to? As Gittelsohn noted, no one in the military setting other than the chaplain had the interest or the time for this task.[5] After describing numerous examples of his crucial role as the friend away from home in his unpublished memoir of the war, he stated definitely, "Don't, for a single second, underestimate the morale value of just having the chaplain around as an available friend at a time like that."[6]

Before long, Gittelsohn quickly realized that although the military services seemed to have adequate numbers of doctors and medical personnel to attend to the physical needs of servicemen, there appeared to be a shocking scarcity of trained psychiatrists available to servicemen. He astutely anticipated the need for increased psychiatric support for combat troops in all military branches, and he saw a role for military chaplains to help remedy this situation.

Gittelsohn realized that there was little he could do for advanced or complex psychiatric cases, other than to try his best to get them to doctors qualified to treat them. Nonetheless, he did see a strong role for the chaplains to counsel Marines who exhibited milder cases of anxiety and stress. Such cases could be handled by chaplains who were professionally trained to listen and offer advice. Their training in Williamsburg had prepared these chaplains well for this sort of challenge.

The nature of his Marine Corps population also contributed to the ability of Navy chaplains like Gittelsohn to succeed in this role. The Marines who came to him were almost all very young and very candid with him. He compared this to the interactions of civilians with their pastors, noting that there was a "threshold of embarrassment and hesitance" that needed to be overcome. In contrast, when military men came to speak with their chaplain, they often wouldn't even wait to sit down before plunging into their stories. Within minutes they would share everything important in their lives with total candor. "In short," he noted, "there is a forthright directness which makes it that much easier for chaplains to know their men, and therefore very much more probable that they can help them."[7]

In his notes, Gittelsohn described the invaluable aid that chaplains provide their men in dealing with emergencies at home. Often this involved the chaplain being proactive and getting involved with the Marine's chain of command in order to facilitate emergency leave. Many young Marines would with great appreciation look back to the efforts of the professorial-looking chaplain who acted as their advocate, stood up to a sometimes rigid chain of command, and helped them deal with intense family issues at home. To Gittelsohn, this was all part of his overall duties as a Navy chaplain, one of his most important tasks in maintaining and improving the morale of his Marines.

A fascinating case that the rabbi dealt with during his tour at Camp Elliott involved a young Marine who came to see him with a problem somewhat unusual for someone who had enlisted in the United States Marine Corps. The young Marine told the rabbi he was not certain he could kill another man, even in combat. Gittelsohn then spent half a day counseling the young man. Here, the chaplain and former pacifist acknowledged that a number of people are constitutionally incapable of killing another human being. Gittelsohn felt that this young man was probably one of those people, but he realized there was no way for the man to transfer out of the Marine Corps. As a chaplain, all he could do was to help the young man adjust to the unpleasant but inevitable future that he would soon encounter.

Turning to the young Marine, he told him that sometimes it is necessary to destroy precisely in order to save. Using the example of building a firewall to stop the spread of a fire, he posed an interesting concept to the young Marine. If, as a Marine, he was to kill a Japanese soldier who would otherwise later murder 10 Americans, "Had he saved ten lives any less clearly than by dressing the otherwise fatal wounds of ten Americans who had already been shot?"[8] The young man had never quite considered the situation from this point of view. With some satisfaction, Gittelsohn felt that he had, at least, provided him a new perspective with which to consider his dilemma.

Like all military chaplains, Gittelsohn quickly learned that his "friend away from home" role often entailed such duties as counseling his Marines on marital and relationship issues, as well as counseling them on "loose women" and venereal diseases. He very much enjoyed getting involved when he felt he could help his young charges with the Marine Corps bureaucracy. Helping Sailors and Marines maintain a sense of individuality within the overall context of a massive military organization was particularly fulfilling for him, and he felt it was extremely important to spend the time to treat everyone as an individual.

At the same time, Gittelsohn and his peers had to balance their compassion as chaplains and advocates with a suspicious eye able to spot potential malingerers trying to get out of duties. In short, they had to separate out real issues from minor ones. At Williamsburg, the student chaplains were warned about rare crusty old sergeant-majors who look upon the chaplains as soft marks for malingerers and weaklings. They would keep a pad of "sympathy chits" with them; if one of their men had personal problems, they would give him one that admitted the bearer to the "mythical order of the bleeding heart," entitling him to thirty minutes of the nearest chaplain's time.[9]

• • •

After entering the United States Navy, Gittelsohn's commitment to civil rights and racial equality remained undiminished. Although these views were espoused by very few chaplains in that era—at least in public— Gittelsohn made his opinions on the subjects known in both his words and actions. While stationed in San Diego, he rarely interacted with the other chaplains assigned to Headquarters, Fleet Marine Force, Pacific Fleet. In his subsequent assignment, he and his family lived off base and he commuted to his job at Camp Pendleton. There, he reported directly to the senior chaplain "to whom I was directly responsible" and his interactions with the other chaplains were "...limited to very rare staff meetings and to those occasions when protocol required that I work through chaplains assigned to specific regiments."[10] He didn't realize it at the time but in San Diego, his views on racial equality, coupled with the antisemitic views of a number of his fellow Christian chaplains, were beginning to make him somewhat of an outcast among his peers.

One evening when he left Camp Elliott, he saw a young Marine standing at the gate, hoping to get a ride into town. Gittelsohn picked him up, along with several others. Sitting in the front next to him, the young Marine spontaneously began spouting out remarks disparaging African Americans. Infuriated, Gittelsohn turned to him and said that it was too bad that he didn't know that the Marine felt that way. If he had, he would have left him standing there and looked for a Black Marine to offer a ride. "My advice to you, when you get into combat," he informed the young man, "is to make sure that if you're ever in a tight spot you don't allow a Negro marine to save your life."[11] He wryly noted that the young man probably stuck to taking the bus from that point on, figuring that bus drivers were not social crusaders.[12]

Gittelsohn maintained his progressive views on issues such as racial

inequality. He still felt that the efforts of the profit-driven armament industries had deleterious effects on attaining world peace. His views subtly
began to isolate him from his fellow chaplains at Camp Elliott.

On a more positive note, Gittelsohn reveled in his and his colleagues'
interfaith efforts. One night while standing the duty at Norfolk Naval Station during his off-site rotation at the Naval Training School for Chaplains,
a young Catholic Sailor came to see him with an issue. The young man kept
addressing Gittelsohn as "Father" and finally Gittelsohn told him, "You
don't have to call me 'Father,' I'm not a priest, but of course I'll be glad to
help you if I can." To which his immediate response was: "O.K., Father!"[13]

On another occasion, Gittelsohn cited two specific incidents during
his tour at Camp Elliott to illustrate his sense of pride in the religious team-
work exhibited by all the Navy chaplains in the area. Because of the large
number of military installations he had to cover as the only Jewish Marine
chaplain in the San Diego area, he was only able to visit the Marine Corps
base once a week. In between these visits, a young Jewish boy needed to see
the chaplain and the chaplain on duty was Lieutenant Commander Walter
Mahler, a Roman Catholic priest. The young man was probably away from
home for the first time in his life—and this was realistically the first time he
lived in a predominantly non–Jewish environment. In short, he was having trouble adjusting to his life in the Marine Corps. In particular, he felt
pitifully exposed as a minority and he "wore his Jewishness with uncomfortable awkwardness."[14] Under the circumstances, a Catholic priest could
have deferred and told the boy to wait for an appointment to see Rabbi Gittelsohn. With pride, Gittelsohn noted, "He could have, and he might have,
but he didn't. For that would have been neither the 'Navy way,' nor Walter
Mahler's way."[15]

Displaying superb counseling skills, Mahler sat the young man down
and patiently said to him:

> Look here, my boy, don't ever let me catch you walking around this base
> ashamed of the fact that you're a Jew! As a Catholic priest, I get down on my
> knees every morning to pray to a Jew, Jesus. I hold a Jewish girl, Mary, to be one
> of the most sacred personalities of my faith. You just walk out of this office and
> hold your head as high as you know how. Being a Jew is something to be proud
> of, not something to hide![16]

To Gittelsohn, Walter Mahler epitomized what an ideal military chaplain should be. He was caring, compassionate, and an effective advocate
for his men. Gittelsohn would later work with the young man Mahler has
counseled and he noted that he had acquired a new sense of self-respect,
largely due to the initial counseling of a Navy chaplain who had happened to be a Catholic priest. The young man also gained a degree of new

knowledge of Christianity and its intimate relationship to Judaism. This, concluded Gittelsohn, was "the Navy way."

In the unpublished memoir of his wartime experiences, Gittelsohn proudly recorded several stories that showcased "the Navy way," as American servicemen of all faiths accommodated their different religions while training for their common crusade against the Axis powers. An article published in the Jewish Telegraphic Agency on December 24, 1943, told how throughout the Army and Navy, Jewish Sailors were requesting duty during the holidays so their Christian colleagues could enjoy their religious observances. The article specifically mentioned Chaplain Gittelsohn reporting how Jewish Marines volunteered to stand duty on Christmas on behalf of their fellow Marines of Christian faiths.[17] Indeed, on Passover 1944, Marine Corps cooks and messmen, none of them Jewish, worked for weeks to prepare a traditional Passover Seder for their Jewish colleagues. These same men also prepared the meal to break the fast after Yom Kippur and wouldn't allow the Jewish Marines to help clean up, stating, "This is your holiday."

• • •

Gittelsohn would describe the most unusual experience of his tour in San Diego in his unpublished memoirs. He described the frenetic activity every Sunday at the chapel of the Marine Corps base, which would conduct two Protestant services alternating with two Catholic services, followed by his Jewish service at 11 a.m. One service would have been barely concluded before the chapel would be set up for the next service, and with surprising efficiency, the chapel would be converted from a Christian sanctuary into a Jewish synagogue.

During one of the Sunday synagogue services he conducted, Gittelsohn noticed a most unusual worshiper. The young man, obviously a Catholic, crossed himself and kneeled in one of the rear rows. He recited his own prayers while Jewish worship proceeded in the chapel. Once his own worship was concluded, he remained in his seat, listening to a large part of the rest of the service with obvious interest. In a while, he stood, crossed himself and quietly left as the Jewish service continued. From his pulpit, Gittelsohn noted the same young man returning for four consecutive weeks.

It was unclear if that Marine's duties actually prevented him from attending Catholic services. It was obvious to Gittelsohn that this young man could enter the chapel during Jewish services and, without embarrassment or self-consciousness, worship God in his own way, while Jews around him worshipped the same God in their way. Gittelsohn described this situation as an inspiring example for civilian life in the future where Americans would learn to worship together because they had learned to live and suffer and rejoice together. He noted that the young man was not less Catholic, nor were they less Jewish, because they were worshiping, in their own ways, the same God at the same time in the same room. As a result, Gittelsohn observed, "...he knew and respected our faith more than he did before, even as we increased our knowledge and respect for his. Thus do men at war learn to pray together."[18]

• • •

After moving 3,000 miles from New York to San Diego, the Gittelsohns settled into housing at Camp Elliott. There, Roland and Ruth established some important friendships, some of them with fellow chaplains and their families. While at the Naval Training School for Chaplains in Williamsburg, he became friends with a Congregational-Christian minister named Herbert Van Meter. By coincidence, both Gittelsohn and Van Meter were assigned to Camp Elliott and would soon after that be assigned together again. Their personalities meshed perfectly soon after arriving at Camp Elliott where both Navy chaplains were serving with the Marines. The Gittelsohns and the Van Meters became close friends and frequently dined together. Their friendship would endure even after the war. The two former Navy chaplains would remain close friends for 37 years until Van Meter's death in 1982.

Gittelsohn wrote several times about 2nd Lieutenant Martin Weinberg. Weinberg was the first Jewish Marine Corps officer who he met after reporting to San Diego. Weinberg was the epitome of the gung-ho Marine. He was an extremely capable officer who was itching to be sent to the combat zone. Gittelsohn noted that Weinberg was one of the most unique individuals he had ever met. They were immediately impressed with each other and became friends.

In fall 1943, Gittelsohn presided at Martin Weinberg's wedding to Miss Yetta Adler of San Diego. It was the first marriage he performed as a Navy chaplain and, in his autobiography, he noted that it may have been "the first and perhaps the only marriage ceremony uniting two Jewish Marines."[19] Soon after that, Ruth and Roland Gittelsohn both became close friends with Yetta and Martin. The Weinbergs attended Friday services at Camp Elliott regularly, and when Weinberg was shipped out to the combat zone, Yetta would maintain her close friendship with the Gittelsohns while attending the Rabbi's synagogue.

Martin Weinberg corresponded as often as he could with Chaplain Gittelsohn. He shipped out with the Replacement Battalion of the 2nd Marine Division heading to Camp Tarawa on the Island of Hawaii. There the Marines prepared for the invasion of Saipan and the rest of the Mariana Islands. In his letters to Gittelsohn, Weinberg discussed his fears and doubts as he prepared to face battle for the first time. He missed Yetta and their friends, but he did take his greatest comfort from the Jewish services conducted on the island. Before leaving Hawaii, he wrote that the services had been a great source of relaxation, release of tension, and enjoyment for he and his colleagues. "There is nothing equal to a Jewish atmosphere," he declared, "and thank God, wherever we Jews are, we are able to gather, to create that atmosphere, to be content beyond words."[20]

Gittelsohn received only one negative letter from his friend. At Camp Tarawa, Weinberg encountered a small number of fellow Marine officers who resented him because he was a Jew. Though they did nothing overt, it became obvious to Weinberg that they wanted nothing to do with a United States Marine Corps officer with an obviously Jewish-sounding name like Weinberg. While this was just a small cadre of antisemites, it still bothered Weinberg and he would share his disgust in his correspondence with his good friend back in San Diego.

In July of 1944, right after the Battle of Saipan, Yetta Weinberg received a telegram from General Alexander Vandergrift, Commandant of the Marine Corps. It contained the devastating news, regretfully informing her that her husband, 2nd Lieutenant Martin Weinberg, was killed in action at Saipan. Gittelsohn would describe the telegram as, "the most final and irrevocable thing I've ever held in my hand or seen with my eye."[21]

Yetta was devastated by the death of her husband. She would write to Gittelsohn, "My only thought & prayer is that Marty's death was not in vain. He held his ideals very high & was willing to die for them; should they ever be destroyed, I would lose all faith & trust in humanity."[22]

Gittelsohn was stunned and shaken by Weinberg's death, a man he admired and loved. He would reflect back with anger when thinking about the antisemitism that his friend, a dedicated Marine officer, had to endure from other Marines he went into combat with. The eloquent rabbi strove for words that could express this discordant expression of American ideals. He would write that anyone who would not welcome Martin Weinberg, regardless of their rank, "…is an enemy of the United States, a faithless betrayer of her most cherished ideals. Whoever understands America—understands her and loves her—must also understand and love Marty Weinberg."[23]

• • •

As the spring of 1944 approached, Gittelsohn neared the end of his tour at Headquarters, Fleet Marine Force, Pacific Fleet. He would reflect back on his tour at Camp Elliott with pride and took great satisfaction in knowing that he had taken care of the Jewish Marines in the San Diego area and had helped all of the Marines who had come to him for assistance. Truly, Gittelsohn had been their "friend away from home." In addition, his relationships with his fellow chaplains had been, by and large, satisfactory.

In May, he received orders to report up the road to the newly formed 5th Marine Division at the newly built Camp Pendleton.

Gittelsohn's notes would take on a darker, more somber tone after he reported to this new assignment. He would inadvertently achieve great fame throughout the United States as a result of his new posting. However, his tour would be tarnished by his fellow chaplain's increasing resentment towards his new job as assistant division chaplain. In addition, his stance on social issues would prompt further hostility along with outright antisemitism.

SEVENTEEN

The Road to Iwo Jima

On May 23, 1944, Gittelsohn reported to the newly formed 5th Marine Division. During this tour the former pacifist would take part in the bloodiest battle in the history of the United States Marine Corps on a largely unknown Japanese island called Iwo Jima.

By mid–1944, the tide had clearly turned during the war in the Pacific. In December 1943, planning began on Operation Forager, the invasion of the Mariana Islands. The capture of Saipan, Guam, and Tinian would be critical to stage America's newly developed, long-range bomber for use against Japan. On June 15, the 2nd and 4th Marine Divisions, along with the U.S. Army's 27th Infantry Division, invaded Saipan. After fierce fighting, the island was secured on July 9. On July 21, Guam was invaded by the First Provisional Marine Brigade and the U.S. Army's 77th Infantry Division. The island was secured by August 10. Lastly, the 2nd and 4th Marine Divisions landed on Tinian Island on July 24 and secured the island by August 1.

With the Marianas conquered and now in American hands, the United States had what it needed to begin the final phase of the war: air bases from which to stage the aerial assault on the Japanese mainland. With airfields on the newly captured islands, America's newest and most advanced bomber, the B-29 Superfortress, was now within flying range of Japan.

The B-29 was introduced into the United States Army Air Forces in 1944. The largest aircraft in the Air Forces inventory, it contained several revolutionary advances. It featured a pressurized cabin and had centralized fire control of its .50 caliber machine guns. Its mechanical systems were so advanced and complex that a new specialist had to be added to each air crew—the flight engineer. The B-29 was capable of flying long-range missions from the Mariana Islands to Japan 1,500 miles away and back. Each mission lasted approximately fourteen hours. The first B-29s reached their bases in the Marianas in October and began their long-range bombing missions to Japan by November 1944.

At first, the bombing results were disappointing. There was relatively little damage inflicted using daylight high altitude bombing tactics and utilizing conventional explosive ordinance. Soon another factor came into play. Often over target, B-29s were damaged by antiaircraft fire and these crippled planes would have to struggle over a 1,500 mile, seven hour return flight to their bases. Halfway between targets in Japan and the Marianas was another island under Japanese control. Japanese fighter planes were often sent up from that island's airfields to intercept returning B-29s. In addition, the Japanese used that island to launch bombing raids on American airfields located on Guam, Saipan, and Tinian. This island's name was Iwo Jima.

While some researchers state that the justification for the invasion of Iwo Jima was to provide the captured airfields for crippled B-29s returning from bombing raids over Japan,[1] the sole reason given by General of the Army "Hap" Arnold and Fleet Admiral Chester Nimitz was to provide a fighter base for the P-51s that would escort the bombers on their missions.[2]

Iwo Jima was the largest in a chain of three small islands, known as the Volcano Islands, that had been under Japanese possession since the mid-nineteenth century. Iwo Jima was first visited by an English explorer named Gore, who called Iwo Jima "Sulphur Island" because it reeked of the vile-smelling mineral.[3] The eight square mile island, shaped like a pork chop, featured two beaches, one on both its east and west shores. It was five miles long, less than three miles wide at the north end, and a half-mile wide on the south end. The Japanese had two functional airfields and were in the process of constructing a third. The most prominent feature of the island was the inactive volcano Mount Suribachi, a 528 foot high mountain on its southern tip. Anticipating that the Americans would need to take the island if it would continue its drive towards the Japanese mainland, Emperor Hirohito ordered an all-out build-up of Japan's defenses on Iwo Jima.

By mid–1944, America's top two military leaders in the Pacific, General Douglas MacArthur and Admiral Chester Nimitz, had a sharp disagreement about what strategy was needed to conquer Japan. MacArthur envisioned a three-part plan: First, the Philippines would be recaptured. Next, Okinawa and Formosa would be conquered, and from there a million-man American force would be assembled on the Chinese mainland. From the mainland, the invasion of the Japanese home islands would be launched.

Nimitz, however, endorsed a different strategy—a direct seaborne assault led by the Marines to establish a beachhead on Kyushu, the southernmost of the Japanese home islands.[4] Part of Nimitz's overall strategy was to invade and conquer Iwo Jima to eliminate the threat it posed to his plan to attack the Japanese mainland.

For either plan to succeed, the United States would require

unchallenged control of the skies of Japan and the thousands of miles of ocean approaches to it. The American Joint Chiefs of Staff, regardless of which plan they would ultimately endorse, had promulgated an immediate strategy which was to completely pulverize the Japanese mainland's war-making capabilities with massive saturation bombing of its industrial centers and military installations. This job would fall to the hundreds of B-29s now stationed in the Marianas and would be greatly facilitated by invading and securing Iwo Jima.

In coming to this conclusion, the Joint Chiefs gave consideration to the length of the B-29 bombing missions, the Japanese fighter attacks originating from Iwo Jima, as well as the Japanese bombing raids, also originating from Iwo Jima. Another crucial factor for capturing Iwo Jima and making it an American air base was the much shorter distance to Japan. Its conquest by the United States would bring Allied forces 700 miles closer to Japan than the Marianas. It was also determined that if the United States had the island in its possession, crippled B-29s returning from bombing raids would have a much shorter distance to fly to return to American airfields. Hence, in early July, General George C. Marshall, Chairman of the Joint Chiefs of Staff, ordered that Iwo Jima must be taken by American forces by mid–January 1945.

Chester Nimitz was able to convince the Chief of Naval Operations, Admiral Ernest King, to endorse his immediate strategy of invading Iwo Jima, versus MacArthur's recommended invasion of Formosa. In his meeting with King at Treasure Island in San Francisco Bay, Nimitz presented his plan, which included the full endorsement of Army Lieutenant General Simon Bolivar Buckner, who had been selected by MacArthur to command the United States Tenth Army in the Formosa invasion, along with Lieutenant General Millard F. Harmon, the ranking Army Air Forces general in the Pacific. Admiral King, though, arrived at the meeting with his mind set on endorsing MacArthur's proposed invasion of Formosa. In addition, he was planning on working to change General Marshall's mind about requiring the invasion of Iwo Jima.

However, in the five-hour meeting, Nimitz and his staff successfully argued their case and were able to change King's mind. Upon his return to Washington, King recommended to the Joint Chiefs that the invasion of Formosa be scrapped, and instead, they recommended an assault on Iwo Jima as ordered by Marshall. The Joint Chiefs unanimously agreed with King's recommendation and back in Hawaii, Admiral Nimitz and his staff were given the green light to begin planning Operation Detachment: the amphibious invasion of Iwo Jima.

In September 1944, the planning for the invasion of Iwo Jima began in earnest. The logistics required for the assault were staggering.

Seventy-three ships would transport the Marines along with all their combat supplies. Each ship would have rations for 60 days, 6,000 five-gallon
cans of water, gasoline for 25 days for all vehicles, as well as medical supplies, spare parts, and general supplies to last approximately 30 days. The
weight for each Marine was 1,322 pounds.[5] The landing of American forces
on Iwo Jima would have a personal, life-long impact on Rabbi Roland Gittelsohn, as he would be part of the planned invasion force.

• • •

The Japanese knew the importance of Iwo Jima to America's war plans.
They had troops on the island since 1943, and they accelerated their efforts
to fortify the island after the fall of the Marianas. They knew that the fall of
Iwo Jima would bring the Americans virtually to the next logical goal: the
Japanese mainland. The island therefore had to be defended at all costs. The
man who Emperor Hirohito hand-picked to oversee the fortifications of
Iwo Jima's defenses, as well as to lead the defense of the island against the
anticipated American onslaught, was Lieutenant General Tadamichi Kuribayashi. Kuribayashi would oversee the around-the-clock efforts of his men,
driving them under horrendous conditions that included intense geother-
mal heat and ever-present sulfur gas, while the men were on half rations
of food and water. They would complete over 11 miles of tunnels and thousands of pillboxes in addition to their living spaces.[6]

Kuribayashi was a brilliant strategist who had served as deputy military attaché at the Japanese embassy in Washington, D.C., in 1928. He was
fluent in English and spent two-plus years traveling around the United
States. He was an admirer of America and Americans, and during his trav-
els around the country, he had written his family: "The United States is the
last country in the world Japan should fight. Its industrial potential is huge
and fabulous, and the people are energetic and versatile. One must never
underestimate the Americans' fighting ability."[7]

On June 19, 1944, Kuribayashi landed at the Chidori airfield on Iwo
Jima to take command of the island's defense against the expected American amphibious invasion. The manner in which he constructed his defenses
made shelling and bombing essentially useless. The positions were master-
pieces of concealment and construction: walls of many of his underground
defensive bunkers and tunnels were more than three feet of steel-reinforced
concrete and impossible to spot from the natural terrain upheavals that
camouflaged them.[8]

The top Marine commander in the Pacific was Lieutenant General
Holland M. "Howlin' Mad" Smith. The brash, outspoken Marine had come
under much criticism because of the large number of Marine casualties suffered during prior Pacific campaigns at Peleliu and particularly Tarawa,

where 3,056 Marines were killed or wounded in the 72 hours of combat. There were loud cries for his dismissal from some family members of killed servicemen, several members of Congress and several newspapers, especially those published by Robert R. McCormick and William Randolph Hearst. In their demand to have General Smith removed, McCormick's *Chicago Tribune* had described him with terms like "Butcher ... cold-blooded murderer ... indiscriminate waster of human life."[9] Other issues such as his age (62) and his medical condition (diabetes), had taken the personal intervention of President Roosevelt himself to keep him on active duty and commanding his men overseas.[10]

In the initial planning phase, General Smith selected three Marine Corps divisions for the amphibious invasion force that would comprise the V Amphibious Corps under the command of Major General Harry "The Dutchman" Schmidt. This would be the largest force of Marines ever sent into combat. It would consist of the 3rd Marine Division, the 4th Marine Division, and a recently formed division that had never, as a unit, been in combat before: the 5th Marine Division.

• • •

On November 11, 1943, the 5th Marine Division was activated. Although it was a brand-new Marine Corps division, it was comprised of many veterans of earlier Pacific campaigns, such as Tarawa and Peleliu. Its division Headquarters Battalion officially began functioning less than a month later, on December 1. In less than two weeks, two infantry regiments (the 26th and 27th Infantry Regiments) and one artillery regiment (the 13th Artillery Regiment) were organized. The official activation date for the 5th Marine Division was January 21, 1944. The acting Division Commander was Brigadier General Thomas A. Bourke. On February 4, Major General Keller E. Rockey replaced Bourke and became the commanding general of the division.

This new Marine division was based at the newly developed Camp Pendleton, located on the California coast in San Diego County. In order to create the large West Coast training base, the Marine Corps acquired nearly 123,000 acres to construct the base in February 1942. The base, named after Major General Joseph Pendleton, was dedicated by President Roosevelt on September 25, 1942.

The urgency surrounding the creation of the 5th Marine Division centered around the grim reality of the Pacific war. The staunch, fanatical resistance exhibited by the Japanese at Tarawa and Peleliu, coupled with high Marine casualty rates, drove home the need to recruit and train large numbers of additional Marines and prepare them for combat.[11] It was at Camp Pendleton that more than 20,000 thousand Marines of the 5th Marine

Division trained for months to acquire the combat skills that would be critical to fight a determined and well-entrenched foe in the Pacific campaigns to come.

When he reported to the headquarters of the newly formed 5th Marine Division in May of 1944, LT(j.g.) Gittelsohn met a man who was to have a profound effect on his military career. The division chaplain was a career Navy officer, Commander Warren C. Cuthriell. He was a 44-year-old Baptist minister, who immediately impressed Gittelsohn with his intellect and his sense of fairness. Cuthriell informed the rabbi that he was the newest and also the last of 17 chaplains who would be assigned to the division.

It was then that Cuthriell delivered a stunning bit of news to Gittelsohn. Division policy dictated that the one Jewish chaplain in the division should have access to every regiment in the division. In order to accomplish this, the Jewish chaplain was automatically designated as Assistant Division Chaplain and placed in Headquarters Battalion. Hence, on his first day after reporting to his new command, Gittelsohn, the newest of the chaplains to report in, became the number two man in the chain of command of the 5th Marine Division's chaplains. It was shortly after the appointment as assistant division chaplain that Gittelsohn would first detect signs of resentment from his fellow division chaplains.

Gittelsohn would write very little about his four months at Camp Pendleton. He had minimal contact with the other chaplains in the division, except for his immediate superior, Commander Cuthriell, unless it was to attend a rare chaplain staff meeting, or if his job as assistant division chaplain required such interaction.[12] He and the family lived off base, and most of the time he was able to leave the base and head home at 4 p.m. In addition to tending to the spiritual needs of all the men and conducting Jewish services on Friday nights, he continued with various other chaplain duties that he performed while at Camp Elliott. The difference in this assignment was the scale of his job which now included chaplain duties for over 20,000 Marines. He was now responsible for four infantry regiments consisting of approximately 3,000 men each, 14 battalions: Headquarters Battalion; Medical, Artillery, Tanks, Engineering Battalions; four Amphibious Tractor Battalions; and various other support battalions that included two Replacement Battalions of 2,650 Marines each.

During the training phase for the upcoming invasion of Iwo Jima, Gittelsohn broke even further away from his strict pacifist roots. He requested a revolver and learned how to competently fire it. He would practice on the firing range on a regular basis and learned how to strip, clean, and maintain his gun in working order. Technically, the Geneva Convention forbade doctors and chaplains from carrying weapons, but almost all did for self-defense. Gittelsohn did not want to take any chances against the

Japanese. "I never had to fire it in combat," he wrote later. "Would I have done so if directly attacked? I think so, but don't really know for sure. Thank God, the choice was never forced on me."[13]

At Camp Pendleton, the Marines participated daily in grueling physical activities, including forced marches in full combat gear and regular calisthenics that transformed many recent civilian recruits into physically hardened Marines. They learned to hone their combat skills with all forms of weaponry, including hand-to-hand combat. They mastered the techniques of climbing over the rails and down the sides of large transport ships and into small landing vehicles that would transport them to beaches on some yet unknown Pacific islands.

They then built on their combat skills required for amphibious assaults on enemy-held beaches. In July of 1944, the 5th Marine Division staged a series of full-fledged mock amphibious assaults. The nine landing teams, each consisting of an infantry battalion with guns, armor, and other support elements, were taken by large transports for practice amphibious landings on San Clemente Island off the California coast. Once the second landing exercise was completed, the troops reboarded the transports and headed for their final exercise—an assault on the California coast, "Pendleton Island."[14] During this planning and training phase for Operation Detachment, the Marines had no idea where they would be fighting. They only knew that they were preparing for amphibious assault on an island they were sure they never heard of before. They also knew that the fighting would be savage.

Eighteen

Going Overseas
with the 5th Marine Division

Three major planning sessions were held to prepare for Operation Detachment and at these meetings General "Howlin' Mad" Smith was not happy. He did not like Nimitz and generally felt that the Navy never gave enough pre-bombardment support to his Marines prior to their landings. Now this complaint again reared its head. "This will be the bloodiest fight in Marine Corps history," General Smith announced. After a dramatic pause, he stated, "The fighting will be fierce and the casualties will be awful, but my Marines will take the damned island." Staring at Nimitz, Smith asked, "How much bombardment will we get before H-Hour?"[1]

Smith had requested 10 days of pre-invasion bombardment at the minimum. Nimitz, however, was under many constraints. The Iwo Jima invasion had to mesh with General MacArthur's Philippines campaign and, also, preparations were underway for the anticipated Okinawa campaign that would follow shortly after Iwo Jima was secured. Nimitz's reply infuriated him. "Three days," he informed the Marine, was all the bombardment they could provide under the circumstances. In an effort to mollify Smith, Nimitz offered a fourth day of naval bombardment, but only if the weather was perfect. Nimitz again explained that their naval resources were stretched too thin to provide any more to Operation Detachment. In the end, Nimitz would request, and the Joint Chiefs would approve, a 30-day delay to the operation. Iwo Jima was now scheduled to be invaded on February 19, 1945.[2]

With the deployment overseas looming shortly, Gittelsohn wrote a letter to all Jewish Marines in the 5th Marine Division on August 8, 1944.[3] After reminding them of regular Friday night services, he instructed them to be sure that their dog tags were properly marked with an "H" (Hebrew) or "J" (Jewish) to indicate their religion. Otherwise, if they became a casualty, fellow Marines would not be able to identify their faith and secure the Jewish chaplain. He promised the men he would visit them as frequently as possible and assured them that he could be reached through Headquarters Company at Headquarters Battalion. He also reminded them that the regimental Protestant and Catholic chaplains could help them in his absence.

After assuring them he would arrange for regular Friday night services once they reached their base in Hawaii, he noted with pride that attendance at their Jewish services had been growing steadily. If any Jewish Marine reading the letter had not yet attended, he asked them to consider the letter a personal invitation from him. "The more interest we show in our religion," Gittelsohn informed them, "the more respect we can expect from others, and, the more consideration we shall receive when the time comes to request special Jewish holiday privileges."[4] He ended his message to the approximately 300 Jews in the division with, "Don't hesitate to call on me for any assistance I can possibly give you. Until I see you again, good luck, and God bless you!"[5]

As summer 1944 came to an end, the stressful knowledge that he would soon be going overseas and into combat began to wear on the entire Gittelsohn family. In one of his regular columns written for the *Nassau Daily Review*, entitled "Somewhere in the Pacific," the Rabbi described the stress of the upcoming deployment on all of the Marine families, using his own children to illustrate to those back home what it was like for a father to leave home and go to war. At the time, David was seven years old, and Judy was four years old.

Prior to leaving Camp Pendleton, he wrote that each time David and Judy visited the base there was the visible presence of war and what it might do to their daddy. Other children's fathers were leaving for overseas on a daily basis and soon they came to realize that one day it would be their daddy's turn. Both children kept asking repeatedly, what would he do if, when he arrived overseas, he encountered a Jap who wanted to kill him. "When they learned that I was to be shipped out by plane rather than ship, one of them said, 'Boy, Dad, am I glad you're going to fly. Now I know you won't drown!'"[6]

In his writings, he would lament the effect of his absence and the effect of the war on his family. "What can I do, dear David and darling Judy, to make up to you this terrible thing that life has done to you? You didn't ask for this war. You don't even understand it…. But you are among its most lamentable victims."[7] Toward the end of his life, he would conclude that the stress of war could well have been the genesis of his wife Ruth's severe emotional crises which began soon after World War II ended.

• • •

Part of the 5th Marine Division left in July for Guam to act as reserve forces for the Marianas campaign. It turned out they were not needed there so instead they reported to the Camp Tarawa, the division training base near Hilo, on the island of Hawaii. Towards the end of the summer, the orders were issued: the entire 5th Marine Division would board transport ships in San Diego and embark for Hawaii where the division would train at Camp Tarawa. They would leave on September 19.

After the operational orders were issued, Gittelsohn had to send the family back to New York. They spent the afternoon together in Los Angeles before Ruth, David, and Judy boarded a train heading to the East Coast. He would describe these hours as the saddest he had ever known. When the moment came to kiss his father good-bye, David sat on the edge of his seat, "almost hypnotized, and as I kissed them he whispered over and over again as if in a trance, 'Good luck, Daddy … good luck, Daddy … good luck, Daddy.' He must have said it at least a dozen times."[8] Gittelsohn was only partially successful in suppressing his tears. After that farewell, he spent several hours wandering around Los Angeles, had dinner and sat through a movie in an effort to take his mind off of the sobering thought that his family might never see him again. He was going to catch a midnight train for San Francisco where he would be flying out to Hawaii.

He had to share a cab to the train station with three businessmen, as wartime conditions made the sharing of taxis mandatory. Stunned, he listened to the three businessmen begin to complain endlessly about all of the hardships being imposed on them by the war. Hotel rooms were almost impossible to get, service and food even at the best restaurants were abominable, etc. They seemed oblivious to the man in the uniform of a Navy lieutenant (the rank Gittelsohn was promoted to September 1, 1944) sitting with them.

Finally, Gittelsohn exploded and sarcastically declared how sorry he was over all their troubles and inconveniences. "I just kissed my wife and children good-bye, not knowing whether I'll ever see them again. Tomorrow I am being flown overseas, sooner or later into combat. But your plight really touches me; my heart bleeds for you."[9] Stunned silence followed in the cab. Gittelsohn then refused their awkward invitation to be their guest for drinks while they all waited for their trains at the station.

• • •

In order to be with the majority of the men in the division, Gittelsohn did not fly over to Hawaii until more than half of them were already at Camp Tarawa. Upon his arrival, he was delighted to again see his good friend Herbert Van Meter, who was assigned as chaplain to the 26th Regiment. Van Meter pleasantly surprised his friend; knowing that Gittelsohn's arrival to Hawaii would be delayed—and concerned with the spiritual needs of the Jewish Marines—Van Meter began conducting regular Friday night Jewish services on the base. Van Meter was so skilled and knowledgeable about Judaism that the Jewish Marines began to call him Rabbi Van Meter.[10] He was one of the few Christian chaplains who liked and respected Gittelsohn. This was partly attributable to Gittelsohn's outspoken personality and liberal, progressive views and his politics. Clearly, antisemitism also factored into other Christian chaplains' disapproval of the rabbi. Lastly, their resentment over his appointment as assistant division chaplain would continue to fester. In later years, Gittelsohn would recall, "Clearly, I was not very popular among the Christian chaplains."[11]

Shortly after reporting to Camp Tarawa, Gittelsohn was presented with a plum perk that came with his job. He and Warren Cuthriell, as members of the Headquarters Battalion, were assigned cabins for their living quarters while at the base. The other fifteen chaplains were billeted in tents. From that point on, he could sense increasing hostility towards him by his peers. In addition, an increasingly obvious reason for their dislike of Gittelsohn was his unapologetic support of the Black Marines in the 5th Marine

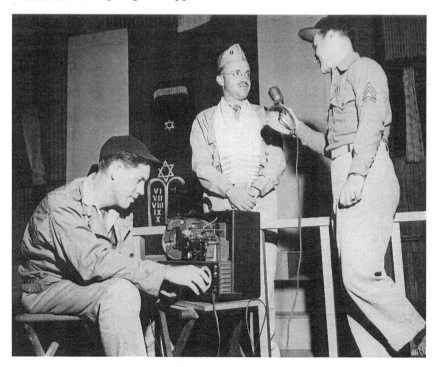

Roland Gittelsohn (with his infamous moustache) doing a radio broadcast from Hawaii, probably in 1944 (United States Marine Corps).

Division. As he would later note, he could sense that the Blacks had quickly learned that there "…were only two chaplains in the division who gave a damn about them, who would take their complaints about discrimination seriously, and do something to defend them."[12]

In his wartime notes, Gittelsohn wrote two entries under the title of "Negroes."[13] In each note, he took pains to document acts of discrimination and humiliation that he had both witnessed or documented from others. In the first entry from Camp Tarawa, he described the problems that the Black Marines were having at USO-sponsored dances. Although there had been no overt words spoken, the Blacks felt unwelcome at the dances and mentioned that there were problems getting girls to accompany them. In general, the Blacks had nothing to do on their days off and would instead hang around the barracks where they at least had some recreational gear. Gittelsohn noted that he spoke to "Chap. C.," presumably Commander Cuthriell, about trying to arrange to bring girls to the men's dances.

In the same entry, written at that time, he described an incident that took place on October 29, 1944, after one of the dances. In detail, he noted that three of the Blacks left the dance to return to their jobs as dishwashers back at the galley, but were harassed and provoked by two White Marines, when one of the three Blacks arrived late. To prevent a brawl from occurring, their supervisor, a Colonel Shipply, promptly intervened, telling them all to forget it, promising them that they'd get a fair break if, "they'd behave and do their job." After Shipply left, "Major A." came on the scene and counseled the Black Marine who had arrived late, stating that, "[You've got] those racial feelings in the back of your head and you think your people are being walked on, but you've got to get this out of your head—You're a Marine now."[14]

The last entry in that section was dated October 31 and concerned a crack made by a Sergeant Morrison upon learning that two of the Blacks were promoted to the rank of sergeant. "Why, if he goes back to South Carolina with those stripes, they'll shoot him."

In another entry under the heading of "Negroes," Gittelsohn described an incident that occurred on Christmas Day, 1944. About midnight, two of the Black Marines from the 26th Regiment came to see him and told him of an incident earlier that evening involving another Black Marine named Booth. They told the chaplain that after an officer gave them a bottle of whiskey as a Christmas gift, Booth was accused of being drunk by Gunnery Sergeant "B." That Gunnery Sergeant then sent someone to get Booth, stating, "Tell Booth he'd better straighten up and come here, and stop staggering around," and that he, "better be walking straight!"

Booth admitted that he (along with everyone else) had a couple of drinks, but was livid at the accusation of drunkenness. At that point Booth pushed away Gunnery Sergeant B's hand when he grabbed him, exclaiming, "Get your God-damned hand off of me!" Gittelsohn's written entry noted that the "other Negroes rushed in to make sure that B. didn't do anything rash," and restrained him, but Gunnery Sergeant B then ordered the MPs to take Booth to the hospital for a sobriety test. The test revealed he had alcohol in his system but was not drunk. He was released shortly after.

The name "Kelley" appears in some of Gittelsohn's wartime notes in this section and in his autobiography, written in 1988, he explains how he intervened on behalf of Jack Kelley, Jr., a Black Marine who had been thrown in the brig. Knowing Gittelsohn's passion on the subject, someone at Headquarters Company asked if he was aware of the situation and that he was imprisoned at the instigation of a Southern warrant officer. Gittelsohn did investigate and was convinced that Kelley's sole offense was to be not sufficiently subservient to a White man. Within a day, Kelley was released. With pride, Gittelsohn noted that after the war, Kelley became a shipyard worker, a dedicated family man, and that he, a rabbi, remained his chaplain to that day.[15]

Gittelsohn's efforts on behalf of the Black Marines of the 5th Marine Division would do little to enhance his standing among most of the other chaplains. Being the only Jewish chaplain already had cast him as an outsider, and his outspoken views on racial equality and other social issues would continue to increase their impression of him as a left-leaning activist and possible communist. The discussion groups that he initiated after his arrival at Camp Tarawa proved to be a source of increasing friction between not only Gittelsohn and the other chaplains, but between him and the command structure of the division.

• • •

In the 1930s, Gittelsohn and his fellow pacifists had disdain for the military, as they felt that a large military organization couldn't possibly be "democratic." The rabbi had now come to embrace the leadership styles of those he felt were unorthodox leaders in the Marine Corps. He had unbridled admiration for Lieutenant Colonel Evans Carlson, leader of the 2nd Marine Raider Battalion, more famously known as "Carlson's Raiders." From 1937 through 1938, Carlson had served as a military observer with the Chinese communist forces under Mao Tse-Tung. Carlson came to admire their organization, and he would use their egalitarian concepts when he formed the 2nd Marine Raider Battalion.

Under Carlson, all the men would embrace an egalitarian, team-building approach. Leadership would entail responsibility, not privilege, and Carlson included the novel concept of giving his men "ethical indoctrination" so that they would know the reasons for which they were fighting. Their exploits on the August 17, 1942, raid on the Japanese-held Makin Island would be memorialized in the movie *Gung Ho*.

Another leader for whom Gittelsohn expressed great admiration was Marine Captain Leon Goldberg. Goldberg's exploits in the Eniwetok campaign were featured in the March 13, 1944, issue of *Life* Magazine. Gittelsohn had the pleasure of meeting Goldberg in Hawaii after he returned from Eniwetok. He was both surprised and impressed to find Goldberg to be somewhat mild-mannered and almost timid-looking. Yet Goldberg had fearlessly led his men after the landings, and they unhesitatingly followed him into the fray. Goldberg called all of his men by their first name; they all called him "Goldy." Gittelsohn recorded his thoughts after meeting Goldberg: "Here was a group of men who knew that democracy was worth fighting for,— knew it because they were themselves living democracy then and there."[16]

It was the influence of Marine Corps leaders like Carlson and Goldberg that inspired Gittelsohn to begin his evening discussion groups. He would conduct an evening discussion group every week. His basic motivation was simply that the American military had done a great job teaching its Marines, Sailors, and Soldiers how to fight. Yet it had done a poor job in teaching these men about why they were fighting. The main purpose of the groups was to answer the question "Why are we fighting?" If the men could truly answer that question, Gittelsohn felt that they would be more motivated and that their morale would be at its peak. The topics centered mostly on issues—social, ethical, political, moral—for which he believed the war was being waged.[17] The discussion groups were open to all and averaged about 15 participants per session.

At first, Gittelsohn thought that by the very fact that these men had willingly volunteered for the group, he would hear extraordinary thoughtfulness from its members about why the war was being fought. Much to his initial disappointment, he heard thoughts such as "To kill Japs before they kill me" and "It's my neck or theirs."[18] He felt that these combat goals were, of course, adequate for initial survival in combat, but he wanted them to consider the long-range picture and see beyond this by thinking forward toward a new world, the one that would be the result of their efforts. The combat skills and the necessary combat engagements were the means; a new, just world that emerged would be the end, the ultimate reason why they strove so hard to defeat the evil of the Axis powers.

In Gittelsohn's view, the inability to realize this end vision was America's greatest failure and potentially its most disastrous defeat. He decried the low level of political awareness in the military. In his view the military in general had failed in this regard. He believed the Marines were probably the least politically aware, since all Marines, regardless of their ultimate specialty, were considered infantrymen. He felt it was not surprising that in an organization which had dedicated itself to sheer fighting skills often would overlook the big-picture goals for which they were fighting.[19]

Gittelsohn had no doubt that America's allies—the Russians, the Chinese, and the British—were more advanced than were American fighting men in their understanding of the goals for which they truly were fighting. Hence, his creation of the discussion groups from which he derived much satisfaction and through which he felt he was doing much to increase his men's awareness. Undoubtedly, the inspiration for these discussion groups was truly the experience of Carlson's Raiders. Gittelsohn would refer to the Raiders many times in his notes about the groups.

The enthusiastic tone with which he wrote about the discussion groups and their purpose in his immediate post-war memoirs contrasts markedly with his reminiscences in his 1988 autobiography. The passage of time seemed to have erased the idealism with which he initially approached the groups during the war and replaced them with bitter memories. In reflection, the groups were an unintended source of pain and conflict for him.

In his autobiography, he revealed that he had, in fact, conducted two evening meetings a week, one on Monday nights, the other on Wednesday nights. The meetings were open to all who were interested. The meetings proved to be a source of dissension and controversy, and Gittelsohn would reflect that he made two "cardinal sins." First, he invited Black Marines to attend, and five or six would regularly come. Secondly, he made the decision that all sides of important issues should be discussed as fairly as possible. His handling of both of his "sins" would do much to isolate him further from his chaplaincy peers and to mark him as a troublemaker in the eyes of his chain of command.

Months later, following the battle of Iwo Jima, the 5th Marine Division was able to return to Camp Tarawa. At that time Gittelsohn would resume his twice-weekly discussion groups. Major General Thomas A. Bourke, who had replaced General Keller Rockey as the Division Commander on June 25, 1945, would send him a message via Division Chaplain Warren Cuthriell. General Bourke suggested that, since there were two weekly meetings, perhaps it would be a good idea to hold separate sessions for Blacks and Whites instead of mixing the races. Finding the suggestion extremely offensive, Gittelsohn responded back through his chain of command via Chaplain Cuthriell. In a response that bordered on disrespect to a superior officer, he promised faithfully never to interfere with the military leadership of the division because he didn't consider himself to be an expert in that field. Hence, he would greatly appreciate it if the general would reciprocate when it came to his area of competence. Describing his response to General Bourke in his autobiography, he sarcastically added, "Dale Carnegie would not have approved."[20]

Gittelsohn tried to present all sides of the various issues that were discussed, but this too became a source of controversy within the division. As an example, to enhance the discussion of labor unions, he acquired union literature for the group. Among those from which he solicited information was the International Longshoreman's Union. At the time, the union was headed by Harry Bridges, an acknowledged Communist who had been ordered deported by the Attorney General of the United States, and this issue was currently being decided by the Supreme Court. Gittelsohn would wryly note, "The fact that I also ordered pamphlets from the United States Chamber of Commerce and the National Association of Manufacturers was apparently considered irrelevant. I was a dangerous person to have around."[21]

In spite of the controversies generated by his discussion groups and the ill will that they engendered between him and his fellow chaplains, Gittelsohn was convinced of their necessity. For him, answering the questions "Where do we go from here?" and "For what are we fighting?" were the keys to the effort to build the morale of his Marines. He sincerely believed that his men should consider the type of world and society they wanted, and consider what they envisioned as the American way of life they felt worthy of possibly sacrificing their lives for. In his own words, "The mere asking of questions, the churning of ideas, the stimulation of clear, honest thinking about goals, will be our most valuable aid in winning a war to obtain those goals."[22]

• • •

Training for the upcoming invasion of "Island X" continued and intensified. During that time, it was perhaps inevitable that the festering resentment the other chaplains felt towards their outspoken assistant division chaplain would begin to be expressed more overtly. The subtle antisemitism that Gittelsohn had perceived up to this time also began to be expressed much more freely. The situation erupted in October of 1944 over printed religious materials that he had obtained for the regimental libraries.

Gittelsohn had learned of two pamphlets that he felt would be important materials for the libraries. One was published by the Anti-Defamation League of B'nai B'rith and was a brief, effective compilation of questions and answers concerning popular misconceptions about Judaism and Jews. The other pamphlet, entitled *Fighting for America*, was issued by the Jewish Welfare Board and detailed Jewish participation in the military history of the United States.

Gittelsohn was no doubt attempting to dispel the negative stereotype that Jews were connivers who often tried to escape military service in World War I as well as in the current war. This was an all-too-common belief, especially in light of the fact that, until 1918, the Army Manual of Instructions for Medical Advisory Boards stated: "The foreign born, especially Jews, are more apt to malinger than the native born."[23] In reality, although Jews comprised only 3.3 percent of the United States population, they accounted for 4.23 percent of the United States armed forces during World War II.[24]

At a staff meeting for all the division chaplains, Gittelsohn brought copies of his two pamphlets for his colleagues, so they could be distributed to the regimental libraries. To his surprise, several of the chaplains refused to accept them. One chaplain in particular made a scene in front of the entire group. Facing Gittelsohn, he angrily objected to both pamphlets. Claiming he had read both, he objected to the Jewish Welfare Board publication because it "made Jews out to be perfect patriots." Complaining about the Anti-Defamation League's publication, he stated unequivocally that the pamphlet was unacceptable because it stated that the Romans had crucified Jesus, while anyone who knows anything at all knows that the Jews were guilty. "If you want your Jewish boys to read this trash, give it to them yourself. I refuse to put it on the shelf for Christians to read!"[25]

On November 9, 1944, a particularly acrimonious exchange took place when Gittelsohn was confronted in a meeting by three of his division chaplains.[26] They were Roman Catholic chaplain Father Paul F. Bradley, the Rev. Glenn E. Baumann, an Evangelical Minister of the Reformed Church of America, and Roman Catholic chaplain Father John L. Ecker. Gittelsohn's notes written on that date described the venomous attacks delivered by his fellow chaplains.

Chaplain Baumann, the Protestant minister, reiterated the complaint about the account of the crucifixion in one of the pamphlets. Why should he put this literature in his regimental library, he asked, when there wasn't any Protestant or Catholic materials in the library? He then went on to complain about a prior chaplains' meeting that they all had sat through. With disdain, he informed Gittelsohn that he had listened to him for an hour talk about "the Negro problem" at the roundtable discussion at that meeting, "a subject which wasn't important in the first place."[27]

Chaplain Ecker, the Catholic priest, proceeded to inform Gittelsohn that most likely the hatred that many people felt towards Jews was something that they brought on themselves. He noted that no child is born with prejudice and then posed the question of where it must come from. To Gittelsohn, he clearly implied that there was something wrong with the Jewish people that "naturally and automatically leads to prejudice."[28]

It was Chaplain Bradley, the other Catholic priest, who was the most opinionated and outspoken at the meeting. Describing Bradley as the most popular priest in the division, Gittelsohn sat in stunned silence as he listened to his tirade. Gittelsohn, according to Bradley, was a poor chaplain because he spent too much time fighting antisemitism and not enough time teaching Judaism. As for the Jews in general, they controlled too much of the government. In Bradley's view, both Washington, D.C., and New York City had both gone too far in appeasing the Jews.

Bradley was just getting warmed up at this point. He began to ramble on with other assorted opinions about Jews in general. He began to lecture Gittelsohn on the Abraham Lincoln Battalion, the group of American volunteers who went to Spain in 1937 to fight in the Spanish Civil War on the side of the Spanish Republican forces against Franco's Nationalist forces. Many of these volunteers were members of the Communist Party as well as other socialist organizations. The battalion, Bradley informed Gittelsohn, was made up mostly of Jews (actual estimates put the percentage of Jews in the battalion at 25 to 30 percent). During his tirade, Bradley expounded his beliefs about certain people he felt were lapsed Catholics. The Basques, he informed the other three chaplains, were actually renegade Catholics who had been excommunicated since the early 1900s. Former New York governor Charles Poletti, a former activist in the Roosevelt administration, was another "lapsed Catholic" and target of Bradley's ire.

In an interesting thread of reasoning, Bradley presented Gittelsohn with this idea: Should the Russians close all houses of worship except for one Catholic church and one synagogue in Moscow, it wouldn't be equal discrimination since there were so many fewer Jews than Catholics there. The labor movement next became the subject of Bradley's lecture. He informed the rabbi that the CIO Political Action Committee, a labor organization formed in 1943 to support President Roosevelt's 1944 campaign, was a communist organization and that "the Jews control and run it."[29]

Bradley continued on with his tirade, next expressing his admiration for two of the most controversial Catholic priests of the era. Father Charles Coughlin, the notorious "Radio Priest," was a rabid antisemite who had a huge following in the United States before the war. Father Edward L. Curran, author of *One Hundred Great Moments in Catholic History*, was known as Coughlin's spokesman in the East.[30] According to Bradley, Edward L. Curran was a man "whose veracity can't be doubted." He went on to describe Father Coughlin, the admirer of fascists and staunch advocate of the notorious forgery *The Protocols of the Elders of Zion*, as "the greatest Catholic priest in the world. I'd kiss the ground he walks on."[31]

To end the confrontation, the two priests demanded to know why Gittelsohn, as one of only 300 Jews in the division, had been appointed as assistant division chaplain when there were no Catholics serving in the division chaplain's office, given their much greater numbers. Gittelsohn patiently tried to explain that his appointment had resulted from 5th Division policy, but the priests weren't satisfied. Ignoring Gittelsohn's point, they went on to state that the assistant division chaplain of the 4th Marine Division was a Catholic priest. One of the regimental chaplains in the 4th Marine Division was Rabbi (Lieutenant) Leon W. Rosenberg who had graduated from chaplains school two weeks after Gittelsohn, but he was not appointed assistant division chaplain.

The following morning another Christian chaplain, who was present when the others confronted Gittelsohn, came to his quarters to speak with him. Obviously embarrassed by the behavior of his colleagues, he looked his fellow Jewish chaplain in the eye and sincerely said, "I just wanted you to understand clearly and directly that far from all of us feel the way … does. If there's anything I can do, now or ever, to cooperate, I want to be called on."[32]

Less than two months later they would all be departing for the invasion for which they had all been training. It had become obvious to Gittelsohn that his fellow chaplains greatly resented him for a number of reasons, and that antisemitism was a large factor behind this resentment. Yet, in spite of all the dissention in their ranks, the chaplains as a team would perform superbly in the upcoming Iwo Jima campaign, displaying courage and working together to minister to all of their Marines. The rancor would once again rear its head after the Marines secured the island.

Nineteen

Invasion

American aircraft launched from the Navy's aircraft carriers had bombed Iwo Jima daily since June of 1944. B-24 bombers from the 7th Air Force flying out of Saipan also bombed the island every day. All this was in preparation for the invasion the Japanese defenders knew would ultimately come. By the time of the amphibious landing, Iwo Jima had suffered the most prolonged bombing campaign of any of the islands in the Pacific war.

The American invasion plans were formulated that fall. The senior Marine Corps officer ashore would be Major General Harry "The Dutchman" Schmidt. He would be designated the Commanding General of the V Amphibious Corps, consisting of the three component divisions. The 4th Marine Division was commanded by Major General Clifton Cates, the 5th Marine Division was commanded by Major General Keller Rockey, and the 3rd Marine Division was commanded by Major General Graves Erskine.

The Marines would land on the southeastern beaches at Iwo Jima. The beaches were divided into seven adjacent landing beaches, each five hundred yards wide. They were color-coded, starting with Green Beach near the base of Mount Suribachi. In sequence going northward, the other beaches were called Red Beach 1, Red Beach 2, Yellow Beach 1, Yellow Beach 2, Blue Beach 1, and Blue Beach 2. The 5th Divisional Marines would land at Green and Red Beaches and the 4th Divisional Marines would land at Yellow and Blue Beaches. Originally, the 3rd Marine Division was to be held back as a floating reserve and would remain eighty miles out at sea. That would change on the first day of the battle when the extremely high casualty rates necessitated using elements of the 3rd Marine Division as part of the landing force.[1]

In addition to the experienced, battle-hardened troops that comprised the three Marine divisions, each division had replacement battalions of 2,650 men each. The vast majority of these replacements had never been in a combat environment. Most of the troops were fresh from boot camp with little advanced combat training, or older men reporting from desk jobs back in the states. Over 250 were new 2nd lieutenants fresh from the platoon leader's school in Quantico, Virginia. These nearly 8,000 men facing a baptism of fire generated deep concern, from General Smith down to the platoon level.[2]

While the 5th Marine Division trained on the island of Hawaii, the 4th Marine Division did its advanced training on the Hawaiian island of Maui. The 3rd Marine Division trained on Guam. Every day these Marines climbed steep slopes and staged frontal attacks against mock pillboxes and bunkers. The combat training realistically simulated combat conditions by using live machine gun and artillery fire, while ordinance was delivered from Marine aircraft. Veterans of prior Pacific island campaigns sensed that this upcoming operation would be "a real man-killer, no pun intended," in the words of a gunnery sergeant who had fought at Guadalcanal. This was evident from the ruggedness of the training, which was always very strenuous as yet another campaign neared.[3] There was no liberty (time off) and no place to go even if there was liberty.

For months the Marines had been training for another amphibious invasion of an island somewhere in the Pacific without knowing their destination. Had they known the name of the island they were training to invade, most of them would have shrugged their shoulders and admitted that they never heard of it. For a few weeks longer, the men of the V Amphibious Corps would only know that they were training to invade "Island X."

It was Christmas Eve 1944. The men of the 4th and 5th Marine Divisions celebrated the holiday with huge Christmas dinners. The following day, December 25, 1944, lead elements of the 5th Marine Division boarded the attack transport *Athene* amid cheers and well-wishes of many local residents. Another farewell celebration was repeated two days later on December 27, when the men of the 4th Marine Division came down from Camp Maui and boarded their transport ships. The last units of the 5th Marine Division pulled out of Hawaii on January 4. The men of the 3rd Marine Division on Guam, located fifteen hundred miles closer to Iwo Jima, would not embark for another five weeks.[4] The three Marine divisions would all rendezvous off Saipan.

Prior to leaving Hawaiian waters, the 4th and 5th Divisions made rehearsal landings on Maui and Kahoolawe. The landings were best described as "chaotic," and by the first week in January, all remaining elements of the 4th and the 5th Divisions had departed Hawaii. On February 14, the V Amphibious Corps made a final dress rehearsal before leaving Saipan. Marines climbed down the cargo nets into their landing craft and made runs to the beaches. Again, realistic combat conditions utilizing live ordinance was the order of the day. Two days later, all of the ships had left Magicienne Bay, headed for Iwo Jima.

Meanwhile the bombing campaign against Iwo Jima intensified. Starting with the December 8 raid where 212 B-24s and fighter aircraft attacked the Chidori Airfield, Iwo Jima would be pounded daily from the skies and from frequent close-in naval shelling by U.S. Navy ships as little as a mile offshore. From their deeply fortified underground caves, bunkers, and tunnels, General Kuribayashi and his men waited for the Americans who they knew were going to use Iwo Jima—if they conquered it—as a stepping-stone to invade their homeland. The orders were issued—General Kuribayashi's men would fight to the death when the Americans landed, and "No man must die until he has killed at least ten Americans."[5]

• • •

In the first week of January 1945, Lieutenant Roland Gittelsohn, assistant division chaplain of the 5th Marine Division, departed Hawaii aboard the USS *Deuel* (APA-160), a *Haskell*-class attack transport ship. Aboard the ship, which would be their home for the next five weeks, all 80 officers lived in cramped quarters in a space equivalent to a five-room apartment. The average bunk had half the headroom of a Pullman lower.[6] Describing himself and his fellow officers as "hot ... nervous, irritated, and lonely," in these living conditions, he also recalled that there was no quarreling and that everyone demonstrated the upmost respect for one another. Noting that there was an unconscious consideration and kindness on the part of these men who knew that in all literal truth they were "in the same boat," he proudly commented on the fact that "…men facing the most uncomfortable present and the most frightening future of their lives were wonderfully human toward each other!"[7]

The deployment from Hawaii to the Iwo Jima took 40 days. After rendezvousing off Saipan in early February, 485 surface ships prepared to get underway for the 600-mile journey to their destination. During the 40-day transit, for the first time the Marines learned the real name of "Island X": Iwo Jima.

As the 70 mile long convoy headed north, the Marines noted the drop in evening temperatures. This was a distinct change for most veterans of earlier Pacific campaigns. The days remained warm enough for the men to sun themselves on the decks during daylight. To pass the time, they played cards, chess and checkers and repeatedly checked their weapons and their ammunition. They talked about anything and everything—their families, women, and their liberty experiences, as they reviewed their training exercises and maps and studied the models of the island. In short, they discussed anything to escape the boredom of their time at sea, as well as to distract themselves from their anxiety over the coming battle that they all knew would be horrific.[8]

On February 16, Rear Admiral William "Spike" Blandy's Task Force 54 arrived off the coast of Iwo Jima. Consisting initially of six battleships, five cruisers, and multiple destroyers, the ships commenced their bombardment of Iwo Jima as planned by Nimitz and staff. The poor weather and limited visibility that day necessitated an additional day of bombardment.

On the morning of February 17, the weather had cleared and Blandy's ships closed to within 3,000 yards of the shore. Advancing toward the beach, Japanese spotters saw a flotilla of rocket-firing Landing Craft Infantry (LCI) ships closing in and General Kuribayashi was placed in a quandary: was this the invasion force? In fact, these smaller ships carried a crew of fifty Sailors and about a hundred frogmen from the Navy's Underwater Demolition Team (UDT). Their mission was to check the beach for landing obstacles and to obtain soil samples for analysis.

Kuribayashi made one of the few serious errors of the Japanese defensive campaign and concluded that this indeed was the invasion landing force approaching. Immediately, all of the Japanese defensive sites opened fire and while they wreaked havoc on the LCIs, by doing so they revealed their positions to Task Force 54's gunners, who proceeded to destroy the exposed Japanese positions.[9]

Meanwhile, many of the frogmen made it to the beach where they took their soil samples. They would be able to report that the bottom terrain at the beach line was firm and clear of obstructions, but the surf just a few yards from the shore was nearly six feet high. In a display of humor that can only be exhibited by men facing deadly combat, the frogmen planted a small sign on the beach that read "Welcome to Iwo Jima."[10]

That night, believing that he had repulsed the initial American landing attempt on Iwo Jima, Kuribayashi radioed the Imperial Army headquarters in Tokyo that he had beaten back the Americans, but he knew that they would be back very soon. To boost the morale of the Japanese people, Radio Tokyo announced that evening: "On February 17 in the morning, enemy troops tried to land on the island of Iwo. The Japanese garrison at once attacked these troops and repelled them into the sea."[11]

Aboard the American warships gathered off the shore of Iwo Jima, the men of the invasion force listened to the Japanese broadcast with both surprise and, no doubt, joy over the misinterpretation of the day's events by the Japanese High Command. Aboard the *Deuel*, Gittelsohn recorded the day's events in his notes. "1–2 underwater demolition and recon. teams went in to within 100 yds.... UDT men swim under w. spec. apparatus to destroy underwater obstacles & mines—Japs reported this as having repulsed 2 landing attempts this day!"[12]

This was tempered by the other broadcast that many of the Americans also listened to that night. With uncanny accuracy, Japan's premier radio propagandist "Tokyo Rose," announced the names of the units that would be involved in the landings and which beaches they would land at. After naming many of the ships involved in the American armada, she went on to assure her listeners that although the Americans had required a huge amount of ships to get them to the island, the survivors would later be able to be fit into a phone booth.[13]

By the morning of D-Day, February 19, two more battleships and three more cruisers had joined Task Force 54. On this third day of the bombardment, Blandy's battleships moved within a mile and a half of the beaches and were able to destroy over two-thirds of the exposed guns and blockhouses in their target areas near the beaches, while stripping away camouflage that revealed even more targets to Blandy's forces. The last three hours of the third bombardment day was effective, but there were still many targets that had been untouched.[14] The reality was that by the time of the bombardment, a veritable city of 22,000 Japanese troops was functioning below the surface of Iwo Jima.[15] As noted earlier, Kuribayashi had his men on half rations of food and water. In addition, American intelligence had mistakenly concluded that the lack of potable water meant there could only be about 13,000 Japanese troops there. Most of the Japanese forces and their weaponry were underground, undetectable by aerial reconnaissance.[16] Clearly more pre-invasion bombardment would have helped eliminate detected targets on the island, but the Americans were out of time. The amphibious landings were to take place as scheduled on the morning of February 19.

• • •

On February 18, the day before D-Day, the officers and men aboard the USS *Deuel* sat through their final briefings. Gittelsohn's wartime notes describe the multiple topics covered. They included "size, relief-maps, … geography, history, S.O.P, no. of enemy troops & units involved & their jobs, beach terraces…. Jap emplacements, results of preliminary bombardments."[17] The officers were told to expect approximately 700 hundred deaths per division. Based on that estimate, the 5th Marine Division staff planned a cemetery to hold 900 bodies. The grim reality would prove much worse than the planners could imagine. After 36 days of combat on Iwo Jima, 2,280 men would be buried in the 5th Marine Division Cemetery alone and several hundred others would be missing in action.[18]

That evening, Gittelsohn and the Protestant chaplain aboard the *Deuel* delivered a joint pre-invasion religious service over the 1MC, the ship's public address system. After the service, he was asked to speak to everyone aboard; Gittelsohn spoke from the heart. "Men," he said, "I'm going to be speaking in these next few minutes quite as much to myself as to you. We're in this thing together. The same fears and doubts and high hopes which fill your hearts tonight are in mine."[19] He proceeded to remind them of the spiritual weapons that he and his follow chaplains could add to their physical arms and ammunition when they hit the beaches the following morning. He spoke of the love of their parents and wives who were with them all despite the many intervening miles. He reminded them of the pride they all felt, not only in the United States Marine Corps, but in themselves and assured them that it is they who would prevail with their tanks and planes, not the enemy. "You may fire the shot that will break the enemy's back. You may, by your own example of courage give strength to fifty other men and they to five hundred more."[20]

Last, he spoke of faith. Faith in themselves, in each other, and in all who supported them. And of course, faith in God—"a Power that makes for righteousness and insures the triumph of righteousness."[21] He offered them no guarantees, only hope. Closing his message, he stated:

> God bless you! May we win our objective with the least possible loss. May we carry through, each of us so that he never be ashamed of himself. And may we return speedily to our dear ones to carry on with them in peace our struggle for the rights of common people everywhere. Amen.[22]

His powerful words resonated with his fellow Marines. In both his wartime memoir Gittelsohn would write in 1945 and in his autobiography written in 1988, he would recall that weeks after ministering to the wounded in the division field hospital after the horrific battle for Iwo Jima, many of his Marines, both Jewish and Christian, told him how much his words broadcast on February 18 meant to them and helped sustain them in the critical hours after they had been hit.[23]

After delivering their remarks, Gittelsohn and the Protestant chaplain were assigned cabins that night so that they could conduct personal consultations with the men. Arriving at his cabin, Gittelsohn was at first puzzled by the long line of Marines waiting to meet with him. Certainly, he noted, there appeared to be many more Marines in line than those that he had identified as being Jewish in the seven weeks they had been at sea since leaving Hawaii. In a very short while, the rabbi figured out what was going on. A number of those who waited impatiently in line to see him had already visited the Protestant chaplain, and still others were planning to see Gittelsohn first and the other chaplain next. The men of the 5th Marine Division were "covering their bases" and taking no chances. The next day, these young men, both Christians and Jews, would be carrying crucifixes or crosses supplied by the Protestant chaplain, *mezuzot* given to them by Rabbi Gittelsohn, and pocket Bibles provided by both of them.[24]

That night Gittelsohn tried to meet each man who had come to see him where he was; this was not the time for theological instruction. He was ministering to the young men's needs, acting all at once as friend, mentor, father figure and spiritual advisor. After all, he was an "older man" of 34, and with his owlish, professorial look, he no doubt reminded his men of their high school teachers and college professors. He was a source of comfort and strength to his Marines, many of them who would not be alive less than a day later. Never before had these young men needed the assistance and guidance of a chaplain more than on the night of February 18, 1945; and, for many, this assistance and guidance would never be needed so badly again.

TWENTY

In the Heat of Battle

At 3 a.m. reveille sounded aboard all the invasion force ships. Marines dressed, prepared their weapons and gear, and had their final breakfast. Daylight soon began to pierce the night sky, and through broken clouds, a clear, sunny day was emerging. At 6:30 a.m., the order was passed, "Land the landing force!" Aboard the landing craft—LSTs—the amphibious tractors were manned, and on larger transport ships, Higgins boats were lowered into the water as cargo nets were slung over the sides. In short order, Marines began descending the netting and to started load the landing craft.

At the same time the Navy began the last shore bombardment. Beginning at 6:40 a.m., battleships and cruisers unleashed a final torrent of heavy shelling on the beach that continued until 8:05 a.m. Next, it was the turn of the carrier-based aircraft. Seventy-two Navy Corsairs, Hellcat fighters, and Dauntless bombers began bombing and strafing runs on the island's beaches. This final murderous bombing assault on the landing beaches served to reassure the Marines as they watched from their ships and landing craft. They felt certain that there could be no one near the beaches who could possibly survive such an onslaught.

At 8:30 a.m., 68 amphibious tractors (amtracs) crossed the Line of Departure 4,000 yards from the shore and began their half-hour run to the beaches. Crewed by three men, the first wave of amtracs carried no assault troops. Their job was to hit the beach, destroy any enemy positions they found, and to fight their way 50 yards inland to set up a defense perimeter for the landing force. Five minutes after they crossed the Line of Departure, the final naval bombardment commenced. In total, 8,000 more shells landed on the beaches in less than a half hour in the final push to clear the beaches just before the amtracs went ashore.[1]

The bombardment ended and the first wave of amtracs landed on the beach and performed their assigned task. Six more waves of amtracs carrying Marine assault troops landed at five-minute intervals. Each wave would have 1,360 men. Hundreds of Higgins boats followed in succeeding waves, landing Marines to consolidate and expand their beachhead. Four regiments—the 23rd and the 25th Regiments of the 4th Marine Division landing on the right (on Yellow 1, Yellow 2, and Blue 1 landing beaches), and the 27th and 28th Regiments of the 5th Marine Division landing on the left (on Green, Red 1 and Red 2 landing beaches), formed the spearhead of the attack.[2]

At 9:02 a.m., the first wave of amtracs hit the beaches, only two minutes behind the planned H-Hour. At 9:05 a.m., the first troop-carrying amtracs came ashore at the beaches. Hell on Earth was about to begin.

• • •

Like virtually all his shipmates, Gittelsohn slept poorly if at all the night of February 18. During the day, he had learned that he would not be going ashore for at least two days. The USS *Deuel* had been designated as a casualty-receiving ship. Once the Marine combat troops departed on D-Day, the ship would be used as a hospital ship. The command element of the division felt he would be more valuable ministering to the casualties that would be brought back to the ship. At that point, he would be the only chaplain on the ship.

At 3 a.m., when reveille sounded, he got out of his rack and got dressed. After eating breakfast with his Marines, he went topside with the men and spent the morning walking back and forth on the deck, talking with and encouraging his men as they were preparing to go over the side. Watching the Marines climb down the cargo net—something they had done many times and had become quite proficient at—it struck him that this time it really was different. This was no longer a rehearsal. And many of them would not be returning to the ship from the island they were about to invade.

He would later recall two young pharmacist's mates to whom he spoke at length that morning. Although Gittelsohn would be unable to recall details of his discussion with the first sailor, two months after the battle the young man wrote to him from the naval hospital where he was recovering from his combat wounds. He thanked Gittelsohn profusely and doubted whether he would have "made it" without the chaplain's words.[3]

The second pharmacist's mate was a young man who was terrified to go into combat. He was red-eyed from the lack of sleep and was trembling with anxiety when they spoke on the morning of the 19th. What could he possibly say to the young man he wrote, other than he understood his fear and shared it, that there would have been something abnormal about both of them if they felt other than they did. "Whatever my words," Gittelsohn recalled, "he managed somehow to do what he had to and forty-eight hours later, when my turn came, I did the same."[4]

For the first three days after Gittelsohn had gone ashore, he had no contact with the young man. On the fourth day he saw the young man's name on a list of men he would be burying that day in the 5th Marine Division cemetery. Later, after talking to the young man's colleagues, Gittelsohn was able to piece together what had happened. In the midst of a savage Japanese counterattack, the young man had taken refuge in a shell-hole. From about 30 yards away, he heard the moans of a wounded Marine, crying for help. He selflessly set out to render medical aid to his wounded brother in arms, despite the carnage all around him. As he reached the wounded Marine, a Japanese shell exploded nearby. The shrapnel killed the brave young man, who less than a week before had shared his deepest fears with his chaplain.

On the morning of D-Day, Gittelsohn spotted a young major he knew from the 26th Regiment. The major, a young officer of about 30 years of age, was, like Gittelsohn, a redhead. Gittelsohn saw him in a landing craft next to the *Deuel*, ready to embark to the rendezvous point just before H-Hour. The two men waved to each other as the boat headed away with the other landing craft. Gittelsohn would next see the major five weeks later on Iwo Jima. His hair had turned completely white.[5]

Soon after the last combat troops had left the *Deuel*, the first casualties began arriving onboard. For the former pacifist, the scene was horrifying:

> Torn flesh ... broken bones ... shattered minds; every man demanded and deserved immediate attention. Neither the doctors nor I, the only chaplain still on board, knew where to turn first. I, who had always felt faint at the sight of blood, who would still turn pale if blood flowed in my presence now, stood by an improvised surgical table, holding a young casualty's hand while hunks of shrapnel were being dug out of his knee. The boy's face was pale with pain; his teeth had punctured his lips with blood; his fingernails dug into my palm so deeply that marks were still visible hours later. But each time I inquired about the pain, his grim answer was the same, "Okay, padre!"[6]

It was here that Gittelsohn first witnessed the horrors of savage combat and the sheer heroism exhibited by the Marines. During the 36 days of the battle for Iwo Jima, Gittelsohn and his fellow Marines would become intimately familiar with death and destruction. That five-week demonstration of courage, valor and love for one's comrades-in-arms would profoundly affect their chaplain. Admiral Nimitz would later summarize the heroism of the United States Marines at Iwo Jima with a short phrase that would later be carved into the pedestal of the Iwo Jima Monument: "Uncommon valor was a common virtue." Gittelsohn's wartime notes and reminiscences would contain numerous instances of individual acts of heroism and his admiration and love for these men was obvious.

Roland Gittelsohn conducting the first Jewish service on Iwo Jima, February 1945 (United States Marine Corps).

His anecdote about Hospital Corpsman Joshua Rosenfeld is one of the many such stories documented by the chaplain. On the first day of the campaign, Joshua saw one of his buddies blown back by a mortar shell explosion. Rushing to his aid, Rosenfeld saw that three of the Marine's fingers had been blown off. Temporarily stopping the bleeding with pressure dressings, the corpsman knew that he needed to get his patient back for surgery. Yet the injured Marine was unable to walk, and mortar shells continued to rain down around them. Having no other options, he picked the injured Marine up on his shoulder and turned toward the beach. Carrying him several hundred yards to the beach where he could receive surgical care from one of the surgeons at an aid station, he dropped off his injured patient and then returned to his duties. For his heroism, he was recommended for a Bronze Star.

Gittelsohn later learned of the incident and went up to Rosenfeld, a young man he had become friendly with, and complimented him on his heroic deed. Rosenfeld looked at him "as if I spoke a language he didn't understand, and said: 'Heroism? What else could I have done?'"[7]

• • •

As the Marines rushed off of their amtracs, they confronted an unexpected obstacle. The surveillance maps of the beaches used for planning the landings were derived from aerial reconnaissance photographs taken in July 1944.[8] The maps accurately documented that about 30 yards from the surf the terrain sloped upward in a series of three terraces, each about eight feet high and 16 feet apart.[9] However, the first terrace off the beaches varied from four to nine feet high. In addition, the maps had indicated that the beaches were volcanic sand. However, the Marines quickly learned that these were not typical, sandy beaches. Instead, they were landing on fine black volcanic ash. With each step, their feet would sink to calf depth in the ash. This also made traction for the amtracs much more difficult, if not impossible.

The volcanic ash, combined with the steeply angled terraces off the beaches, made departure off of the beachhead much more difficult than anticipated. Even Gittelsohn would comment on this in his wartime notes under the title "Mistakes Discovered": "Sand wouldn't hold vehicles, many more caves than expected, more underground protection from naval gunfire, no scrub typhus, 1100 civilians evacuated in Nov., grades up from beaches much steeper, over 20,000 Japs instead of 14,000."[10] However, remaining on the beach was not an option, and the Marines would have to get organized and proceed on with their mission.

The 4th Marine Division landing on the Yellow and Blue Beaches and the 5th Marine Division, 27th Regiment landing on the Red Beaches were tasked to go forward and take the nearby Chidori airfield, then designated as Airfield Number 1. From there, the Marines would swing right and methodically take the other two airfields and push to the far end of Iwo Jima, killing all Japanese forces who resisted. Confident that the Japanese knew that Iwo Jima was the last major obstacle to unlimited American bombing of their homeland, the Marines didn't anticipate taking many prisoners. In the end, of the more than 22,000 of Kuribayashi's men on Iwo Jima, only 1,083 would be taken prisoner and survive the battle, and many of them were Korean forced laborers and not Japanese, who rarely surrendered.

On the far-left side of the landing beaches, 1st and 2nd Battalions of the 28th Regiment, 5th Marine Division, had a different D-Day mission. After landing on Green Beach, the 2,000 men of the 28th Regiment, commanded by Colonel Harry "The Horse" Liversedge, would advance forward, cut across the neck of the island to the western shore and cut off Mount Suribachi from the rest of the island. Next, they would swing to the left to scale and conquer Mount Suribachi, code-named "Hot Rocks" by the mission planners.

But first they all had to get off the beaches. Tanks, artillery, and amtracs were getting bogged down in the volcanic ash of the beaches. More and more troops were landing, but the beach was getting too crowded to land more equipment. Offshore, more boats carrying troops and heavy equipment began circling, waiting for the beaches to clear. Bulldozers were landed to attempt to carve a path for the tanks. Meanwhile, the troops were getting organized and forming into fighting units. Luckily, the resistance was very light, with only scattered small-arms fire. The Marines began to believe that maybe the naval bombardment had broken the Japanese defenses.

They were wrong. This was all part of Kuribayashi's plan to lure the enemy ashore and then, from the hidden and underground machine-gun fire and artillery, unleash massive firepower and destroy them. Kuribayashi had waited until the beaches were jammed with immobile tanks and trucks. By 10 a.m., there were 6,200 Marines ashore on the small 3,000-yard beachhead. The Japanese hidden forces then opened fire, reigning death upon the Marines. The volcanic ash made it impossible to dig foxholes for protection. The trapped tanks and artillery pieces became prime targets for Japanese gunners. The Marines were initially unable to clear the clogged beaches, unable to land more gear, and unable to evacuate casualties. Their situation appeared grim by afternoon.

But Kuribayashi had waited too long to spring his trap, and there were six thousand Americans ashore—proud, well-trained, disciplined, and determined United States Marines. While they had but a few tanks and some artillery, they had their traditions and their beliefs. The Japanese were about to learn something about the Marines that Gittelsohn already knew: They had everything they needed to fight and survive for the time being. And they had faith that help would soon come; faith that, because they were Marines, they would pull through and win again.[11]

By late afternoon, the Marine infantrymen had cleared the beaches and advanced against the murderous Japanese counterattacks. The original D-Day objective had been to secure the southern half of the island, including Mount Suribachi and the two operational airfields. But the savage Japanese defenses, coupled with the onerous landing beach conditions had made this impossible. The Americans had pushed across the southern neck of Iwo Jima and had isolated off Mount Suribachi. In addition, they had reached the southern edge of the primary airfield. By 7:00 p.m. it was dark and the Marines dug in the best they could as they fought off the chill of a cold night. They were hyper-vigilant, expecting *Banzai* attacks throughout the night, consistent with Japanese tactics in the past.

This was not to be—General Kuribayashi had other plans for the Marines. Shelling of Marine positions continued throughout the night. Very few Marines got much sleep with shells exploding all around them.

Offshore, naval gunfire provided by U.S. Navy battleships and gunboats pounded suspected Japanese positions, adding to the nonstop noise. On the beaches, shore parties worked nonstop unloading gear and supplies while bulldozers continued to carve out roadways for tanks and artillery. Casualties piled up on the beaches awaiting transport to hospital ships and transport ships with medical facilities.

As dawn broke the following morning, General Holland Smith met with reporters aboard the USS *Eldorado*. After expressing surprise that there had been no *Banzai* attacks during the night, he paid a compliment to Kuribayashi. "I don't know who he is, but the Jap general running the show is one smart bastard."[12] He also realized that the large number of casualties would require that he bring in the 3rd Marine Division, which then landed on Iwo on February 24.

In Washington, D.C., President Franklin D. Roosevelt was briefed at the White House on the results of D-Day of the Iwo Jima campaign. At the end of the briefing, he was given the grim news: The Marines had suffered 2,341 casualties, including 548 killed and 18 missing. Author Jim Bishop reported, "It was the first time in the war, through good news and bad, that anyone had seen the President gasp in horror."[13]

Twenty-One

Uncommon Valor

For the first two days of the Iwo Jima campaign, Gittelsohn remained on board the *Deuel*, ministering to the wounded and dying. He, like all the crewmembers, was astonished and sickened by the number of casualties they received. Yet, every one of them did their jobs and none faltered. A sadly typical experience was that of Lieutenant Commander J.H. McCauley, a Navy surgeon aboard one of the attack transports that was designated as a casualty-receiving ship once the Marines went ashore. Their ship had expected to handle 20 casualties at most on D-Day. They ended up handling 74.[1]

Gittelsohn would theorize how the doctors, corpsmen, and chaplains could do their jobs day in and day out and not seem to let that affect them. He attempted to explain this in a letter to his sister after she wrote to him and expressed her admiration for his bravery under fire. In his reply to Natalie he wrote:

> You know, it's strange reading that you think I was strong on Iwo. Somehow I don't impress me that way at all. The feeling one has in combat is hard to describe. All I know is that no one was weaker or more utterly frightened than I on the way up to Iwo, and now in recollection I wonder whether I was really able to go through the things the papers say I did. During our actual days on the island no one had time or energy to ask questions or to analyze whether he is weak or strong. It was almost like being under the influence of anesthesia: you had a job to do, so you did it. It was as simple as that. You didn't dare sit or stand in one place too long because you didn't want a sniper to get a "bead" on you. So you kept rushing around, I suspect quite as much to get away from yourself as to avoid the snipers. Now in retrospect some of the things I had very little trouble living through bother me now more than they did then. But whatever you do, don't credit me with being strong in combat; no one but a fool is. The rest of us just acted like a bunch of marionettes whose strings were being skillfully manipulated.[2]

Gittelsohn would refer to this as "combat anesthesia" and he compared notes with other Iwo Jima veterans to see if his experience was similar to theirs in this respect. Not surprisingly, he noted that, "We felt at the time almost as if we were doped."[3]

On February 21, Gittelsohn went ashore to Iwo Jima. Embarking on a landing craft, his arrival on the beach with other Marines was delayed by wreckage blocking their original landing site. The sea was choppy on the half-hour run to the shore and the chaplain felt slightly seasick. As they approached the beach, he noted that they were lucky that they weren't greeted with mortar fire; but as soon as they hit the beach, sniper fire buzzed all around them. Gittelsohn's notes indicate that he landed on the beach with a Marine named Sanders and Dr. Daniel McCarthy, the 28th Regimental Surgeon. A half-hour after they landed on the beach, both of these men were killed by enemy fire. McCarthy was killed by an enemy shell near the beach as he was heading over to help identify the body of a hospital corpsman.[4] Soon after, the 28th Regimental Chaplain, Father Paul Bradley would write to McCarthy's uncle and namesake, Father Daniel McCarthy of Savannah, Georgia, offering his condolences to the young surgeon's family.[5]

His first night on Iwo Jima, Gittelsohn settled in a foxhole just off the beach. Mortar fire continued all around him throughout the night, as it would his entire first week ashore. That first night, he witnessed combat on the beach that he would write about in his wartime notes as well as his autobiography. On the beach, he watched shore parties unload much-needed supplies and equipment from a Landing Ship Tank (LST). About 50 yards away from the LST were a hundred drums of gasoline and ammunition that had been offloaded from other ships and were awaiting transport inland. Gittelsohn and his colleagues watched with horror as deadly accurate gunfire suddenly began raining down on the LST. The source of the Japanese shell's accuracy became apparent to them—they were able to see Japanese forward observers with binoculars on a partially sunken barge near the beach who were directing fire on the LST. The accuracy of the Japanese gunners was impressive. Eleven straight salvos hit the LST directly. To the Americans' astonishment and gratitude, none of the shells hit any of the drums nearby. In his notes, Gittelsohn acknowledged his appreciation for the gunner's accuracy, stating, "Jap F. O.'s so accurate 11 consec. shots hit the LST, with none over on drums—hit there would have wiped out whole left flank of the beach."[6]

Gittelsohn would later ask several of the men who had offloaded the LST how they felt on that nerve-wracking night. "Felt? They didn't have time to feel," he noted. They had a mission to accomplish and "in their crowded, benumbed consciousness at that moment there was room for nothing else."[7] Later, when Gittelsohn would discuss with them the close call they had experienced, he noted that their faces would perceptibly pale when they realized the full measure of what they had been through almost unwittingly. This, he would explain, was another instance of "combat anesthesia."[8]

Like all chaplains in times of combat, Gittelsohn's mission was to minister to the needs of his fellow warriors, to be there during their time in battle and encourage, counsel, support them. As he learned very quickly, the chaplain's job was also to be with his wounded men, visiting them and comforting them in battalion aid stations and field hospitals. And the toughest task of all—to be with his men, preparing them to meet their God, as they lay dying before him. All of the chaplains with the Marines at Iwo Jima performed these tasks exceedingly well. Having their chaplains at the front lines right alongside of them provided an immeasurable boost to the Marines' morale. Gittelsohn's wartime notes indicated "Gratitude of men on seeing them either at hosp. or in front lines—Talked of latter weeks afterward—"[9]

For the remainder of his time on Iwo Jima, Gittelsohn, like all the Marines, was faced with the possibility of his own death. In several instances, his life would be spared in intervals that could be measured in inches or minutes. Once ashore, all the Marines had to dig foxholes to sleep in, and their chaplains were no exception. The rabbi learned to sleep as best as he could with intermittent to constant shelling taking place throughout the night. One morning, he awakened to a stunning surprise. Less than a foot from the edge of his foxhole lay a foot-long piece of shrapnel. Had it landed only a few more inches closer, it probably would have killed him.[10]

There were no rear areas at Iwo Jima. Every single inch was a front line—a lesson that Gittelsohn learned very quickly. On several occasions, it seems that fate intervened to spare his life. On the beach one morning, he noted, "I once stood talking to a Marine not more than ten yards away; a sniper's bullet struck him and instantly killed him."[11] Just as it had been a matter of inches that saved him from the shrapnel killing him in his foxhole one night, it was a matter of minutes that spared him on other occasions. In his wartime notes, he recorded: "W. O. Stelburg killed by mortar on beach where we were before and after." In the same note he documented that on his tenth day ashore: "Boy hit by mortar 15' from us on hill."[12] Towards the end of his life, he would reflect on the 36 days of combat on Iwo Jima and succinctly distill his thoughts thusly: "How a single one of us left Iwo alive is a miracle."[13]

• • •

During the first two days of combat on Iwo Jima, most of the dead Marines were left where they fell. Not only was there no place to bury them, but the Marines on the beachhead were facing continual machine gun, small arms, and mortar fire from the determined Japanese defenders. These unburied dead raised serious health—as well as morale—issues. The invasion planners had factored this into the overall battle plan. Late in the afternoon of D-day plus one, the Graves Registration Officer of the 4th Marine Division and his team landed on Yellow Beach to begin the gruesome but necessary task of burying the dead as soon as possible. The following morning, D-day plus two, their counterparts from the 5th Marine Division landed on Red Beach.[14]

The cemetery for the 5th Marine Division was located furthest west, close to the base of Mount Suribachi. The 3rd and 4th Division cemeteries were located side by side near the north-south runway of Airfield Number 1, now designated as Motoyama Number 1. All three cemeteries were studded with land mines that had to be defused or detonated before the burials could actually begin. Additionally, cemetery workers had the constant threat of small arms and mortar fire when they established the burial grounds.[15]

Gittelsohn spent much of his time ashore on Iwo Jima in the 5th Marine Division Cemetery. It proved to be harrowing work. It was not possible to know the religion of every man buried because sometimes all they had to bury was a burlap sack containing fragment of bones and flesh; in many instances this was all that remained of a young United States Marine. Accordingly, it was division policy to have a Catholic, a Protestant, and a Jewish Chaplain on hand. Gittelsohn, of course, was the only Jewish chaplain in the 5th Marine Division.[16]

In writing about his work in the 5th Marine Division Cemetery, Gittelsohn repeatedly reflected on two thoughts. The first was the day-to-day horror of working in the cemetery and having to bury young men who only a few days before were living, dedicated Americans and had bright, hopeful futures. The other was the fortitude, courage, and inner strength that all the Marines who worked in the cemetery displayed every day. Just as he would think about the doctors and corpsmen, he would remember the men who worked with him at the cemetery and wonder, "Where did they get the strength?"[17]

The 5th Marine Division assigned 50 Black Marines and 25 White Marines to duty at the cemetery. This became their fulltime job for almost a month. They worked all day, every day for the duration of the battle, performing such grim tasks as trying to identify body parts and going through the pockets of their dead fellow Marines. Not infrequently, they would discover the body of a friend, often burned, maimed, and mutilated. And last they had the solemn duty of digging graves and burying their fallen comrades. Gittelsohn spent two to three hours a day at the cemetery, and his experiences there profoundly affected his emotions. "I found as a chaplain that my two or three hours a day in the cemetery taxed more than the last ounce of my endurance and strength."[18]

The sheer number of casualties required that the internments be a mass and somewhat impersonal affair. Bulldozers cut long trenches in the ground—eight feet deep and thirty yards long—as graves. The shrouds were green GI blankets or ponchos. Cemetery workers placed the bodies in the ground in accordance with Marine Corps regulations: "Three feet from center line of body to center line of body, fifty bodies in a row, three feet between rows." Each grave was listed on a master location chart with the dead man's name, rank, serial number, and unit. Pre-manufactured crosses and grave markers had been brought with the graves registration personnel.[19]

Gittelsohn paid glowing tribute to the men of the cemetery detail. To him, they were heroes in every sense of the word. Describing their performance on Iwo Jima, he wrote "No task from tip to tip of Iwo Jima called for greater or nobler courage." Feeling that it took a special kind of bravery to be able to accomplish what they had to do, he summarized his feelings for these men by writing, "Courage? I bow before it humbly."[20]

Perhaps Gittelsohn best summarized the spectrum of the stressful duties that the workers at the cemetery experienced day in and day out when he wrote in one of his wartime notes: "At cem., hand, piece of foot & 12 [inches] of torso for identification—Going thru pockets, fingerprinting & dental exam of corpses—bodies burnt, bloated stumps—looking at shrouds impersonally until realizing someone's son!"[21]

In his unpublished wartime memoir, he reminisced in a similar vein when he noted it was only later—in his foxhole at night or on a ship returning to rest camp—that a sudden wave of nausea came over him with the dread realization: "My God! These were not empty shrouds or quarters of beef! Yesterday these were the sons of mothers and the husbands of wives!"[22]

On the morning of February 23, Gittelsohn was standing in a mass grave at the division cemetery, tending to the grim routines that his duty there required. At 10:31 a.m., he happened to look up towards Mount Suribachi when he saw a group of Marines on the summit hoisting a small American flag on a thin pipe. He was witnessing the planting of the first flag on Mount Suribachi. In his later years he would write, "Never since have I witnessed an American flag fluttering in the wind without reliving that scene."[23]

• • •

On the morning of February 22, the 5th Division Marines waited for the rains to cease. Rain made the volcanic ash a slogging mess, and again tanks and heavy equipment began to back up on the beach. In addition to dealing with enemy fire and horrendous weather conditions, the Marines almost became casualties of friendly fire when Navy carrier-based aircraft arrived and began bombing Mount Suribachi. Assuming that the planes mistook them for Japanese troops, they frantically radioed back to have the planes stop the bombing of their positions. Fortunately, the planes were alerted and broke off, avoiding Marine casualties on the ground. There was another near-catastrophe Gittelsohn commented on later that day: "During fight for 1 ridge, elements of 28th got on it—One plane, not knowing they were there, attacked—1 dropped 500 lb bomb on it—Dud, didn't go off."[24]

Even though the tanks and heavy equipment remained bogged down on the beach, the Marines continued to assault up the sides of Suribachi, taking out foxhole after foxhole, pillbox after pillbox that hid heavily armed Japanese soldiers. By 6:30 p.m., they stopped for the evening. Three Marine battalions surrounded the sides of the volcano. The Japanese defenders were greatly hampered by the poor weather and the reduced visibility. The Americans clearly had a foothold on the volcano and the Japanese knew it. That night, in a very unusual action for the Japanese military, 150 Japanese soldiers, about one half the remaining force, attempted to flee the volcano fortress and link up with their fellow defenders on the northern part of Iwo Jima. They were acting on the orders of Colonel Kanehiko Atsuchi. All but about 20 of these men were cut to ribbons by the Marines as they attempted to escape.[25]

The Marines proceeded with their own plan. Earlier that afternoon, Colonel Harry Liversedge received orders from General Holland Smith that Mount Suribachi must be taken the next day. He then went to pay a visit to the 2nd Battalion headquarters and sought out the battalion commander, Lieutenant Colonel Chandler Johnson. Johnson was a short, cigar-chomping, aggressive warrior who was all Marine. Liversedge gave short and succinct orders to his battalion commander: "Tomorrow we climb."[26]

Offshore aboard the USS *Auburn*, General Smith tallied up the casualty reports. Once again the figures were grim. By the end of the third day of the invasion, 4,574 men were killed and wounded. In its push eastward to take the airstrips, the 4th Marine Division had lost 2,517 men. The 5th Marine Division, in its drive to take Mount Suribachi, had suffered 2,057 casualties.[27]

The following morning, February 23, Chandler Johnson was up before dawn, briefing his company commanders. Their objective, he informed them, was to be on top of the volcano by sundown. At 8:00 a.m., he sent for First Lieutenant Harold Schrier, leader of the 3rd Platoon, Easy Company,

2nd Battalion, 5th Marine Division. The 3rd Platoon would be the lead element of the assault. Just before the 40-man platoon embarked, Johnson turned to his adjutant and asked him to hand him something from his map case. "Take the platoon up the hill," Johnson instructed Schrier, "and when you get to the top, put this up."[28]

Johnson handed him a small American flag, measuring 54 by 28 inches, that the battalion adjutant had brought ashore from the USS *Missoula*.

Scouts from two different companies were already climbing up the steep sides of Suribachi, looking for the best path to the summit. The men were surprised by the lack of Japanese resistance as well as the good footing as they ascended the mountain. It took them 40 minutes to reach the top and they encountered no Japanese troops. It was 9:40 a.m. They rapidly descended back down to the 3rd Platoon to make their report.

Upon being briefed by the scouts, Schrier and his men collected their supplies. They stocked up on ammunition, hand grenades, demolition charges and fueled their flamethrowers. Once geared up, Platoon Sergeant Ernest "Boots" Thomas turned to the men and barked out, "Patrol, up the hill! Come on, let's move out!" In addition to their 40-man patrol, they also took a radioman and two stretcher teams. Also added to the team was Staff Sergeant Louis R. Lowery, a photographer for *Leatherneck* magazine.[29]

They departed in single file, ascending the slopes. Every few minutes, the men would have to stop to catch their breath as the angle of the sloping paths increased. All the while, Marines on the beaches and offshore followed their progress with binoculars. As the men passed the entrances to caves, they would toss grenades in to kill any possible Japanese troops inside. At all times, the platoon was expecting an attack by the Japanese defenders, an attack that never occurred.

At 10 a.m., the platoon reached the rim of the volcano. Not one shot had been fired against them. Peering down into the crater, Schrier noted unmanned machine guns, several destroyed rocket launchers, a number of mortar pits, and five artillery pieces.[30] Several of the artillery pieces were fused together by the heat of American bombing. "Where the hell are the Nips?" he wondered as he signaled for his men to follow.[31]

Upon arriving on the crest, Sergeant Thomas ordered his men to find a pole to attach the flag to. It was at that moment when several Japanese soldiers flung grenades from camouflaged cave openings. The Marines answered their attack with a barrage of fire and hurled grenades back at the cave. The skirmish quickly ended and while it was ensuing, two of the Marines found a seven-foot length of pipe from a rainwater cistern and attached Colonel Johnson's the flag to it. Lou Lowery captured the moment on camera as the Marines posted it in the ground. It was 10:31 a.m., the very moment when Gittelsohn, standing in a mass grave in the cemetery, raised his eyes and looked up at Mount Suribachi.

Just as Lowery snapped the shutter, several Japanese soldiers leaped out of hiding at them and were cut down by the Marines. More Japanese grenades flew out of camouflaged cave entrances and the Marines answered with heavy fire, finally burning out the caves with flamethrowers. This encounter, too, was quickly over.

On Green Beach, General Smith was watching the flag as it was planted on Mount Suribachi. Standing next to him was a very important guest, Secretary of the Navy James Forrestal. "Holland, this means a Marine Corps for another five hundred years," Forrestal said. Smith nodded his head with pride, tears clouding his eyes.[32]

Watching from his command post, Chandler Johnson turned to his assistant operations officer, Lieutenant Ted Tuttle and said, "Some sonuvabitch is gonna want that flag but he's not going to get it. That's our flag. Better find another one and get it up there and bring ours back." Tuttle was sent to the beach to find another flag.[33]

Lieutenant Tuttle returned in a short while, out of breath from his climb back to the command post. He had gone aboard LST 779 and was able to obtain the ship's rarely used ceremonial flag. This flag was much bigger, measuring eight feet by four feet eight inches. As Tuttle burst into the command post, three men were about to depart for the summit. Thirty-three-year-old Joe Rosenthal was a longtime photographer for the Associated Press who came ashore every day and took a multitude of photographs of the Marines in combat. Also with Rosenthal were Marine photographers Sergeant William Genaust, a motion picture cameraman, and Private Robert Campbell. Tuttle handed the flag to Johnson, who in turn handed it to 19-year-old Private First Class Rene Gagnon and told him, "When you get to the top, you tell Schrier to put this flag up, and I want him to save the small flag for me."[34] Gagnon, accompanied by the three photographers, immediately left and began the climb up to the top.

It was around noon when Gagnon reached the top. After Gagnon handed the flag to Sergeant Michael Strank and conveyed Johnson's message to him, Strank in turn explained to Lieutenant Schrier, "Colonel Johnson wants this big flag run up high so every son of a bitch on this whole cruddy island can see it!"[35] Nearby, Private First Class Ira Hayes and Private First Class Franklin Sousley were dragging a heavy iron pipe toward them. Schrier ordered that the new flag should be raised simultaneously as the old flag was lowered. Strank attached the new flag to the heavy pole while he, Hayes, Sousley, Corporal Harlon Block, Corporal Harold Keller, and Private First Class Harold Schultz planted the new flagpole into the ground. Nearby, Sergeant Bill Genaust was filming the flag raising, and Joe

Rosenthal snapped the shutter of his Speed Graphic camera. Rosenthal's photograph of the second flag raising was a masterpiece that would win the 1945 Pulitzer Prize and would become the official symbol of the Seventh War Bond Drive. It would become one of the most famous photographs of all time.

• • •

By D-Day Plus 5 the Americans had pushed northward from Suribachi and were on the outskirts of the second Japanese airfield, not that far from the original D-Day objective. It was at that time that the situation on the beaches finally improved. The combined efforts of the Marines, the Seabees, and all the support troops resulted in the gradual clearing of the beaches, which allowed more gear and more fighting men to come ashore. The adverse topographical conditions and the determined Japanese defenses had made the situation nearly untenable. In addition, the beach had to be adequately cleared of mines before the equipment could move off the beach. Gittelsohn noted "1,000 mines collected on 1 beach up to airfield #1."[36]

Much of the credit in sorting out the chaos on the beach and coordinating the landing force logistics in any Marine amphibious invasion must go to the men in charge of the process—Navy beachmasters. In this case, the beachmasters deserved particular recognition, for the situation at Iwo Jima was different from previous Pacific campaigns.

In prior amphibious landings, the shore parties remained offshore until the beachhead perimeter had been secured—usually a few hours after H-Hour—and the attack had started to move inland.[37] This was not the procedure for Iwo Jima. Nimitz's planners were thinking ahead to future landings on the Japanese home islands and wanted to test out new techniques. The beachmasters went ashore in the assault waves with the Marines. By noon of D-Day, 77 beachmasters were ashore on the landing beaches, beginning their critical work. To coordinate the landings at the seven color-coded beaches, gasoline-powered generators, amplifiers and loudspeakers were dragged through the surf and set up in and around sand-bagged shell holes so that the beachmasters could direct the landing craft traffic.[38]

One of the Navy beachmasters Gittelsohn observed on the beaches those first few days was Captain Carl E. Anderson, a very forceful individual with a strong Swedish accent. He had a loud voice that bellowed constantly over the loudspeakers which added to his mystique of being a man who never slept. In a very short time, Anderson's beach work force became depleted and raw replacements were sent in to work under his command. These men had never seen combat before and most were right out of basic training. Many were cooks, bakers, musicians, and clerks, sent into the deathtrap of the beaches of Iwo Jima, where 20 of Anderson's fellow beachmasters would be killed or wounded before the battle ended. Yet, under Anderson's direction, they got the job done.

Gittelsohn's wartime notes recorded an incident he observed on the beach shortly after he himself landed. The incident he described occurred on Yellow 1 Beach on approximately D-Day plus 4. That night the Japanese launched an intense mortar attack on the beach. The men, including Gittelsohn, leaped into shell holes and whatever foxholes they could fashion in the black ash of the beach. With machine gun fire piercing the air, the men could hear Anderson yelling over the loudspeaker, "Dig a hole! Dig a hole!" After a while, the mortar fire dropped off and Carl Anderson took charge again. It was time to get back to work.

Much to his surprise and disgust, Anderson couldn't get his men to move out of their foxholes. They were simply too scared to come out and resume unloading the supplies arriving on the beach. Spewing profanity, Anderson screamed at them, begging them to come out and resume work. Even after he threatened to put them on report, the men remained too scared to emerge from their foxholes. "All right," he yelled, "stay in your holes. Try me. See if I don't put you on report!" It was to no avail.

Gittelsohn concluded his note by revealing the ultimate leadership skills of Captain Carl Anderson, who, "Finally sneered into mike: 'And you guys call yourselves Marines!'—[and with that sarcastic declaration] Every last man came out."[39]

TWENTY-TWO

Coping with Hell on Earth

As the casualties mounted on Iwo Jima, stateside, General Smith and Admiral Nimitz confronted continuing criticism. They faced increasing public furor over the heavy Marine casualties that had begun with the landings at Peleliu and Tarawa. Back home there was a movement by prominent media persons to have General Douglas MacArthur named as overall United States Commander in the Pacific. Highly critical of Smith and Nimitz, *Chicago Tribune* publisher Robert R. McCormick decried what he felt was the needless and tragic waste of Marine lives. William Randolph Hearst, the powerful head of Hearst Publications, strongly opposed General Smith while becoming a staunch supporter of General MacArthur.

The February 27, 1945, edition of Hearst's flagship newspaper, the *San Francisco Examiner*, featured a front-page editorial with a heavy black border. It was personally written by Hearst, who explained that while the Marines would ultimately conquer Iwo Jima, "there is awesome evidence in the situation that the attacking American forces are paying heavily for the island, perhaps too heavily." He continued in his attack by stating that it was the same thing that happened at Tarawa and Saipan. "If it continues the American forces are in danger of being worn out before they ever reach the really critical Japanese areas."[1]

The next day, Hearst published another editorial heavily criticizing Smith and Nimitz and strongly supporting MacArthur. The accolades, which included key words in capital letters, included "GENERAL MacARTHUR is our best strategist" and "HE SAVES LIVES OF OUR OWN MEN." He concluded his editorial by stating, "Why do we not use him more, and indeed, why do we not give him the supreme command in the Pacific war, and utilize to the utmost his rare military genius of winning important battles without excessive loss of precious American lives?"[2]

Controversy over mounting Marine casualties at Iwo Jima continued to spread throughout the United States as the editorials were printed nationwide by Hearst's many newspapers. The evening the first editorial appeared, more than a hundred enraged United States Marines stormed into the editorial offices of the *San Francisco Examiner,* demanding to speak to the controversial newsman. Hearst, who was ensconced in his palatial estate in San Simeon, declined to speak to them. The San Francisco Police Department, as well as the Navy shore patrol, was called in to disperse the Marines.

On Iwo Jima most of the Marines were engaged in deadly combat and were largely unaware of the firestorm that was brewing back home. A few months after the battle, Gittelsohn would record his feelings concerning what his Marine and Navy colleagues had accomplished at Iwo Jima:

> Let anyone who doubts that stand as three of us did a few days after Mt. Suribachi had been secured, on top of Iwo Jima's southern-tip volcano, and look down on the sea lanes through which we approached and the ugly black beaches where we made our landings. From there, believe me, the wonder is not that we suffered such grievous losses, but that we succeeded in taking the island at all! In the face of what American marines and sailors accomplished against the impossible odds of Iwo, the cheap prattle of a William Randolph Hearst about unnecessary losses is nothing less than blasphemy.[3]

Gittelsohn's pride in his fellow Marines, as well as his contempt for Hearst and other critics of the Iwo Jima campaign was unequivocally stated. He would conclude that part of his memoirs by stating that no one would ever again be able to use the words "American" and "impossible" in the same sentence to him. "Along with a humble respect for the average American's courage, I carried back with me from Iwo an admittedly egotistical pride in the fact that for him, nothing is impossible!"[4]

• • •

The heavy casualty rate suffered by the Marines on Iwo Jima was a testimony to the defensive strategy employed by General Kuribayashi. His strategy was to allow the Americans to land on the beaches relatively unopposed, then to annihilate them there. His troops were virtually invisible to the invading enemy and their defensive positions were heavily fortified and relatively invulnerable to the daily heavy enemy bombardment. Perhaps most important of all was the *Bushido* code that Kuribayashi lived and breathed and no doubt further instilled into his troops. They all knew that surrender was not an option and they must die defending the island if necessary.

Months before the invasion, General Kuribayashi had issued a proclamation to his men exhorting them to fight to the death. He called it, "The Iwo Jima Courageous Battle Vows," and copies of this document were found by the Marines in destroyed bunkers, pillboxes, tunnels, and caves. It read:

Above all else we shall dedicate ourselves and our entire strength to the defense
of this island.
We shall grasp bombs, charge the enemy tanks, and destroy them.
We shall infiltrate into the midst of the enemy and annihilate them.
With every salvo we will, without fail, kill the enemy.
Each man will make it his duty to kill ten enemy before dying.
Until we are destroyed to the last man, we shall harass the enemy by guerrilla
tactics.[5]

Kuribayashi's proclamation clearly expressed the fanaticism and murder-
ous/suicidal mindset of the Japanese soldier in World War II. His philosophy was simple: Every soldier must be a focused, killing machine without
regard for himself or his comrades' welfare, and obey all orders without
question.[6]

• • •

As the Marines drove northward and casualties mounted, Gittelsohn's work at the 5th Marine Division Cemetery remained extremely busy.
When he wasn't spending several hours a day there, he found himself split-
ting his time between visiting his Marines in forward combat areas and
spending time with wounded Marines at the field and evacuation hospitals.
The carnage he witnessed would stay with him forever. As he would recall
towards the end of his life, "...on the island itself, I saw enough blood to
float a yacht."[7] The personal courage and the fortitude displayed by both the
wounded Marines and their medical caregivers would astound him.

It struck Gittelsohn that he never heard a wounded man cry during
the Iwo Jima campaign. To be sure, many men cried when their buddies
were killed or when they would visit the grave of a buddy at the cemetery.
But like the young Marine he supported during surgery aboard the *Deuel*
on D-Day, Gittelsohn never observed a wounded Marine cry. In five weeks
of intensive combat, through many hundreds of contacts with men who
were badly hurt, the only men he ever heard cry were those who were telling of a buddy who had been killed before their eyes, or those who had
struggled mentally under a strain too great to bear. Gittelsohn succinctly
described this situation thusly: "Quentin Reynolds expressed more than
the title of a [1941] book in his sentence: 'THE WOUNDED DON'T CRY.'"[8]

One afternoon, Gittelsohn remained at the Corps evacuation hospital tent, waiting for one of his wounded Marines to regain consciousness.
As he waited for over three hours, he observed the duty corpsman performing his tasks. Gittelsohn was struck by the corpsman's youthful appearance,
guessing that since he had "no fuzz yet on his face or hair on his chest,"
he couldn't have been older than seventeen. Yet with the self-assurance of
a man much older than he, the young corpsman would go from patient

to patient, administering care to his wounded fellow Marines. The young man's poise and professionalism made a lasting impression on Gittelsohn. He would comment on the young man both in his wartime notes and in his autobiography written years later. "Where did this boy," he asked himself, "who should have been bending over school books, not broken bodies— where did he get such strength?"⁹

In a letter that he wrote to his congregants on March 17, 1945, Gittelsohn described the horrors of human destruction along with the incredible courage that he had witnessed on Iwo Jima. Towards the end of the letter, he described an example of this courage (one that he also mentioned in his wartime notes). Again, he was in one of the medical tents with wounded Marines, where he observed a corpsman attending to his patients' combat injuries. He reverently wrote his congregants in New York that, "I know the courage and pride of a hospital corpsman who continued to administer whatever aid he could to the wounded [Marine] even after both his [the Marine's] legs had been blown off!"¹⁰

There was little respite from the violence and fighting even in a field hospital. One night during the third week on Iwo Jima, five Japanese soldiers entered one of the field hospitals. Spotted immediately, one was killed but four escaped. For the next few days tensions were high among the medical personnel. Finally, all the Japanese intruders were caught and killed. Gittelsohn also described an incident involving a wounded Japanese soldier who was brought to the division hospital. "1 Jap patient in Div Hosp tried to escape, shot up several Div. patients in Wards before killed."¹¹ In contrast to these anecdotes, Gittelsohn also recorded a note under the heading of "Dem(ocracy) vs. Fascism." Here he described an event that took place at one of the hospitals at 1:00 a.m., while visiting one of his men. At that point he witnessed a wounded Japanese soldier being treated by a Navy doctor and two corpsmen who were "pumping plasma & blood into [the] Jap to save him."¹²

Like all the Americans at Iwo Jima, Gittelsohn was profoundly affected by the deaths of close friends during the fighting. In both his unpublished memoirs and his autobiography, he recalled the death of a young Marine in the 5th Marine Division that he had grown very close to and who had become a dear friend. The Marine was named Don Fox, "a nice, decent kid," who was one of the division's photographers. One afternoon, Gittelsohn received word over the field phone that Fox had been hit by sniper fire in the head and was in the battalion aid station.

Gittelsohn grabbed a jeep and rushed to be with his friend. He searched for Fox at several aid stations but kept missing him as the wounded Marine was transported back to the beach. Gittelsohn finally caught up to his friend at the beach evacuation hospital. It was there that the neurosurgeon immediately told him that there was no hope—Don Fox would die shortly. The rabbi spent the next two hours with his dying friend in the hot, sweaty tent. Fox never regained consciousness. As Gittelsohn sat next to his friend, he watched as Fox's respirations became shallow and finally ceased. With tears in his eyes, the chaplain watched as another comrade died.

Shortly afterward, Gittelsohn wrote, "His face will haunt me the rest of my life,—the face of a good, sweet boy,—his eyes so horribly black- ened, his throat so gasping for breath, his life's blood so freely flowing onto the deck."[13] There was nothing he could do for him except just sit there, pray, and watch his fine young friend die. And there was very little he could do later for his grieving parents. It was painful for him to acknowl- edge the desire to do so much for his friend, and the ability to do so little. He somberly reflected that, "A chaplain suffers that feeling of futility not infrequently."[14]

One night before blackout, Gittelsohn was in his foxhole when a tele- gram was delivered to him. The return address surprised him—it was from the wife of one of his fellow Marines, a young man named Herman Pod- zeba. Podzeba had grown close to his chaplain and had revealed that his wife was pregnant with their first child. Because the Red Cross was unable to clear cables to men in active combat, she had written it to Gittelsohn, requesting that he deliver her husband the joyous news. She had just given birth to a baby girl. Gittelsohn would remember—"I felt happy to have such a mission. It was good, in the midst of carnage and death, to bear the blessed tidings of a new life."[15]

The following morning, Gittelsohn set out to find Herman Pod- zeba to relay the joyous news revealed in his wife's telegram. Podzeba had recently been transferred to a new unit, making him difficult to locate; but just before noon, Gittelsohn found him. He was at the cemetery—a corpse awaiting burial. He never knew he had become a father.[16]

• • •

The Marines on Iwo Jima bore witness to the continued savagery of the Japanese soldiers. Their inhumane brutality towards Allied prisoners of war was already well known, as was their disregard for the Geneva Con- vention rules of warfare. Unlike the European Theater, Navy corpsmen at Iwo Jima quickly learned that distinguishing themselves on the battlefield with a red cross on their helmet or on their sleeve simply provided cross- hairs for Japanese soldiers to target. Although technically noncombatants, all Navy corpsmen and other medical personnel in the Pacific had been issued .45-caliber pistols for both self-protection and the protection of their patients. As they were also noncombatants, Navy chaplains were sup- posed to be unarmed. Most of them did, in fact, carry side arms.

On Iwo Jima the Japanese soldiers had special instructions for dealing with Navy corpsmen. They were trained how to recognize him and make him a priority target. The idea was that if they could kill a corpsman, more Marines would be unattended, bleeding into the sand. Even better for them was to wound a corpsman. Since the Marines were very protective of their corpsmen, often three or four would rush to help them when injured, making them inviting targets.[17]

Even though they did not have distinguishing uniform markings, the Japanese would be able to identify each corpsman by his medical pouch, called the Unit 3, and would specifically target them. Gittelsohn would observe this every day and angrily recorded his reaction in his wartime notes: "Japs esp. shot at corpsmen & stretcher bearers, no doubt of this— So much so that many corpsmen swore to carry gear in future operations in gas mask case, not corpsmen's unit bag!"[18] As another Marine observed, "Jap snipers seemed to take a special delight in trying to kill Marines trying to recover bodies of Marines already dead."[19]

Japanese atrocities at Iwo Jima left many the survivors with indelible images they would never be able to erase from their memories. As an example, years later Hospital Corpsman John Bradley would not be able to speak of his experiences at Iwo Jima. Towards the end of his life he would finally share some of the repressed memories with his son, author James Bradley. His father described one incident that involved a friend of his from Milwaukee with whom he was pinned down under intense Japanese fire. Bradley ran off to render aid to a wounded Marine, and when he returned his friend was gone. Bradley would recall:

> A few days later someone yelled that they had found him. They called me over because I was a corpsman. The Japanese [had] pulled him underground and tortured him. His fingernails ... his tongue.... It was terrible. I've tried hard to forget all this. And then I visited his parents after the war and just lied to them. "He didn't suffer at all," I told them. "He didn't feel a thing, didn't know what hit him," I said. I just lied to them.[20]

The horrendous torture and mutilation of U.S. Marines by their Japanese captors was sadly not uncommon. Many American servicemen who would observe the brutally sadistic actions of the Japanese towards their prisoners would be unable to speak about the atrocities they observed for the rest of their lives.

After John Bradley died in 1994, his son James researched his father's life and interviewed Cliff Langley, one of John's fellow corpsman at Iwo Jima. Bradley and Langley had retrieved the body of a good friend, Ralph "Iggy" Ignatowski. Langley grimly related that, "Both his arms were fractured. They just hung there like arms on a broken doll. He had been bayoneted repeatedly. The back of his head had been smashed in."[21]

But this was not the complete story. In 1974, twenty years before John died, James Bradley was living in Japan. He invited his parents to come visit him there, but his father refused. Years later James' brother Steve explained their father's reaction. "He didn't say anything for a long while. Then he blurted out, 'Jim wants us to come visit him. They tortured my buddy. The Japanese stuffed his penis in his mouth. I'm not too interested in going to Japan."[22]

Gittelsohn was stunned by the horrors he had observed at Iwo Jima, and his wartime notes contain some cryptic references to these actions. A young Marine he knew named Sokol was captured along with another Marine who Gittelsohn did not name in his note. The Marines recovered the body of Sokol's colleague. It had been mutilated. His ears had been cut off and his bones were broken. In addition, his body was covered with cigarette and acid burns.[23]

Gittelsohn recorded his anger in finding watches and bracelets taken from dead Marines on the bodies of Japanese soldiers they had killed. He also revealed his revulsion in observing some of the Marines' actions in the heat of battle, as Gittelsohn noted, "Horror of Marines stealing Jap teeth, ears-"[24]

In a somewhat ironic entry, Gittelsohn expressed his frustration with what was to him another form of atrocity that he personally loathed: capitalistic wartime profiteering. This was demonstrated to him when he found out the Japanese were using American-made arms.[25]

He would vent his disgust and frustration once again at the end of the war. His anger is evident in his writing, the writing of a clergyman who has witnessed the horror of man's inhumanity to man and the seeming triumph of good over evil—only then to receive a slap in the face by sideline observers who invested money, and not their lives in the conflict. It wasn't easy, Gittelsohn wrote after the war, after one has watched that sort of thing for day after harrowing day, "…to remain calm and rational when you find 'Carnegie Steel' stamped on the metal of which Jap field pieces were made, or when you see Jap rifle ammunition marked WRA (apparently, Winchester Repeating Arms) 42!"[26] Gittelsohn felt that he and his colleagues found it easier to control their sorrow on Iwo than it would be to harness their anger if ever again American corporations attempted to seek profit at the expense of American boys.

• • •

For five weeks the Americans were locked in savage combat with a Japanese foe determined to fight to the death. The level of casualties was horrific, far beyond the predicted levels. Yet the Marines fought on, day after

Roland Gittelsohn (far right) conducting Jewish service on Iwo Jima, March 2, 1945 (United States Marine Corps).

day. Alongside of them, their Navy corpsmen and chaplains shared their burden in conditions that were unthinkable to most of them only a short time before. How could they cope with the death and destruction, watching their friends be wounded or die in front of their eyes? How could they go on day after day and do their jobs? Gittelsohn theorized that one of the large factors enabling the men to carry on as they did was "combat anesthesia" as mentioned earlier. Another major coping mechanism that allowed them to get through the battle was a not-so-secret weapon he mentioned frequently in his wartime notes: humor.

He wrote about numerous events that provoked some laughter and forced his fellow Marines to smile. This provided a much-needed counterbalance to the horrors to which they were subjected on a daily basis. One of these events occurred at a regimental command post, when about a dozen Marines sat down to lunch of K-rations and sardines. As the men cracked open their tins, they suddenly heard the unmistakable sinister sputter of a grenade less than a foot away from them. All twelve men, including Chaplain Gittelsohn dove to the ground to protect themselves the best they could. Knives, crackers, mess gear went flying in every direction as the cry of "Incoming!" rang out. The men covered their heads and braced for the explosion. Seconds passed and there was none. As the men slowly began to lift their heads, they suddenly heard hysterical laughter coming from one member of their group, the chaplain's clerk. He proceeded to unravel the mystery of the "dud grenade."

The young Marine had grown tired of the culinary drabness which he and his colleagues were subjected to every day. So he hit on a novel idea to spice up the Marine Corps' cuisine—why not liven up the rations and improve the taste with grilled cheese? Putting the can of cheese on the fire to melt, he had forgotten only one thing: to pierce the tin can first with a few holes. When the heated can burst its seams, three unanticipated events occurred simultaneously: the hapless chef was sprayed with a thick coating of cheese, twelve men ranging in rank from private to lieutenant colonel moved faster than they ever had before, and to the American arsenal of secret weapons was added something new—the cheese grenade.[27]

Most of the activities on Iwo were very grim, but nonetheless, were still occasionally punctured by humor. Gittelsohn's good friend Chaplain Herb Van Meter had an unenviable task. He was in charge of the burial detail for his regiment and each morning, he would take a working party to the front lines and retrieve the bodies of dead Marines to be brought back for burial. As he related to Gittelsohn, one morning he and his men received the shock of their lives. They had moved one body only a few yards when the "corpse" sat bolt upright on the stretcher and demanded, "Hey, where the hell do you guys think you're taking me?" A Marine who was very much alive had laid down for a much-needed nap and wrapped a poncho around himself. To the weary work detail, any human form lying prone under a poncho with only two feet showing meant a "customer." Both the stretcher bearers and the "corpse that sat up and talked" would laugh heartily more than a few times in retelling the story afterward.[28]

On another occasion, one of the advancing Marine platoons overran a Japanese site and captured a number of military items, among them a bugle. At the time, Gittelsohn was nearby in a foxhole with his Marines. All of the men were still under heavy fire with the enemy surrounding them on three sides. All around, the air crackled with machine gun and carbine fire. Suddenly from a nearby foxhole, the men could hear the captured bugle signaling the most improbable of all bugle calls that were standard in the Navy and Marine Corps, indicating time liberty and time for movies![29]

One humorous anecdote Gittelsohn recorded involved a wager he made before he went ashore on Iwo Jima. It was well known in the 5th Marine Division that Chaplain Gittelsohn's favorite food was ice cream. In a moment of levity before heading for the beaches, he made a bet with the division chaplain, Warren Cuthriell, that he would manage to find ice cream even in combat. After four weeks on the island, he had not succeeded in finding any of his favorite food. Then, suddenly, he was stuck with an inspired idea. A hospital ship was only a half-mile offshore. He contacted Cuthriell and quickly convinced him that there had to be Jewish casualties aboard.

Cuthriell agreed with his assistant, so with official authorization Gittelsohn commandeered a small landing craft and visited the Jewish men who were recuperating from serious wounds, bringing them whatever comfort he could. However, before he headed back for shore, he visited the officer's wardroom. A short while later, he was able to hand-deliver a note to Warren Cuthriell from the wardroom's chief petty officer attesting to the fact that, after completing his visits, he had enjoyed a delicious dish of chocolate ice cream.[30]

One morning when he left the evacuation hospital on the beach, Gittelsohn observed several enlisted men with a rare captured Japanese soldier. The prisoner was a senior enlisted man, a sergeant major, who didn't appear to understand English. Obviously worried that he might have weapons on him or even a small explosive device, the Marines were trying to get him to take off his pants. For ten minutes, six Marine linguists tried every known dialect to get him to remove his pants but weren't able to convey their message to their prisoner. It seemed to no avail when a gruff Marine gunnery sergeant who spoke no Japanese, walked up to the prisoner and loudly said in English, "Take off your God-damn pants!" The language barrier was apparently overcome, as Gittelsohn next wrote, "Off they came."[31]

Shortly after Mount Suribachi was taken, the Seabees bulldozed a narrow roadway up the side of the volcano. Almost immediately after completion a hand-written sign appeared along the road, 50 yards up from the base of the hill. It read:

SURIBACHI HEIGHTS REALTY COMPANY
Ocean View
Cool Breezes
Free Fireworks Nightly![32]

Other chaplains also noticed the effective coping mechanism that humor provided in helping the Marines deal with the horror of combat on Iwo Jima. Navy Lieutenant Louis H. Valbracht, a Lutheran minister serving as the 27th Regimental Chaplain, was also amazed at the humor exhibited by men who were facing death. On the way to the beach, he watched a young private hang over the side of the landing craft, looking at enemy shells exploding all around them. "Boy, what a place to go fishing," he said. "Look at those babies jump." Another young Marine cried out in mock hysteria: "Someone lied to me. The natives on this beach *ain't* friendly."[33]

When his landing craft arrived on the beach, Valbracht, along with the rest of his boat mates, ran up the terraces off the beach. As he ran, he saw a corporal walking towards him from a previous landing wave, heading back to the beach. He had been hit by shrapnel that had torn his boot off along with several of his toes. As he limped past the chaplain heading to an evacuation boat, he commented, "Short war, no?"[34]

TWENTY-THREE

Endgame

The 4th and 5th Marine Divisions, joined by elements of the 3rd Marine Division, continued to fight their way northward throughout February and March. Their casualties mounted as they fought the well-entrenched, fanatical Japanese defenders. Cave by cave, pillbox by pillbox, and tunnel by tunnel, the Marines battled for every square foot of Iwo Jima. During the entire time, the expected and dreaded nighttime *Banzai* charges the Japanese had utilized in all prior Pacific campaigns never materialized. The changed tactics employed by Kuribayashi, namely to wear down the American Marines from well dug-in Japanese tunnels and caves, had proved devastatingly effective.

On March 4, 1945, D-Day plus 14, the Marines had advanced only to the line they were anticipated to reach on D-Day plus 1. The casualties had been appalling: Colonel Harry Liversedge's 28th Regiment had suffered 1,952 casualties, nearly 60 percent of its landing force.[1]

In all three divisions, the high casualty rates necessitated the insertion of replacement troops. These troops were not like the experienced, battle-hardened Marines who had landed on the beaches on February 19. They were rear echelon noncombatants—clerks, cooks, bakers, truck drivers, carpenters, mechanics, and musicians, anyone who could carry a rifle. These men now had to fill the ranks of front-line units.[2] Many of the green troops were 2nd Lieutenants new to combat and fresh from the States, not trained to the standard that they needed to be in the hell-like environment they were about to enter.[3] Accordingly, in his wartime notes, Gittelsohn expressed his concerns about these replacements who, by necessity due to the high casualty rates, were thrown into combat. "Replacements very badly trained—High mortality. Some didn't know how to throw grenades or operate weapons they were put on."[4]

Late that afternoon, generals Cates, Erskine, and Rockey received orders from V Amphibious Corps: "There will be no general attack tomorrow. Except for limited adjustment of positions, each division will utilize the day for rest, refitting, and reorganization in preparation for resumption of action on 6 March."[5] The following day, assault plans were finalized for the three divisions. The 5th Division would be on the left, fighting its way northward, past Motoyama Number 2 and onto the west coast of the island, over the deadly Nishi ridge. The 3rd Division would fight its way up the center of the island, past Motoyama Number 3 airfield, which was under construction. They would link up with the 5th Division at Kitano Point on the island's northernmost point. It was here that General Kuribayashi's headquarters was located. The 4th Division would fight its way north up the east coast of the island, through defenses that were so heavily fortified that the Marines would refer to the area as the "Meat Grinder."

It would take the Marines nearly three more weeks and many more casualties to secure Iwo Jima from the Japanese defenders determined to fight to the death.

• • •

Just before noon on March 4, the B-29 Superfortress named *Dinah Might*, under the command of 1st Lieutenant Raymond Malo, dropped its bomb load over Japan at an altitude of 35,000 feet. As they began their return leg to Saipan, the bombardier announced that they had a problem: their bomb bay doors were frozen open. Determined to avoid any potential Japanese fighter aircraft in their compromised condition, Malo elected to remain at that altitude. He knew that this would greatly increase *Dinah Might's* fuel consumption. After several hours of flying, the fuel in their main tanks was exhausted and Malo threw the switch that opened his reserve fuel tank. Unfortunately, it malfunctioned. *Dina Might* had only several more minutes of flying time before it was totally out of fuel.

Lieutenant Malo's options were limited to three choices: bail out, ditch, or attempt to land on Iwo Jima which they were rapidly approaching. The first two options were unpalatable, and *Dina Might* radioed Motoyama Number One, requesting permission to land. Although combat was raging less than two miles to the north, permission was granted. After two low level passes, *Dina Might* landed on Motoyama's north-south runway. The Marines watched the B-29 land and observed with amusement while one hatch opened and four or five men jumped out and fell to their hands and knees. It provided quite a contrast to see men so glad to be on the island that they were kissing it, while a mile or two north were three Marine divisions that thought the place was hell on earth, its ground not even good enough to spit on.[6]

Before the fighting died down on March 26, more than 40 B-29s made successful forced landings on the island, potentially saving 440 crewmembers.[7] War correspondent Robert Sherrod stated that to the Marines, Iwo looked like the ugliest place on earth, but B-29 pilots who made emergency landings months later called it the most beautiful. "One pilot … said, 'Whenever I land on the island, I thank God and the men who fought for it.'"[8]

On March 14, D-Day plus 23, heavy fighting continued in the northern sector of the island. However, this was the day Admiral Nimitz proclaimed that Iwo Jima was secured. A formal ceremony began at 9:30 a.m. On a patch of land two hundred yards north of Mount Suribachi, Marine generals and Navy admirals assembled along with an honor guard of 24 Marines, eight from each division. As the men stood at parade rest, Colonel David A. Stafford read the words that Admiral Nimitz had written, declaring that, "United States forces under my command have occupied this and the other Volcano Islands. All of the powers of the government of the Japanese Empire in these islands so occupied are hereby suspended…."[9]

The flag on Mount Suribachi was lowered as the color guard raised the American flag at the ceremony site to the top of the newly installed flagpole. As the generals and admirals saluted the Stars and Stripes, Iwo Jima officially became a United States territory. Nimitz would soon after come under criticism for the timing of this proclamation. "Who does the admiral think he's kidding?" asked one Marine upon hearing of the proclamation. "We're still getting killed!"[10] In fact, they would suffer more than 6,000 additional casualties before leaving the island.[11]

• • •

After Iwo Jima was formally secured, planning began for the departure of the V Amphibious Corps, despite the fighting that still raged. Originally the planners had anticipated transferring the 5th Marine Division to Saipan to prepare for the invasion of Okinawa, scheduled for April 1, 1945. However, the heavy casualties suffered by the division had greatly reduced their combat capacity and they were not deemed ready for the invasion under the circumstances. They would instead be returning to Hawaii for rest and recuperation and to begin training again once they were fully augmented with replacements.

The date of departure was announced to be March 26. Looking at his calendar, Gittelsohn realized that the division's change in plans would impact preparations he had made for the Passover holidays, which were to begin the evening of March 28. They would now be at sea, bound for Hawaii, and the Passover Seders would be held at sea on various transport ships. As per the original plans, Gittelsohn had arranged for all the Passover supplies, including *matzoh*, gefilte fish, wine, and *haggadot* to be sent to Saipan. Luckily, he mentioned his dilemma to his good friend, Chaplain Carl Elder.

Elder was an Army chaplain whom Gittelsohn had befriended on Iwo Jima and with whom he grew very close. Chaplain Elder made it a point to round up all of the Jewish Marines and bring them to Friday night Jewish religious services. He would attend the services with them in addition to conducting his own Christian services every Sunday. He epitomized the collegial interfaith mission of the military services that Gittelsohn had grown to enjoy so much at Williamsburg.

About four days later, Gittelsohn received a call on his field telephone and was surprised to hear Carl Elder's voice. "Roland? This is Carl. Get yourself over here to my area with a jeep or truck. I have half-a-ton of Passover gear for you and the other Jewish chaplains."[12] Elder had co-opted a cargo plane, flown six hundred miles to Saipan, and brought back all of the Passover supplies that Gittelsohn had arranged to be sent there. Gittelsohn had actually forgotten the conversation he had with his Christian colleague and was delighted and humbled by this act of kindness, an act that guaranteed surviving Jewish Marines from Iwo Jima would be able to truly celebrate Passover Seders.[13]

Several years after the war, Elder was in the New York area during Passover time. Gittelsohn invited him to his synagogue to be the guest of honor at their Seder. During the Seder, he told the congregation of the selfless act of kindness that his Christian colleague had performed on behalf of the Jewish Marines at Iwo Jima. When he finished relating the story, the entire congregation rose to their feet and gave the Rev. Carl Elder a standing ovation.[14]

TWENTY-FOUR

The Purest Democracy

After Iwo Jima was officially secured on March 14, planning began for Marine combat troops' departure and their replacement with U.S. Army occupation troops. One of the major preliminary items on the V Amphibious Corps' agenda was dedicating its three division cemeteries. Division chaplain Commander Warren Cuthriell was responsible for planning the 5th Marine Division cemetery dedication.

Cuthriell's original intention was to use the same format for dedicating each of the three division's cemeteries. First the division commander would speak at a secular ceremony. Then the chaplains of the three major faiths would unite in a single religious memorial service, with each briefly speaking. The service would culminate with one of the division's chaplains delivering the memorial sermon for their departed comrades in arms.

It would have seemed logical for Cuthriell, as the senior chaplain, to be the chaplain delivering the memorial sermon at the end of the religious service. However, he had different plans for the ceremony. Once General Keller Rockey, the 5th Marine Division Commander, finished speaking, the chaplain delivering the sermon at the religious ceremony would be Lieutenant Roland Gittelsohn. Cuthriell made the decision because Gittelsohn represented the smallest religious denomination of all the chaplains—a fact that appealed to Cuthriell's sense of democracy. Cuthriell was also aware that Gittelsohn was an excellent speaker and preacher.

For Cuthriell, having his assistant division chaplain as the speaker seemed to be an inspired choice. He did not anticipate the firestorm of outrage that his selection of Gittelsohn would cause among many other 5th Division chaplains.

Immediately after Cuthriell announced his plans, the firestorm erupted. Two of the Protestant chaplains went to see him and expressed their extreme displeasure with the proposed arrangements. They were highly offended that a rabbi would be the one to preach over the graves of men who were predominantly Christians. That argument highly offended

199

Cuthriell, who countered that the right of a Jew to preach on such an occasion was precisely one of the ideals for which the war was being fought. As Gittelsohn would later admiringly note of Cuthriell, this counterargument to his fellow Christian clergymen had come from a Southern Baptist who had probably met no more than a dozen Jews in his life.[1] Cuthriell would not give in to his colleagues' demand: Gittelsohn would remain the designated speaker for the combined religious service.

Cuthriell believed that the problem would end after his confrontation with his fellow Protestant chaplains. He was wrong. Shortly after the first confrontation, the six Catholic chaplains of the 5th Marine Division came to him and they were livid. They expressed their unanimous and vociferous objection to any joint service, and most especially to one that would feature the sermon of a Jew. Cuthriell was stunned by their next threat: if the service was to proceed as Cuthriell planned, they all would refuse to participate and, more ominously, they would urge all of the Catholic Marines to boycott the ceremony.

By his own admission in his autobiography, Gittelsohn was not popular among many of the Christian chaplains. While Cuthriell may have not realized the extent of the animosity towards the Rabbi, he almost certainly was unaware of the venomous confrontation between the Jewish chaplain and the three Catholic chaplains that took place the previous November while they were still in Hawaii. For days Cuthriell did not share any of what was expressed to him at these meetings with Gittelsohn, who proceeded to work on the sermon he was planning to deliver after General Rockey would conclude the secular service. During this time frame, Cuthriell became progressively angrier at his fellow Christian chaplains.

After several days had passed, and as the cemetery dedication planning had progressed, Cuthriell sent for Gittelsohn. After inviting him to sit down, Cuthriell told his assistant division chaplain what had transpired since the initial ceremony planning. Gittelsohn listened in silence as Cuthriell revealed the dilemma facing him. While he wasn't happy about it, he could live with the protests of two of his fellow Protestant chaplains. However, the protest and possible boycott of the Catholic clergy and all the Catholic Marines was a threat Cuthriell was having a difficult time ignoring. To Gittelsohn's utter amazement, Cuthriell then announced to him that he had no intention to buckle to the demands. He was going to proceed as he originally planned.

After Cuthriell finished speaking, Gittelsohn absorbed all of the information that had been laid out before him. The pain of Cuthriell's dilemma was obvious to him. The utter discrimination and disrespect hurled at Gittelsohn by his fellow chaplains stung him deeply. Cuthriell was a man Gittelsohn respected and he knew there would likely be career ramifications for him. The scandal that would erupt if Cuthriell held fast against his fellow Christian chaplains would likely stain his record and greatly dampen any potential for future promotions for this highly competent career naval officer. Gittelsohn felt he had no moral right to expose his friend to this kind of embarrassment. He thanked his friend profusely for his efforts and withdrew his name from the combined service.[2]

Cuthriell no doubt appreciated the insistence by his assistant that he be removed as the speaker for the combined memorial service. It was probably the only logical way to avoid an extremely awkward situation, not only for himself, but for the entire 5th Marine Division. However, he was still angry over the whole situation and he made a decision that was his prerogative as division chaplain and overall planner of the ceremony. He announced that there would be no combined religious memorial service. After General Rockey's speech, each of the three denominations would have their own separate religious service in separate parts of the cemetery. Gittelsohn, meanwhile, had written a speech that he intended to deliver at the combined religious service. Now he would be speaking to a considerably smaller audience and there was little time to revise his talk. He decided that he would deliver the sermon that he had already written despite the much smaller audience that would be in attendance for the Jewish memorial service.

This account of the conflict leading up to Gittelsohn's sermon at the 5th Marine Division cemetery was recounted in his autobiography. Another version was offered by two other Marines, Sammy Bernstein, who worked with Gittelsohn at the cemetery, and Ken Brown, who was the chaplain's assistant for the division. They recalled the events somewhat differently in a documentary film, *In the Shadow of Suribachi—Sammy's Sto*ry (2017).[3] As they recalled, Bernstein drove Gittelsohn up to the podium where he was prepared to deliver his sermon to the entire assembled 5th Marine Division. However, Gittelsohn was turned away by the other Christian chaplains. At that point Gittelsohn instructed Bernstein to gather up as many Jewish Marines as he could find for their smaller ceremony, where he would deliver his famous speech.

It is difficult to determine which version of events is the accurate one, but the mystery seems to have been clarified by a film posted on YouTube by the Marine Corps History Division on April 26, 2016.[4] Entitled "*Dedication of the 5th Marine Division Cemetery on Iwo Jima, 1945*," the 10 minute and 48 second video has no sound, but in the segment showing the main ceremony with the entire assembled division, there are four speakers, clearly including Roland Gittelsohn. His presence on the podium supports his version of the events. The other speakers were likely other chaplains, who each recited a blessing on behalf of their respective religious denominations. The film also shows segments shot at the separate religious ceremonies that followed, although there is no film of the Jewish ceremony. It was apparently at the conclusion of the main ceremony that Sammy Bernstein drove Gittelsohn to the corner of the cemetery where he conducted the separate Jewish service.

In 1947, Gittelsohn wrote an article entitled "Brothers All?" that was published in *The Reconstructionist*. In the original typewritten draft, Gittelsohn hand-wrote two additional words in brackets. The passage then read:

> I do not remember anything in my life that made me so painfully heartsick. We had just come through nearly five weeks of miserable hell. Some of us [chaplains] had tried to serve men of all faiths and of no faith, without making denomination or affiliation a prerequisite for help. Protestants, Catholics, and Jews had lived together, fought together, died together, and now lay buried together. But we the living could not unite to pray together! My chief consolation at the moment was that another Jew besides myself [Jesus] would have been unacceptable as dedicator of the cemetery—even though these very men professed to teach in his name![5]

Two years later it still clearly pained him to recall the hurt he felt when Cuthriell revealed to him the other chaplains' objections and proposed protests.[6]

On the morning of March 21, 1945, Marines started assembling at the three cemeteries for the formal dedications. That morning, the surviving remnants of the 5th Marine Division stood as Major General Keller Rockey spoke to them from the heart. He said, "We are here today to dedicate the 5th Marine Division Cemetery on Iwo Jima. Under these white crosses lie 1,876 officers and men who gave their lives in the capture of this island." Paying tribute to the fallen warriors under his command, he concluded his short speech by saying, "The finest tribute which we can pay these men who lie here is in dedicating ourselves to maintain in our organizations the high standards of courage and devotion which they have so nobly set."[7] After Rockey finished, the Catholic chaplain, the Protestant chaplain, and Gittelsohn each came up individually and delivered a short prayer. After completing this first part of the dedication ceremony the men began to walk over to the different parts of the cemetery that were designated for the Protestant, Catholic, and Jewish memorial services.

Between 40 and 50 Marines assembled in the corner of the cemetery that was designated for the Jewish service. Unbeknownst to Gittelsohn, three of the Protestant chaplains from the 5th Marine Division attended the Jewish cemetery service. The three had been so disgusted with the treatment accorded to Gittelsohn by their fellow Christian chaplains, that they decided to boycott their own Protestant service and instead attend the Jewish service. Once all had assembled, Lieutenant Gittelsohn began to speak:

Roland Gittelsohn delivering his famous sermon that would come to be known as "The Purest Democracy at the 5th Marine Division cemetery on Iwo Jima, March 21, 1945" (United States Marine Corps).

This is perhaps the grimmest, and surely the holiest task we have faced since D-Day. Here before us lie the bodies of comrades and friends. Men who until yesterday or last week laughed with us, joked with us, trained with us. Men who were on the same ships with us, and went over the sides with us as we prepared to hit the beaches of this island. Men who fought with us and feared with us. Somewhere in this plot of ground there may lie the man who could have discovered the cure for cancer. Under one of these Christian crosses, or beneath a Jewish Star of David, there may rest now a man who was destined to be a great prophet … to find the way, perhaps, for all to live in plenty, with poverty and hardship for none. Now they lie here silently in this sacred soil, and we gather to consecrate this earth in their memory.

It is not easy to do so. Some of us have buried our closest friends here. We saw these men killed before our very eyes. Any one of us might have died in their places. Indeed, some of us are alive and breathing at this very moment only because men who lie here beneath us had the courage and strength to give their lives for ours. To speak in memory of such men as these is not easy. Of them, too, can it be said with utter truth: "The world will little note nor long remember what we say here. It can never forget what they did here."

No, our poor power of speech can add nothing to what these men and the other dead of our division who are not here have already done. All that we even hope to do is follow their example. To show the same selfless courage in peace that they did in war. To swear that, by the grace of God and the stubborn strength and power of human will, their sons and ours shall never suffer these pains again. These men have done their job well. They have paid the ghastly price of freedom. If that freedom be once again lost, as it was after the last war, the unforgivable blame will be ours, not theirs. So it is we "the living" who are here to be dedicated and consecrated.

We dedicate ourselves, first, to live together in peace the way they fought and are buried in this war. Here lie men who loved America because their ancestors generations ago helped in her founding, and other men who loved her with equal passion because they themselves or their fathers escaped from oppression to her blessed shores. Here lie officers and men, Negroes and whites, rich men and poor … together. Here are Protestants, Catholics and Jews … together. Here no man prefers another because of his color. Here there are no quotas of how many from each group are admitted or allowed. Among these men there is no discrimination. No prejudices. No hatred. Theirs is the highest and purest democracy.

Any man among us "the living" who fails to understand that will thereby betray those who lie here dead. Whoever of us lifts his hand in hate against a brother, or thinks himself superior to those who happen to be in the minority, makes of this ceremony and of the bloody sacrifices it commemorates, an empty, hollow mockery. To this, then, as our solemn, sacred duty, do we the living now dedicate ourselves: to the right of Protestants, Catholics, and Jews, of white men and Negroes alike, to enjoy the democracy for which all of them have here paid the price.

To one thing more do we consecrate ourselves in memory of those who sleep beneath these crosses and stars. We shall not foolishly suppose, as did the last generation of America's fighting men, that victory on the battlefield will automatically guarantee the triumph of democracy at home. This war, with all its frightful heartache and suffering, is but the beginning of our generation's struggle for democracy. When the last battle has been won, there will be those at home, as there were last time, who will want us to turn our backs in selfish isolation on the rest of organized humanity, and thus to sabotage the very peace for which we fight. We promise you who lie here: we will not do that! We will join hands with Britain, China, Russia—in peace, even as we have in war, to build the kind of world for which you died.

When the last shot has been fired, there will still be those whose eyes are turned backward, not forward, who will be satisfied with those wide extremes of poverty and wealth in which the seeds of another war can breed. We promise you, our departed comrades: this, too, we will not permit. This war has been fought by the common man; its fruits of peace must be enjoyed by the common man! We promise, by all that is sacred and holy, that your sons—the sons of miners and millers, the sons of farmers and workers, will inherit from your death the right to a living that is decent and secure.

When the final cross has been placed in the last cemetery, once again there will be those to whom profit is more important than peace, who will insist with the voice of sweet reasonableness and appeasement that it is better to trade with the enemies of mankind than, by crushing them, to lose their profit. To you who sleep here silently, we give you our promise: we will not listen! We will not forget that some of you were burnt with oil that came from American wells, that many of you were killed by shells fashioned from American steel. We promise that when once again men seek profit at your expense, we shall remember how you looked when we placed you reverently, lovingly, in the ground.

Thus do we memorialize those who, having ceased living with us, now live within us. Thus do we consecrate ourselves, the living, to carry on the struggle they began. Too much blood has gone into this soil for us to let it lie barren. Too much pain and heartache have fertilized the earth on which we stand. We here solemnly swear: this shall not be in vain! Out of this, and from the suffering and sorrow of those who mourn, this will come—we promise—the birth of a new freedom for the sons of men everywhere. AMEN.[8]

Thus, with powerful eloquence, Roland Gittelsohn expressed the American ideals for which he and his fellow Marines had fought for and many had died for. Despite the difficulties he experienced with his fellow chaplains in the 5th Marine Division, Gittelsohn's vision of America, a vision highlighted by individual dignity, respect, and tolerance towards one's fellow man, never dimmed. He envisioned a country that would look forward to a great future for all Americans, paid for by people like his fellow Sailors, Soldiers, and Marines.

His stirring sermon, destined to be the most famous speech of World War II, was heard by only a handful of men and it was highly probable that its message would have not reached beyond the small corner of the 5th Marine Division Cemetery. But fate had a different plan for Gittelsohn, and his speech, which came to be known as "The Purest Democracy," was about to be heard around the world.

After the three chaplains finished their respective religious services, the men of all three Marine divisions walked again among the graves, visiting their departed fellow Marines, perhaps for the last time. As always at the cemeteries, tears flowed freely from the eyes of men, many of them teenagers, who had witnessed death and destruction that would live with them for the rest of their lives. At the 5th Division cemetery, the three Protestant chaplains were thoroughly enamored of the eloquence of Gittelsohn's words and the heartfelt message that he had delivered just minutes before. They had boycotted their own Protestant service out of principle, but the sermon that they had just heard transcended religious differences. It was a message for all Marines regardless of faith, a message for all Americans.

One of the three chaplains had a plan. After the ceremony he sought out Gittelsohn and complimented him on his sermon. With gratitude, the rabbi told him that the speech they had just heard was the one he had intended to give at the combined service; he had not changed it for the smaller Jewish service. Stating he wanted to read it over, Gittelsohn's colleague asked to borrow the speech and, feeling flattered and gratified, Gittelsohn gave him his copy so he could read it at his leisure. He didn't give it a second thought when his Protestant colleague left with the onion-skin sheets in his hand.

Walking over to the division headquarters, the chaplain sought out a mimeograph machine. Unbeknownst to Gittelsohn, he proceeded to make several thousand copies of the speech. He felt this was one of those rare speeches that anyone would ever hear in a lifetime, so he distributed it to all the men in his regiment. Many of the Marines, most of whom were not at the Jewish ceremony, read it and were also touched by the message it conveyed—one of purpose, brotherhood, and "pure democracy." Most of them proceeded to mail their copy of the speech home to their families. Roland Gittelsohn was about to become a name known throughout America.

• • •

Gittelsohn's recollection of his experiences at the cemetery triggered some of the most heart-wrenching memories of Iwo Jima. Such experiences were a burden that all surviving Marines would take away from the island. Gittelsohn witnessed many sad moments when Marines just back from the advancing front lines would come to the cemetery and look for their buddies. The non-sectarian nature of the cemetery made a huge impression on him as he observed the behavior of the men visiting their fallen comrades in arms. Typical of this was the morning he observed two Christian Marines praying over the grave of a Jewish buddy. They noticed the Jewish chaplain's insignia on his collar and asked him to pray with them.

On one of the last mornings on Iwo Jima, Gittelsohn saw one of the Jewish Marines, Sid Randall from Boston, crying over the grave of a Catholic buddy. Gittelsohn would next see Randall eight years later when he moved to Boston to assume the rabbinic leadership of Temple Israel in Boston. Sid Randall was among his new congregants and they remained close for years. In his autobiography Gittelsohn noted, "We seldom talk about our shared combat experience; Sid still finds it difficult to ventilate his pain."[9]

Before leaving Iwo Jima, he recorded, "1 of most touching things—before we left several hundred graves marked w carved stones by buddies—1 inscription: 'Zeke—God bless you—Your childhood buddy.'"[10] He embellished on this in both his unpublished post-war memoir and in his autobiography. Many of the Marines had discovered that the sandstone on the north end of Iwo Jima could be smoothed and carved. The men began to carve headstones for the graves of their friends to supplement the identical white wooden crosses and stars. On the last evening he was on Iwo Jima, Gittelsohn walked through the cemetery. That night, he observed three to four hundred of these spontaneously carved monuments, each carved by a man who had already expended his last ounce of strength in combat but "...could not leave without a final tribute to someone he loved. No one bothered to inquire whether the faith of the carver matched that of the deceased."[11]

Describing this incident in his post-war memoir, he said, "I don't know when any single experience in my life has touched me so deeply."[12] He ended the chapter by describing his Marine colleagues in such a way that his love for them is evident. "Marines tough? Don't let them ever kid you! They're tough only when they face a bitter, ruthless enemy. But in their innermost heart of hearts they're soft. And decent. And profoundly, everlastingly good!"[13]

• • •

Early on the morning of March 26, the remaining Japanese were desperate. Kuribayashi knew he was defeated and the end was obvious, but the Japanese *Bushido* code demanded that they not surrender and instead die fighting in defense of the emperor. On that morning, in the predawn darkness, Kuribayashi finally unleashed a suicidal *Banzai* attack. Unlike prior *Banzai* attacks which were characterized by shouting, drunken Japanese soldiers attacking with bugles blaring, this final, desperate attack was different. It was a silent, well-organized raid that began at 5:15 a.m. near the second airfield, Motoyama Number 2.

About 300 Americans were asleep in their tents when the Japanese attacked from three directions, slaughtering their unsuspecting enemy. These American troops were shore party personnel, aircrew, supply troops, Army antiaircraft gunners, and Seabees. However, when the brunt of the attack hit the 5th Marine Division's Pioneer Battalion, the tide began to turn. By 8:00 a.m. it was over. Nearly 60 Americans were killed in the attack. Strewn around the battleground were 262 Japanese bodies.[14] In his own notes, Gittelsohn would record, "Banzai our last night on Iwo—65 casualties, 197 Japs killed."[15]

Later that day the men of the 5th Marine Division boarded transport ships for the transit back to Hawaii. It had taken 22 transport ships to bring them to Iwo Jima. The survivors would fit into eight transport ships.[16] In all, nearly 6,800 Marines were buried on the island. Gittelsohn's notes indicate that in the 5th Marine Division cemetery they had buried 2,280 Marines.[17] After 36 days of sustained combat, they were finally leaving the site of the bloodiest battle in Marine Corps history.

Before getting underway, Gittelsohn had one more mission to perform.

He was determined to deliver the Passover supplies to the other ships in the task force that had Jewish Marines and Sailors aboard. His friend Carl Elder had certainly gone above and beyond the bonds of true friendship by procuring 850 pounds of supplies from Saipan and now, before the ships got underway, Gittelsohn was determined to deliver the Passover Seder supplies to about 20 ships while they were anchored a short distance offshore.

Gittelsohn and his sergeant commandeered a small landing craft and packed several cartons for each ship. On that sunny and windy day, they set out on their delivery mission and soon ran into difficulties that Gittelsohn would find very humorous in retrospect. Once his landing craft came alongside each ship, to board he had to climb a Jacob's ladder, grasping each rung of the ladder with one hand and carrying the carton under his other arm. By his own admission, Gittelsohn was not known for his "kinetic dexterity." On his final delivery of the morning, he was struggling up the Jacob's ladder when suddenly a gust of wind lifted the ladder—and the rabbi—several yards away from the side of the ship. The wind caused him to sway dangerously back and forth and then twisted him around so that he was caught between the ladder and the ship, facing out. With much struggle, he finally was able to untangle himself and get aboard to deliver his package. He realized at the time that he very well could have been killed, ironically as they prepared to depart the island. However, as he recalled years later, "I wish I had a movie to establish just how I managed to deliver my package and save my skin."[18]

Soon after, he arrived back on his own transport ship and they got underway, departing for Hawaii. It was over. Five weeks of hell had finally ended. During the entire campaign Gittelsohn had not let the stress hinder him in performing his work. "We moved about as robots, automatically performing the motions that had been programmed into us," he had written of their actions on Iwo Jima.[19] He had lived through the horror which he recorded in his private notes. Perhaps it was "combat anesthesia" that had steeled him through the ordeal. Whatever the source of his strength, it suddenly left him on the day they departed from Iwo Jima. That night at dinnertime, he sat down in the officer's wardroom and as a mess steward placed a bowl of hot soup in front of him, he would recall that, "I burst into the most uncontrollable explosion of tears in my whole life. Everything I had somehow managed to absorb for five weeks finally caught up with me."[20]

Like many combat veterans, he suffered from what is now known as post-traumatic stress disorder (PTSD), although his was a mild case. In the weeks that followed his departure, he suffered two horrifying combat nightmares. As the years passed, he explained that his wartime experiences increasingly receded to the point where it was almost as if they were incidents he had read about in a book rather than having actually lived through.[21]

For a long time new experiences reminded him of his time on Iwo Jima. Any unpleasant or earthy odor would bring to his mind the stench of the decaying bodies of his dead Marine comrades. While on Iwo Jima one morning, his clerk, Sergeant Julius Abramson, had returned to their foxhole "as pale as a ghost." It took Abramson a few minutes before he could describe what he had just seen when he walked by the hospital operating rooms a few minutes before. "Outside one of the ORs, he saw two feet cut off at the ankles, still clad in socks and shoes.[22] In a cryptic note written during the campaign, he described a similar experience and wrote "1 a.m.— had seen 2 feet, in shoes, outside O.R."[23] This gruesome sight stayed with him for the rest of his life. As he noted in his autobiography, "The sight of bare feet protruding from a blanket—even in the most benign of settings— evoked nightmarish memories of corpses lined up in neat rows, entirely covered except for their feet."[24]

Easter Sunday fell on the sixth day on the task force's journey to Hawaii. That morning, Gittelsohn stood on the fantail of the ship during Catholic Mass. Partly out of curiosity but also after the Marines' experiences on Iwo Jima, he felt the urge to share companionship and religious reinforcement with others. Memories of his fellowship with the other Christian clergymen students during his days at the chaplains school no doubt came to mind as he listened to the mass. To his astonishment, he heard the ship's Catholic chaplain, preaching on the theme of Resurrection, repeating several times as a litany, "Remember, men, it was the Jews who crucified our Lord! Remember ... remember ... remember...."[25] It was a harbinger of things that were to come when they arrived back in Hawaii.

TWENTY-FIVE

Aftermath

The 5th Marine Division arrived back in Hawaii in mid–April. The Marines all felt good to be ashore in a familiar, friendly, and safe environment once again. They knew they would not be participating in the invasion of Okinawa, but their immediate futures were uncertain beyond that. For Gittelsohn, it was a return to his familiar duties as assistant division chaplain. Along with his fellow Marines, it was a time of rest and recuperation, as well as a time of reflection.

Back home in the United States, the American public began to digest the reports of the entire Iwo Jima campaign and the price paid in blood by the United States Marine Corps: 26,000 casualties, of which 6,800 were buried in the three cemeteries. In addition, the American public was learning of a sermon delivered by a Navy chaplain at the dedication of one of those cemeteries. All across the country, families were receiving letters from their Marine sons and brothers, telling them they had survived and were okay. Thousands of these letters contained a copy of the speech given by Gittelsohn, and the readers were struck by the power of Gittelsohn's message.

A copy of the sermon was sent to *Time* Magazine, which published parts of the speech on April 30, 1945. In a short article entitled "Religion: The Purest Democracy," three excerpts were given after the short introduction: "When the 5th Marine Division cemetery was dedicated on bloody, windswept Iwo Jima, the sermon was delivered by the division's Jewish chaplain, Roland B. Gittelsohn."[1] The news of the powerful speech, which came to be known as "The Purest Democracy," spread like wildfire across the United States.

• • •

Back at the 5th Marine Division headquarters on Hawaii, awards were issued for the members of the American invasion force that conquered Iwo Jima. As a combat veteran of the campaign, Gittelsohn earned the Asiatic-Pacific Campaign medal. The V Amphibious Corps was awarded a Presidential Unit Citation, and all its members were entitled to wear the accompanying ribbon. The 5th Marine Division was awarded a Navy Unit Commendation. In addition to these three campaign ribbons, the former pacifist was also recognized for his individual contributions to the Iwo Jima campaign. That summer, Lieutenant Roland Gittelsohn was awarded a Navy Commendation Medal in recognition of his meritorious service with the United States Marine Corps at Iwo Jima.

• • •

Back on Hawaii, Gittelsohn once again conducted twice-weekly discussion groups on Monday and Wednesday evenings. Just as before Iwo Jima, these meetings were again open to all Marines, including of course those who were Black. These discussion groups again seemed to create friction between Gittelsohn and his fellow chaplains. Although he did not know it at the time, Christian chaplains' resentment of him continued to grow. Much of the renewed resentment seemed to coincide with the increasing acclaim accorded to Gittelsohn as more and more Americans became aware of "The Purest Democracy" speech.

As mentioned previously, not long after Gittelsohn had re-established his discussion groups, he received a "suggestion" from the new 5th Marine Division commanding general, Major General Thomas Bourke. Bourke recommended that he hold separate discussion groups for the Caucasian Marines and the Black Marines. Gittelsohn's previously mentioned none-too-subtle and borderline disrespectful reply, conveyed via Warren Cuthriell, had no doubt infuriated Bourke. There would be consequences for the outspoken chaplain.

A short time later, while at the Headquarters Company, Gittelsohn was approached by a young lieutenant working in the intelligence division (G-2). The young lieutenant, a Christian whom Gittelsohn casually knew, asked him if they could take a walk together. Gittelsohn was flattered and quickly agreed, suspecting there was a personal issue that the young man wanted to discuss. They walked outside the camp limits, exchanging small talk and pleasantries, when the young Marine suddenly turned to him and asked him whether he knew that he was being investigated by G-2. Gittelsohn stared dumbfounded at the lieutenant, who proceeded to tell him that all his mail, both incoming and outgoing, was being scrutinized. After absorbing this disturbing news, Gittelsohn thanked his fellow officer because he realized the risk the man had just taken. The young man risked court-martial and other possible severe punishments by speaking to Gittelsohn about an ongoing intelligence operation.

Walking back to Headquarters Company, Gittelsohn decided his course of action: He would not change his behavior in any way. He would continue to write his letters as he always had, continue to expose the men in his discussion groups to contrasting ideas and points of view, and continue his outspoken ways.[2] It seemed to him that the right to free expression and exchange of points of view, as well as the concepts of equality of all men, were the very ideals that the Marines had fought and died for. Investigative efforts concerning the outspoken chaplain continued behind the scenes as he continued to fulfill his daily duties.

• • •

After *Time* magazine published its article on "The Purest Democracy," the exposure that Gittelsohn's the speech received skyrocketed. One American who was extremely impressed with the sermon was famed journalist Robert St. John, a noted author and world traveler, who had a regular radio program on NBC. He would later become the first journalist to announce the end of World War II, seconds after the Japanese surrender. After reading Gittelsohn's speech, he was convinced that it truly evoked the American ethic and provided the answer to "Why we fight." To Robert St. John, Gittelsohn's speech needed to be heard by all Americans. On Memorial Day, May 30, 1945, he introduced the sermon to the nation when he announced that he was going to do something unusual and asked his audience to bear with him. He was going to read them a memorial address delivered at the dedication of the 5th Marine Division cemetery on Iwo Jima by Chaplain Roland Gittelsohn. He assured his listeners that "…when I get through, I'm sure you'll understand why I've done it."[3]

St. John went on to declare that the words he was about to read should be documented in every history book and that millions of copies of the address should be distributed across the land. "When I get through," he asked his audience, "you tell me what you think of it. Here are the words of the chaplain, as he stood at the side of those American graves on the island of Iwo Jima."[4]

St. John proceeded to read Gittelsohn's sermon and the entire NBC listening audience nationwide was introduced to "The Purest Democracy." For many years afterward, St. John would include a reading of "The Purest Democracy" during his Memorial Day broadcasts.[5]

A competing radio network, CBS, decided that Roland Gittelsohn's sermonic address at Iwo Jima needed the widest dissemination possible. Accordingly, the distinguished Hollywood actor Fredric March read the entire sermon on air for CBS's national audience. In addition, United State Army officials were impressed with the power of Gittelsohn's speech. The Army then arranged to have the speech released for shortwave broadcast to American troops stationed around the world.[6]

Several members of Congress read the speech and were duly impressed with the power of its message. One member of Congress had the entire speech inserted into the *Congressional Record*. Over the next six decades, "The Purest Democracy" would be read aloud on the floor of the House of Representatives and inserted in the *Congressional Record* on many occasions. All this was in tribute to the valor of the United States Marine Corps at Iwo Jima and to one of their chaplains, Rabbi Roland Gittelsohn.[7]

• • •

A few weeks after his reply to General Bourke concerning his discussion groups, Gittelsohn received Temporary Addition Duty (TAD) orders transferring him to duty as a staff chaplain at the headquarters of Fleet Marine Force, Pacific Fleet at Pearl Harbor, while he awaited orders to return stateside. He was no longer supervising other chaplains as the assistant division chaplain, but he performed his duties with enthusiasm and remained an effective advocate for his men in the performance of his chaplain duties. During this time, Gittelsohn stumbled upon evidence of the investigation of him conducted by the 5th Marine Division G-2.

One Sunday morning, when he was the duty chaplain, he returned to the duty office to find his service jacket (personnel file) on the desk, along with other papers that the duty chaplain would normally work with. He was taken aback—normally his personnel file, along with all other similar personnel files, was kept secured under lock and key with access granted only to a limited few. Now he was staring at his own file, which he noted was strangely left among papers to which the duty chaplain always had access. He acknowledged that it could have been an innocent mistake but he concluded, "I'm more inclined to think it was the deliberate act of my new senior chaplain, who wanted me to see the file."[8]

Gittelsohn was now working for Captain Herbert Dumstrey, a career Navy chaplain who was a minister in the Reformed Church of America. Included in the file were the results of the investigation of Lieutenant Roland Gittelsohn by the G-2, military intelligence staff of the 5th Marine Division. The final endorsement was by General Thomas Bourke who wrote, "There is no evidence that LT Gittelsohn is an actual Communist, but he favors many of the causes supported by the Communists. It is requested that he be transferred out of the Division."[9]

In his autobiography, Gittelsohn would sarcastically comment that he was flagrantly guilty, noting that at the time the Communists were our military allies and favored a victory over Japan, just as he did. He added, "By the way, my 'punishment' for this offense was being returned to the United States and my family six months earlier than I would otherwise have been."[10]

Whether or not antisemitism played into General Bourke's negative endorsement is impossible to ascertain. As mentioned earlier, the increasing publicity received by "The Purest Democracy" served to further infuriate the chaplains who originally protested that Gittelsohn had been selected to give the sermon at Iwo Jima. One of those chaplains wrote to Captain Dumstrey to complain vociferously about Gittelsohn and to accuse him of being "anti–Christian." The letter containing Dumstrey's response to the accusing chaplain was in Gittelsohn's personnel file that Dumstrey had left for him to find.

In his letter dated May 11, 1945, Dumstrey had replied to the complaining chaplain, noting that he (Dumstrey) had looked at both sides of the issue and that the accusing chaplain himself was not entirely without fault. Dumstrey informed him that in both word and deed, "...you have contradicted the high standards of a Christian gentleman and the principles of freedom of religion so dear to the hearts of American citizens, which have been at stake in the European conflict." Dumstrey's anger and disappointment was evident as he concluded the letter by expressing regret over the actions of his fellow Christian chaplain:

> I deeply regret that one of your calling should take the stand which it appears you have taken. It serves no good purpose, especially in the service. We are a conglomerate group, a mixture of racial, religious and national antecedents. All have their constitutional rights and privileges. As a minister of religion, you should be among the first to champion rather than scorn them.[11]

As Gittelsohn no doubt noted, the letter speaks volumes about the character of Captain Herbert Dumstrey.

• • •

While he was in Hawaii, Gittelsohn began receiving mail from United States citizens who had read "The Purest Democracy," as well as from Marines he had served with at Iwo Jima. He saved much of this correspondence with his wartime notes. Many pieces are inspiring and on the other hand, gut-wrenching. The outpouring of emotion to a total stranger that was revealed in many of these letters is a tribute to the powerful message that his speech conveyed to many Americans. Representative of the correspondence Gittelsohn received was a letter written on May 6, 1945, by Mary McNeal of Kissimmee, Florida.[12] She began by citing the *Time* magazine article of April 30 and Gittelsohn's sermon at the cemetery dedication, and then continued:

> Our son, PFC William J. McNeal, HqBn HQbr, 5th Marines, sleeps there with his buddies "forever young" and at peace; no more suffering, no more fighting. It was his first action, I think. He was killed Feb 20.... Surely you spoke a great truth when you told what they might have given the world had they been

spared. "Theirs is indeed the highest and purest democracy." [Mrs. McNeal went on to lament the futility of war, noting that it is] "man-made misery," [and not God's punishment] "for our misdeeds." [As in virtually every letter he received, she asked Gittelsohn if he could perhaps find out details about how her son died. As the *Time* Magazine article contained only brief excerpts of the speech, she wrote,] "I wish that I might read all of your sermon—it would be like a service in honor of the boy we love so well. May I have a copy please? ... Thank you for these beliefs—when these become the creed of the earth, there will be real lasting peace. May God guide you in teaching them." [In the rest of the letter, she revealed that William's brother Bernard was serving in the Navy somewhere in the Pacific at that time. In a heart-wrenching remembrance of her son William, she wrote] He never got home on furlough after enlisting in August 1942. He went on until he could no longer endure there—now we can do no less here.

The letters Gittelsohn received confirmed the impact his sermon had on the American public back home. Family members of Marines who gave their lives at Iwo Jima were especially affected by the stirring principles articulated by Gittelsohn in "The Purest Democracy." Their letters to Gittelsohn served to acknowledge that if these Marines had died fighting for the principles he so eloquently expressed then perhaps they had not died in vain.

• • •

Gittelsohn's wartime files also contain several letters from Marines with whom he served, thanking him for his friendship and compassion. Reading them, one can only conclude that he effectively served his Jewish and Christian Marines with equal care, despite the pre- and post-battle conflicts with his fellow chaplains. When he was still at the 5th Marine Division, he received a telegram dated June 12, 1945, from Private Walter Mirschinger.[13] Mirschinger was writing from Springfield, Massachusetts, where he was recovering from a severe combat injury he received on Iwo Jima. He wrote, "It seems like a lifetime ago since our last meeting under very different circumstances." He remembered how the door of their Higgins boat jammed as they were ordered over the side. As Mirschinger scurried up the beach, his heavy equipment load caused him to fall on his knees. "As I was about to get up a very assuring voice said, 'Hello Walter.' I'd like to say that those two words were about the most encouraging words I heard on that hell hole."

After updating Gittelsohn on his recovery from his surgeries, Mirschinger closed by wishing him well and "...that you and the rest of the boys [word unclear] anything like that to go through again before we meet again in the states. Thanks for everything. God speed and may He bless you all."

In addition to the Private Mirschinger's original telegram, Gittelsohn's notes contain the cryptic entry: "Never saw this boy on beach! Said goodbye to him on ship just before he went over the side!"[14]

His wartime file also contains part of a letter from another Marine named Harold Gross.[15] The first page is missing so the date that he wrote to Gittelsohn is unclear. It is, however, apparent from the letter that Gross was from New York and was a member of Gittelsohn's synagogue. He described a religious experience that to him was a tribute to his rabbi. He and some fellow Marines went to a local church to listen to another colleague play the organ. While he stood there in the church, listening to the organ playing beautiful hymns, he couldn't see the church before him. Rather, the experience transported him back to their own temple where he realized "…once more how much those services you gave, and worshipping with my own family and friends meant to me." It seemed strange to him that one had to travel hundreds of miles from home, go to a different church before he realized what his own meant to him. He rhetorically pondered, "Why must it be that way?" Gross closed his letter with news from home. His wife had reported that the Gittelsohn children were cuter than ever, "…and I can readily imagine how anxious you must be to get home and share the joy of raising them with your 'swell' wife. Do hope it won't be much longer now."

TWENTY-SIX

Why Pacifism Failed

The petty jealousies of his fellow chaplains over the nationwide acclaim for "The Purest Democracy" continued to fester after Gittelsohn and his fellow chaplains returned to Hawaii from Iwo Jima in April 1945. His controversial discussion groups had aroused the ire of the 5th Marine Division's commanding general, who would recommend his removal from the division and transfer back to the staff of Fleet Marine Force Pacific Fleet. As noted previously, permeating throughout his tenure in the Pacific was the specter of antisemitism, both subtle and overt.

On August 7, 1945, Gittelsohn received orders transferring him to the Sampson Naval Training Center on the shores of Lake Seneca in upstate New York. Soon after, he learned about the atomic bombs that were dropped on Hiroshima and Nagasaki. The specter of nuclear war totally disgusted him. In his notes he jotted, "Utter insanity/war system. Nuclear destructive overkill. No life on planet. Disintegration, decay/our civ, No $ for schools, human needs, only for war."[1]

Sampson Naval Training Center was one of the Navy's Boot Camps. Gittelsohn worked with new recruits for the few months he was there. He would look back with some bitterness at this assignment, recalling he was there "to waste time for two months doing virtually nothing at Camp Sampson in upstate New York while collecting enough 'points' for discharge."[2]

Soon after arriving at the training center, Gittelsohn received an invitation from Dr. Julian Morgenstern, president of Hebrew Union College in Cincinnati, Ohio, where he was ordained. The college was beginning a series of events to commemorate the seventieth anniversary of the school's founding, and the first event was a three-day seminar to be held from October 16 through October 18, entitled "Judaism and American Democracy." In his invitation, Morgenstern asked the school's distinguished alumnus to be one of the featured speakers.

Gittelsohn wrote back on October 19, expressing his sincere gratitude for the invitation. He would, however, not be able to attend. He explained

217

to Morgenstern that his naval duties would make it impossible for him to accept the invitation to speak in Cincinnati that week. In closing, he noted, "I hope … that in the future it will be possible for me to do so; you know that I shall be delighted to do anything within my power for the College."[3] In the letter, he also took the time to compliment the work of rabbinical student Harold Waintrup for his fine work. Waintrup, who was studying at Hebrew Union College, had recently been filling in for Gittelsohn at the Central Synagogue of Nassau County. Gittelsohn was able to attend the Rosh Hashanah services that Waintrup had conducted when he was on Long Island taking rehabilitative leave after arriving home from the Pacific theater. He was very impressed with the young man's performance of his duties and Gittelsohn felt compelled to let Morgenstern know that Waintrup was doing a "splendid job."

Several weeks later Gittelsohn received another speaking invitation from the college. The school was planning a special 70th anniversary dinner to be held on Saturday, December 8, and once again they were hoping that Gittelsohn would be able to be one of the principal speakers. Gittelsohn replied to Rabbi Samuel Wohl in a letter dated November 12 in which he outlined the circumstances that would in all probability prevent him from attending. He explained that as of 1 December, he would be eligible on points for discharge from the Navy. It was then necessary for him to make formal application on that date, and to await return of his papers from Washington. "The probability is that I shall not be released before the dates of the Cincinnati celebration; my guess is that the middle of the month is the earliest I can expect to get out."[4] Among the guest speakers who were able to attend the December 8 dinner were Henry Morgenthau, Jr., former Secretary of the Treasury and Rabbi Steven Wise, the prominent Zionist and personal friend of the late President Franklin D. Roosevelt.

Gittelsohn submitted his paperwork for discharge from the service on December 1 and it took several weeks to work its way through the bureaucracy, along with millions of other discharge requests. His official discharge date from the United States Naval Reserve was January 27, 1946.

• • •

After the war, the popularity of "The Purest Democracy" continued to resonate with the American public and would continue to do so for decades. In a February 1947 article published in *The Reconstructionist*, Gittelsohn described the controversy over his invitation to speak at the proposed joint religious service at the 5th Marine Division cemetery dedication. Over the years, the speech would also be referred to as the "Gettysburg Address of World War II."[5] In his 1988 autobiography, he pondered about how his sermon received such wide distribution in a quote that is now universally linked to the story of his famous speech. "I have often wondered whether anyone would ever have heard of my Iwo sermon had it not been for the bigoted attempt to ban it."[6]

• • •

At the end of World War II, Gittelsohn wrote a memoir about his wartime experiences, but he never published it. It had three proposed titles: "Pacifist to Padre," "Pacifist in Uniform," and "Pacifist No More." In the preface he explained that it was not a "war book," or an account of the fighting on Iwo Jima. Instead, his reasons for writing the book were two-fold. Firstly, he wanted to trace the seemingly overnight changes that converted average citizens, pacifists, and anti-war activists into a highly effective fighting force. Lastly, there was an emotional story to be told from the memories and files of the chaplain. "He has an unparalleled, unequaled opportunity to observe ordinary human beings, under far from ordinary circumstances, at close quarters."[7]

The memoir is nearly 200 pages long and begins on December 7, 1941, with his initial reaction of "I don't believe it!" He ended his book with a postscript entitled, "Now I Believe It." In the postscript, he traces his evolution from pacifist to combat veteran. The reading provides a compelling story of a complex man, an intellectual faced with a moral dilemma. It traces how that man, Roland Gittelsohn, evolved over the four-year period between 1941 and 1945.

He began the postscript by noting:

> I suppose the story could have ended with the last chapter. That, however, would have left at least the author with a strange feeling of unfinished business. Sometimes, as I look backward and inward upon myself, I wonder whether I am the same "I" who found it so hard to believe on that fateful Sunday afternoon when, for an electric instant, the universe shook and God stopped breathing. I don't know which surprises me more, the stubborn pacifist of 1940 or the military chaplain of 1944. Perhaps the trouble is that I can't entirely forget the one, and I am not altogether adjusted to the other. But whatever the real cause, there are moments when, thinking of myself then and myself now I wonder if I have not suffered from a sort of spiritual schizophrenia.[8]

Here Gittelsohn succinctly described the inner turmoil experienced by many former staunch pacifists who went on to serve honorably in the military during World War II. He pondered the question of what happened to the pacifism that was at the core of his identity. Where had it gone, and why did it fail? After his military experiences and an inordinate amount of thinking, he came up with some definitive ideas about why and how his beloved philosophy of pacifism failed so dismally. It was, he concluded, compromised from the beginning and never had a chance. To use

Gittelsohn's analogy, pacifism perished like a man whose food was withheld from him until he weakened and finally died. As he wrote, "We allowed the nourishment it needed to be withdrawn from the world up to the point where we had on our hands an ideal which was no longer relevant in our new circumstance of international life."[9]

He stated that pacifism could have been saved if, at any point along the way, they had put their foot down stubbornly and said: "'No! We will not yield another inch! Inches add up to feet, and feet make yards. When yards are reached, it will be too late!'"[10] Gittelsohn embellished this idea with an analogy to a building that has an adequate fire extinguisher. Over years the building is greatly expanded, but there is still only one original fire extinguisher to handle possible fires. And when the building burns, who, he asks rhetorically, is to blame?[11]

By 1939, Gittelsohn had concluded that pacifism was forced into a corner where it could not work. The cards, he claimed, were stacked against it. Among the "cards" he referred to, was the indifference to the slaughters in Manchuria and Ethiopia, the civil war in Spain, and the appeasement of Germany at Munich. "Against such odds as these," he declared, "what chance did pacifism or pacifists stand? In a world where two and two made four, we could have succeeded. But not in the world of Munich."[12]

He was still a pacifist down to the marrow of his bones, but by the time of the Dunkirk evacuation in May 1940, he realized that there were limited choices to deal with the reality of the situation. "By then, every choice but two had been eliminated.... It was then either slavery or war. What use, at such a time, to lament what might have been? Too late!"[13]

During the interwar years, men of "prophetic vision and faith" had been warning the world that, "If this and this and this is done, the sum total will unavoidably be war!" Then Gittelsohn added, "Their words went unheeded. Their warnings were ignored."[14] Gittelsohn commented how these people who had issued the warnings faced a dilemma. What must they do? While it may have represented some form of historic justice for these people to stand off, detached from the situation and say, "I told you so," or "We warned you," the reality was much harsher than the theoretical finger-pointing. Gittelsohn expressed the sad irony of the situation. "And so—the grim irony of fate!—they who more than once had tried to stop this thing, they to whom the others would not listen, became colonels and corporals and chaplains."[15]

In a much broader sense, Gittelsohn concluded that the failure of pacifism was religious. "Professing the beliefs of Christians and Jews, we pacifists had acted as though we were Romans and Greeks."[16] Noting that these ancient peoples believed that each separate human virtue could be deified by itself and followed for its own sake, "each became, if an end at all, purely an end by itself, without regard for the others." This he contrasted with the virtue of modern religions that view life as a whole. "Our God is a God of all these virtues, not of any one or two or three. He is a God who combines and expresses all of our human ideals in one great pattern of perfection."[17]

Gittelsohn proceeded to brilliantly summarize the crux of his reasoning about why pacifists had failed in their mission. For this, he harkened back to the 2,000-year-old teachings of Rabbi Simeon ben Gamliel, whom he first discussed in his powerful sermon of October 1, 1938:

> Our mistake as pacifists was that we held peace up as our God and forgot that peace can come only along with the rest. Peace among nations, like the happiness of individuals, is something of a by-product, not a goal to be sought directly for itself. Our rabbis knew that. "On three things does the world stand," they said. "On truth, on justice, and on peace." So! First on truth! Second on justice! And only then on peace! Establish a world in which truth prevails, in which justice is triumphant, and then you shall have peace. Without truth and justice, your leagues will be empty shells, your pledges will be hollow mockeries, your pacifism will be a ghastly joke![18]

It was a sobering lesson, not only for former pacifists, but for the entire world. Let the truth prevail, let justice triumph, and then the world will have peace. As he wrote this postscript, the war was still being fought. "The war will end, and peace—of a sort—will come again. Then our task will only have begun."[19] The sacrifices of those who had died in the war must not be in vain. Gittelsohn used Yetta Weinberg's last thoughts about her late husband to express his feelings concerning the responsibility of mankind from this point forward. A world without war must be the ideal that every nation must strive for. "He held his ideals very high, and was willing to die for them. Should they ever be destroyed, I would lose all faith and trust in humanity!"[20]

Gittelsohn added an addendum to his postscript—a paragraph from Pearl Buck's book *Tell the People*. In it, Buck concluded, "To work for peace, as though it were a thing in itself, without relation to causes, is the crowning folly of our foolish age."[21]

• • •

Like most anti-war activists of the 1930s, Gittelsohn felt that his knowledge and understanding of the "lessons" of World War I helped him understand the international conflicts of the 1930s. Peace activists like him had never stopped to consider that the insights gleaned from that war might not be relevant to the new and different international situation that prevailed during the Depression decade.[22] They tended to see the First World War as a product of economic imperialism, and they assumed that should war again break out, it would be a repeat of 1917, only accomplishing "the transfer of mines, mills and trade routes from one set of capitalists to another."[23] This rigid "economic determinism" left the antiwar activists unable to see the real nature of the upcoming war in Europe: a struggle not over capitalist spoils, but over whether the world would fall under Nazi totalitarianism.[24]

Gittelsohn weighed absolute pacifism against what he had learned over the years, in light of his experiences during World War II. In his 1988 autobiography he summarized these lessons:

> As the threat of nuclear catastrophe has loomed larger and more ominously on the horizon since 1945, I have been increasingly tempted to return to my erstwhile absolute pacifism. Yet I see that now as a puristic position that cannot prevail. It is too late—after a lifetime of heavy smoking has produced lung cancer—to resist surgery as a wastage of blood. The way to deal with cancer is to prevent it; the time is long before it appears. Judaism teaches that the sword comes into the world because of the denial of justice. We approach the perilous brink of war due to a multitude of factors—psychological, political, economic, ethical; because we have allowed monstrous immoralities to fester instead of eradicating them. The only way to prevent the ultimate explosion is to avoid or erase the inequities that cause it. I am afraid that once these inequities have mounted, not even the refusal to fight by ten times Einstein's quota will help, especially as war becomes more and more fiendishly technological, with fewer combatants producing many more casualties.[25]

Gittelsohn's views on absolute pacifism were echoed during the Vietnam War when Rabbi Maurice Lamm expressed a similar view that elucidated the failure of rigid dogmatic pacifism from a religious perspective. Lamm stated that pacifism *absolutizes* the concept of peace and in in Judaism no value is absolute. Only God is absolute. "Everything else in the world is relative to the absolute that we call God. When we transform a relative into an absolute we create an idol."[26]

Viewed from that perspective, the pacifist activists of the 1930s had truly created an idol—one that was toppled and destroyed by Nazi Germany and Imperial Japan.

Twenty-Seven

Once a Marine ...

When examining Gittelsohn's writing, how is the reader able to interpret his true feelings concerning his service with the United States Marine Corps? Which more truly captures what he felt: his memoir written at the end of the war, in which he seems enthusiastic and positive about his wartime experience; or his autobiography written in later years, which provide a narrative of his experiences but seems somewhat darker and at times resentful and bitter? The reality is that, to a degree, both accounts tell a true story. But as he aged and reached his 70s, he focused on some of the darker aspects of his Navy and Marine Corps service.

In any event, both accounts lead us to some definite conclusions concerning his experiences. The former pacifist was proud of his service, and this pride is evident throughout all his writings. "Even as a pacifist," he wrote, "I noted more than once with manifest discomfort, that a good military band parading down the street set my foot a-tapping and my spirits a-marching."[1] Another illustration of Gittelsohn's pride in serving with the Marine Corps was his inspiring pre-combat sermon, reminding his fellow Marines that they were about to become members of the most honorable fraternity on earth, "the fraternity of those who have suffered and sacrificed so that humanity could move forward instead of backward.... Tonight you and I become members of that fraternity!"[2]

He was very candid in describing how his experience as a military chaplain had a positive effect on his religious outlook after the war. While wishing to avoid glibness and easy optimism, he wrote, "...there is little doubt in my own mind that men by the tens of thousands will return to civilian life after the war with a new respect for synagogue and church."[3] He enthusiastically described his belief that servicemen discovered a new freshness and directness in religion, a new type of faith which helps them meet practical problems. They had listened to sermons that were short, simple, and to the point. He believed that was a positive development and

223

that returning servicemen would only respond in later years to similar kinds of religious expression.[4]

Gittelsohn was buoyant over the positive impact of chaplains' interactions with American servicemen. He remained convinced that the chaplains had reintroduced religion into their lives, an important "brand" of religion that would be more relevant to these men:

> Anyone who reads such views with understanding intelligence will see in them not only the greatest promise, but equally the highest challenge that organized religion has faced in a long time. Men will not return from wars willing to accept just any kind of religion. They will return ready to listen, ready to give civilian religion a chance. They will return ready to see if their minister, priest, or rabbi is a "good Joe," as their chaplain was, whether he speaks the same language and faces the same problems as they. If he does, and if toward the solution of those problems he brings them religion's message of eternity clothed simply in the language and needs of today, men will turn to religion in civilian life just as eagerly and hopefully as many of them have done in uniform.[5]

Gittelsohn and his fellow chaplains had evolved from their strict pacifist beliefs and become part of the American war effort. In doing so they created a bridge connecting them with their Soldiers, Sailors, and Marines that would endure upon their return to civilian life.

Gittelsohn observed a benefit to Judaism during his military serve. In civilian life he observed the longtime bickering between members of the Orthodox, Conservative and Reform branches of Judaism. In contrast, all branches of the military, there were no Orthodox, Conservative, or Reform Jews. There were just Jews. Some prayed with their hats on, some prayed with their heads uncovered. Some prayed wearing the tallit (prayer shawl), and some did not. But all of them prayed together in the military. Gittelsohn, a Reform rabbi, wore a tallit and yarmulke at his services for the first time since his ordination. With enthusiasm, he noted, "We are learning from each other and with each other. Unless we muff the greatest opportunity either of us has had in centuries, out of this war we shall together forge a new unity in the religious life of the Jew!"[6]

Gittelsohn's admiration for the Marine Corps is obvious in his writings. Describing the courage that he had witnessed at Iwo Jima, he stated, "Major General Julian Smith did not exaggerate in the least when he said: 'I can never again see a United States Marine without experiencing a feeling of reverence.'"[7] Describing the performance of the Marines on Iwo, he knew he would never be able to use the words "American" and "impossible" in the same sentence. Near the end of his memoir, he would proudly record that, "Along with a humble respect for the average American's courage, I carried home with me from Iwo an admittedly egotistical pride in the fact that for him, nothing is impossible!"[8]

The more somber reflections of his later years in no way diminish the fact that Gittelsohn took pride in his performance as a military chaplain. The reflections on the antisemitism he experienced and his conflicts with fellow chaplains that are prominent in his autobiography in no way negate the fact that he believed that he performed critically important work during

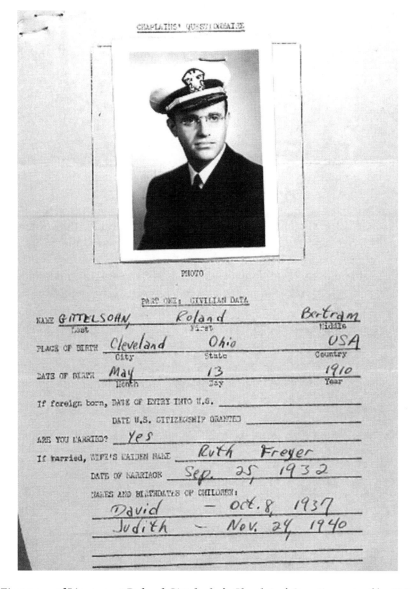

First page of Lieutenant Roland Gittelsohn's Chaplains' Questionnaire file, 1945 (courtesy St. Louis Personnel Records Center).

his military career, and that he and his fellow military chaplains performed their duties in an extremely effective, positive manner. Significantly, he would conclude that overall, his experience as a Navy chaplain was a very positive one. At the end of World War II, he would write, "I have learned more about human behavior in twenty-four months as a chaplain than in an equal number of years as a student of psychology,"[9] and "I think it would not be immodest or inaccurate to say that we shall—most of us—return one day to our civilian congregations considerably changed. We shall be better ministers, priests, and rabbis, because we have been chaplains."[10]

Gittelsohn's feelings about his military experience are best summarized in his autobiography when he wrote, "On the day of my return to civilian life, I said that I wouldn't take a million dollars for the military experience but wouldn't willingly repeat it for five million."[11]

As part of his out-processing from the Navy to the civilian world, Gittelsohn completed a "Chaplains' Questionnaire." Attached to the top of Part One was a formal photograph, a head and shoulders portrait showing Lieutenant Roland Gittelsohn in his service dress blue uniform, his "cover" nattily angled on his head slightly to the right. He didn't appear at all like a fierce warrior or a Hollywood version of a naval officer. Rather, with his wire-rimmed glasses and scholarly expression, he appeared more like a college professor, a man of letters.

Gittelsohn returned home to his wife Ruth, son David, and daughter Judy in early 1946. He promptly resumed his duties as the head of Central Synagogue of Nassau County in Rockville Center, New York. He had experienced both the glory and the horror that only people in combat can ever experience. Now it was time to resume his peaceful life. The pacifist warrior had returned home.

Twenty-Eight

Post-War Years

Shortly after his return from military duty to resume his duties at his synagogue, Gittelsohn's fame as the author of "The Purest Democracy" led to his taking on a highly significant national mission.

On December 5, 1946, President Harry S. Truman issued Executive Order 9808, creating the President's Committee on Civil Rights. Gittelsohn was one of 15 individuals invited to join this prestigious group, chaired by General Electric President Charles E. Wilson. He was the only Jew and rabbi to be appointed.

For nearly a year the civil rights committee met twice a month in Washington, D.C., each session lasting two days. President Truman joined the committee for the first and final sessions. The committee issued its final report, entitled "To Secure These Rights," in December of 1947. Many of the committee's recommendations set the stage for significant future accomplishments of the civil rights movement. About 40 years later, Gittelsohn would ponder, "In how many of these areas have the goals of our committee been fully achieved? None. In how many has substantial progress been made? Nearly all."[1]

• • •

Gittelsohn's tenure at the Central Synagogue of Nassau County would continue another seven years until 1953. That year he was offered a job as senior rabbi at Boston's Temple Israel, then one of the largest Reform synagogues in the country. He had previously been offered the position in 1948 but declined it. When the position opened again five years later, he accepted it because he was ready to move on.

His departure from the Central Synagogue was bittersweet as he had been its only rabbi since its founding in 1936. He took great pride that during his 17 years there, the congregation had grown from 58 families to over 900 under his leadership.

After moving to Boston, Gittelsohn continued his outspoken ways

President Harry S. Truman with the President's Committee on Civil Rights, January 15, 1947. *From left*: the Rev. Henry Knox Sherrill, Bishop Canning Tobias, Richard Potters, Rabbi Roland Gittelsohn, Francis P. Matthews, Morris Ernst, John S. Dickey, James B. Carey, Dr. Sadie Alexander, C.E. Wilson, President Harry Truman, the Rev. Francis J. Hass, Mrs. M.E. Tilly, Boris Shishkin, Dr. Frank P. Graham, Charles Luckman, Tom Clark (AP Photo).

in his new congregation. He encouraged his congregants to be agents for social change and pushed them to engage in social action through education and community activities.[2] He insisted on his right to remain a "crusading rabbi" who would sermonize about pressing issues "in the context of the moral principles of Judaism." As he explicitly announced, "I do not promise to preach always what you want to hear. I believe that there is a two-fold function of a preacher: to comfort the troubled and to trouble the comfortable."[3]

One of the innovations Gittelsohn introduced was adding televised services to complement the synagogue's monthly radio broadcasts. He also instituted a more formal atmosphere during services, stressing decorum, behavior, and courtesy.

During his tenure as rabbi at Temple Israel, Gittelsohn became one of the first clergymen to consistently and vigorously oppose American policy in Vietnam. "We who fought in World War II, however, had little reason to doubt that an abiding purpose was being served," he wrote in his autobiography, noting that the preservation of freedom and the survival of the Jewish people were at stake. In contrast, "Many of those who warred in Vietnam ... saw themselves as helpless pawns in a maelstrom without meaning or aim."[4] His views on the war in Vietnam led to a very public display of his beliefs, consistent with his strong pacifist roots.

In September 1965, the American Legion Crosscup-Pishon Post in Boston designated Gittelsohn as one of three recipients of its annual Good Government Award. Other clergy who were honored with him were Cardinal Richard Cushing and Episcopal Bishop Anson Phelps Stokes, Jr. Two months later, on November 27, Gittelsohn joined 57 other national leaders in sponsoring a peace march in Washington, D.C., in opposition to U.S. policy in Vietnam. The next day the American Legion withdrew its invitation.

Bishop Stokes, while not agreeing with Gittelsohn's beliefs, refused to attend the award ceremony in support of Gittelsohn's right to dissent. This left only Cardinal Cushing to accept the award. Moreover, a group of Catholic, Protestant, and Jewish clergymen issued a statement supporting Gittelsohn's right to dissent. Gittelsohn noted some grumbling within his congregation about his "radicalism," but the Temple's Board of Trustees never attempted to limit his freedom of expression.[5]

Apart from protesting against America's involvement in Vietnam, Gittelsohn, in December 1968, became a strong advocate of Cesar Chavez and his national grape boycott in support of migrant farmworkers. He did so with the strong endorsement of the Massachusetts Board of Rabbis.

In subsequent years, Gittelsohn was involved in many nationwide Jewish organizations in which he played an active role. He served as president of the Massachusetts Board of Rabbis from 1958 to 1960; was the president of the Jewish Community Council of Metropolitan Boston from 1961 to 1963; served as president of the Central Conference of American Rabbis (CCAR) from 1969 to 1971; and served as Vice Chairman of the Union of American Hebrew Congregations from 1973 to 1977.

Gittelsohn was particularly proud of his role as a Zionist, as he noted in his autobiography. As a Zionist his efforts culminated in 1977 when, he was elected as founding president of the Association of Reform Zionists of America (ARZA). In his autobiography he noted that the Orthodox religious parties in Israel exerted a "highly disproportionate political influence as well as a near-monopoly over the nation's religious life."[6] As such he vigorously supported ARZA's two-fold mission, namely, to center a connection to Israel in the American Reform community, and to strengthen the Reform movement on the ground in Israel.[7] Gittelsohn led ARZA for the next seven years until 1984.

• • •

Several years after World War II ended, Roland Gittelsohn's wife Ruth suffered the first of an agonizing series of emotional crises from which she never really recovered. Over the next two decades these episodes recurred.[8] Initially they were emotional/psychiatric, but as the years went by Ruth developed many physical ailments. Her overall health status as well as her mental faculties continued to decline. She suffered from advanced "degenerative dementia" (most likely Alzheimer's disease) and was institutionalized in 1975. During the remaining five years of her life, Roland ruefully noted in his autobiography that the "skills of psychiatrists were not enough to divert her from the womb to which she was determined to return."[9]

In late 1975, Gittelsohn travelled to Israel with members of his congregation. Among them was Hulda Tishler, a widow with two grown sons. She and Roland grew close and fell in love. Upon returning to Boston, Gittelsohn noted that Ruth was now in a vegetative state. Roland obtained a divorce so he could marry Hulda, rather than living together as an unmarried couple. As noted in the book *Becoming American Jews: Temple Israel of Boston*, many in the congregation sympathized with his dilemma, but others "…were dismayed that their rabbi, who had always held his congregants to a high 'moral' and behavioral standard—would have a 'girlfriend,' even though his wife was 'reduced in most respects to infancy.'"[10]

Accordingly, in September 1976, Gittelsohn announced he would retire from his position as senior rabbi a year later in August 1977. Once he retired the board of Temple Israel agreed to offer him the position of Rabbi Emeritus. Roland Gittelsohn and Hulda Tishler were married in 1978. Roland continued to support Ruth in the nursing home until she passed away in 1980.

• • •

In 1988 Gittelsohn reflected on his congregants' perception of him during his years as their spiritual leader. He wrote, "I have infuriated and threatened some, encouraged and inspired others…. My guess is that very few members of my congregation have felt neutral towards me; my kind of personality engenders vigorous support or bitter opposition, seldom mild indifference."[11] To emphasize his point he quoted the influential nineteenth-century scholar Rabbi Israel Salanter, who said: "A rabbi whose community does not disagree with him is no rabbi; a rabbi who fears his community is no man."[12]

• • •

After he left his post as spiritual leader of Temple Israel, Gittelsohn remained busy. On occasion he still conducted services at the synagogue in his capacity as Rabbi Emeritus. He continued to be active in many organizations, especially the ARZA and the Union of American Hebrew Congregations (UAHC). The UAHC recognized Gittelsohn with two awards for his outstanding service: the Maurice N. Eisendrath Bearer of Light Award in 1983, and the Jay Kaufman Award in 1984. He traveled extensively to Europe, Africa, and Israel. Gittelsohn also continued writing, culminating with the publication of his 1988 autobiography, *Here Am I, Harnessed to Hope.* All in all, Gittelsohn wrote twelve books that were published in the course of his life.

• • •

February 19, 1995, was a cloudy, gloomy day as nearly 4,000 people assembled at the Iwo Jima Memorial in Washington, D.C., for the 50th anniversary commemoration of the battle for Iwo Jima. The master of ceremonies was actor Robert Conrad, who portrayed Marine Corps legend Gregory "Pappy" Boyington in the television series *Baa Baa Black Sheep.* The nearly one-hour formal ceremony included speeches by Marine Corps Commandant General Carl Mundy and President Bill Clinton, who noted, "To all of you who served at Iwo Jima, we are the children of your sacrifice and we are grateful."[13]

With less than ten minutes remaining, it was time for the benediction. Conrad introduced the man who would deliver the benediction—Rabbi Roland Gittelsohn. The elderly rabbi was approaching his 85th birthday and was in failing health. Due to his short height, he could barely be seen behind the lectern. However, in a steady, powerful voice, he delivered key portions of his famous sermon from March 21, 1945, that had come to be known as "The Purest Democracy." After he was finished, the Marine color guard retired the colors and the ceremony was ended.

Gittelsohn's health had begun to fail while in his eighties. In 1991 he had been diagnosed with prostate cancer that was treated with radiation therapy. Not long after the 50th anniversary commemoration for Iwo Jima, he developed abdominal pain and was starting to lose weight. That August he received the diagnosis from his doctors and it was grim, declaring he had gastric cancer (cancer of the stomach). Soon thereafter, he underwent surgery followed by chemotherapy.

Although he had advanced cancer and his prognosis was poor, Gittelsohn approached his death philosophically as he explained in an article he wrote for *Reform Judaism Online.*[14] Did he feel that God had inflicted this disease specifically on him as some sort of punishment for something he had done wrong? His answer was an emphatic no. He referred to Maimonides who in the twelfth century asserted that, "God sustains nature in its larger operations and designs, not in each immediate instance. Which means: God determines the general conditions that bring rain, not the specific occasions when rain will fall."

Roland Gittelsohn died at the age of 85 on December 13, 1995.

Although he was slightly under five-foot-six-inches tall, it can truly be said that on that day a giant died. He was buried at the Temple Israel Cemetery in Wakefield, Massachusetts. Under his name, his gravestone reads "Prophet, Scholar, Chaplain U.S.M.C., Author, Champion of Civil Rights, Zionist, Man of Hope."

It is an apt description of who he had been and what he had accomplished.

Epilogue

Rabbi Roland Gittelsohn was a great American leader and thinker. He was one of the most prominent rabbis the United States has ever produced. His life teaches us much about what it means to be an American and to be an ethical person. With remarkable humility and flexibility, he demonstrated his capability to align the convictions of his youth to ever-changing harsh realities. He realized that his initial commitment to total pacifism, although idyllic and optimistic, proved to be unrealistic and immoral, when faced with the likes of Hitler, Mussolini, and Hirohito.

In the course of his life a more mature Gittelsohn intuited the conclusion of philosopher Sam Harris, who wrote in 2005 that pacifism is a difficult position to maintain in practice, and while it is perceived as noble and never described as immoral, he believed that it is indeed immoral. "While it can seem noble enough when the stakes are low," he observed, "pacifism is ultimately nothing more than a willingness to die, and to let others die, at the pleasure of the world's thugs."[1]

Western pacifism between 1933 and1941 reinforced the resolve of immoral hooligans like the three above to take over vast swaths of the world and subjugate millions to the evils of fascism. In the face of such evil, Gittelsohn realized that his total pacifism was unrealistic. Faced with their immoral and barbaric acts worldwide, Gittelsohn knew that the only message these dictators would understand was military force that would be applied in fighting a "just war." As a result, Gittelsohn displayed a strong emotional and intellectual maturity upon realizing the false promise of absolute pacifism, which holds that peace can endure even if we are unwilling to go to battle against oppressive regimes. It was this realization that led to his decision to volunteer for service in the United States Navy.

Once Gittelsohn made the decision to put on a military uniform and serve, he saw another aspect of humanity that was brave, courageous, and democratic. With this revelation he learned that these traits were uniquely

American. While the world was killing each other over ideology and race, Americans from all walks of life, ethnic origins and diverse religious outlooks, came together to fight and destroy fascist warmongers around the world. Although Americans still had problems with segregation and racial discrimination in the United States, those concerns were a far cry from the machinations of Nazi Germany, fascist Italy, and Imperial Japan—the notorious alliance that murdered multiple millions of innocent people.

Although it was an unforeseen outcome during the World War II, Americans' joint war efforts helped blend the American melting pot in an unparalleled manner. All of this occurred in boot camps and officer candidate schools, and in action on the battlefields. Military clergy added to the process of democratization. By ministering to Marines and Sailors of various faiths and ethnicities, Gittelsohn and his fellow Christian and Jewish chaplains showed the greatness of America as the "purest democracy," although he knew America was still far from becoming a totally "pure democracy."

In light of these issues, one can conclude that Rabbi Roland Gittelsohn was far ahead of his time when he served in the military. He saw the racial injustice of segregation and countered it by creating study groups to bring these Americans together so they could learn from each other. With remarkable progressive foresight, he guided his Marines to explore the democratic ideals that represented exactly what it was they were fighting for. He got them to consider that, if they were indeed fighting for their country, then what type of country did they actually envision having in the future? Despite the opposition he received from his commanders, Gittelsohn's tireless nature never wavered when it came to the pursuit of justice and morality, especially in terms of how we should treat our fellow man and woman.

Gittelsohn's beliefs and outlook were succinctly summarized when he delivered his "Purest Democracy" speech at the dedication of the 5th Marine Division's cemetery at Iwo Jima on March 21, 1945. His speech came near the war's end after millions of Americans had risked their lives, and hundreds of thousands had actually given their lives, to prevent the triumph of fascism.

However, as Gittelsohn reminds us, many Americans still harbor various prejudices. As we now know from his life story, this was exemplified by his experience with other clergymen when the 5th Marine Division cemetery was about to be dedicated.

As the reader will recall, several Catholic and Protestant chaplains of the division tried to prevent Gittelsohn, "the Jew," from giving the eulogy because of his Jewish religion and their personal animosity towards him. In spite of his fellow clergymen's bigoted and racist behavior toward him,

Gittelsohn's speech became famous across the land. Paradoxically this was the result of the efforts of some of the other Christian clergymen in the 5th Marine Division that prevented Gittelsohn from speaking at the proposed combined religious service. This treatment encouraged three Protestant ministers to attend the Rabbi's speech in protest.

One of these ministers ended up making numerous copies of the speech, distributing the copies to hundreds, if not thousands, of Marines on Iwo Jima. So impressed were those young Marines, that many of them sent their copy of the speech to their parents and loved ones back home. This enabled the speech to make the rounds with prominent people, especially in the broadcast world where it was soon heard by millions of Americans. This speech would soon be referred to as "The Gettysburg Address of World War II," and would make Gittelsohn one of the most famous military chaplains in the history of the United States.

As noted earlier, President Harry S. Truman was so taken with Gittelsohn's vision that he appointed him to his Committee on Civil Rights in 1946. As Truman and millions of Americans realized, the powerful words of "The Purest Democracy" revealed Gittelsohn's vision for America. This was a vision that eventually presaged the establishment of the civil rights movement and the legislation that accompanied it.

After the war, as Gittelsohn continued his duties as the leader of two synagogues, he helped his congregations become better educated and informed about the important issues facing America. He never shied away from telling people what he thought they needed to hear. He was not there to entertain, but to educate. He was resolute in getting people to think, while making the complacent feel uncomfortable. He did this because he knew America's best was never the best it could be. It could always do better in its pursuit of justice and peace.

President Reagan once said, "Many people live their whole lives wondering if they made a difference in the world. Marines don't have that problem."[2] In the end, this perfectly describes Roland Gittelsohn, the first rabbi to serve as a chaplain with the United States Marine Corps.

Rabbi Gittelsohn made a difference in the lives of the Marines and all Americans, in encouraging them to live up to their democratic values. He left the world a better place. He was there for his countrymen during times of war, when he participated in one of the bloodiest battles of World War II. He was also there when their swords were pounded into plowshares. He guided his countrymen to continue their pursuit of creating an even stronger democracy and a more humane society.

Gittelsohn himself summed up his life's work and his mission at the end of his autobiography: "I live and pray and work for the time when the circle will be closed for all humankind, the circle of integrity within each

person, the circle of love binding us to one another, the circle encompass-
ing ourselves and God."[3]

What inspiring words from Rabbi Roland Gittelsohn! He truly was a
"Prophet, Scholar, Chaplain U.S.M.C., Author, Champion of Civil Rights,
Zionist, Man of Hope."

Inspired by biblical prophets and rabbinic sages, Gittelsohn's evolving
insights and wisdom still provide guidance for us in our pursuit of justice,
harmony, and peace.

Chapter Notes

Chapter One

1. Gittelsohn, R. (1957) *The Little Town That Is No More: The Letters of Reuben Gittelsohn, M.D.* Unpublished manuscript. RBG Files, Box 64, Folder 4, 6.
2. *Ibid.*, 4.
3. *Ibid.*
4. *Ibid.*, 5.
5. *Ibid.*, 6.
6. *Ibid.*, 17.
7. *Ibid.*, 46.
8. Gittelsohn, R. (1988) *Here Am I, Harnessed to Hope.* New York: Vantage, 7.
9. *Ibid.*, 15.
10. Gittelsohn, R. (1957) *The Little Town That Is No More: The Letters of Reuben Gittelsohn, M.D.* Unpublished manuscript. RBG Files, Box 64, Folder 4, 21.
11. *Ibid.*, 22.
12. *Ibid.*, 47.
13. *Ibid.*, 48.
14. Avner, Jane. (2007) "Cleveland." *Encyclopedia Judaica.* Ed. Michael Berenbeim and Fred Skolnik. 2nd ed. Vol. 4. Detroit: Macmillan. 755–759. *Gale Virtual Reference Library.* Web. 8 January. 2013. Accessed 24 March 2013.
15. *Ibid.*
16. Cline, Scott. (2008) "Jews and Judaism." *Encyclopedia of Cleveland History.* Web. 1 July. Accessed 24 March 2013.
17. U.S. Census Bureau. (1900) http://www.ancestry.com. Accessed 16 October 2012.
18. "Congregation Oer Chodosh Sfard Records, 1910–1994." Western Reserve Historical Society. 10 October 2012.
19. "Benjamin Gittelsohn." (1997) *Encyclopedia of Cleveland History.* Web. 10 July. Accessed 20 October 2012.
20. *Ibid.*
21. Gittelsohn, R. (1988) *Here Am I, Harnessed to Hope.* New York: Vantage, 6–7.
22. *Ibid.*, 6.
23. *Ibid.*, 9.
24. *Ibid.*, 7.
25. *Ibid.*, 8.
26. *Ibid.*, 12.
27. *Ibid.*, 12; *Cleveland Jewish Independent*, 8 January 1932.
28. Gittelsohn, R. (1988) *Here Am I, Harnessed to Hope.* New York: Vantage, 14.
29. *Ibid.*
30. Gittelsohn, R. (1957) *The Little Town That Is No More: The Letters of Reuben Gittelsohn, M.D.* Unpublished manuscript. RBG Files, Box 64, Folder 4, 8.
31. *Ibid.*
32. Gittelsohn, R. (1988) *Here Am I, Harnessed to Hope.* New York: Vantage, 17.
33. Gittelsohn, R.B. (1957) *The Little Town That Is No More: The Letters of Reuben Gittelsohn, M.D.* Unpublished manuscript. RBG Files, Box 64, Folder 4, 9.
34. *Ibid.*
35. Gittelsohn, R.B. (1988) *Here Am I, Harnessed to Hope.* New York: Vantage, 18.
36. *Ibid.*, 19.
37. *Ibid.*, 22.
38. *Ibid.*, 23.
39. *Ibid.*
40. *Ibid.*, 24.
41. *Ibid.*
42. *Ibid.*, 28.
43. *Ibid.*, 30.
44. *Ibid.*
45. *Ibid.*, 31.
46. *Ibid.*, 26.
47. *Ibid.*
48. *Ibid.*, 27.
49. *Ibid.*, 30.

Chapter Two

1. Gittelsohn, R. (1988) *Here Am I, Harnessed to Hope.* New York: Vantage, 32.
2. *Ibid.*, 33.
3. *Ibid.*
4. *Ibid.*
5. *Ibid.*, 34.
6. *Ibid.*, 147.
7. *Ibid.*, 34.
8. *Ibid.*
9. Baird, A.C. (1946). *Representative American Speeches: 1945-1946.* New York: H.W. Wilson, 17.
10. Gittelsohn, R.B., op. cit., 35.
11. *Ibid.*
12. *Ibid.*
13. *Ibid.*, 36.
14. *Ibid.*, 17.
15. *Ibid.*, 43.
16. *Ibid.*
17. *Ibid.*
18. *Ibid.*, 44.
19. *Ibid.*, 9.
20. *Ibid.*
21. Gittelsohn, R.B. (1957). *The Little Town That Is No More: The Letters of Reuben Gittelsohn, M.D.* Unpublished manuscript. RBG Files, Box 64, Folder 4, 92.
22. *Ibid.*
23. Gittelsohn, R.B. (1988) *Here Am I, Harnessed to Hope.* New York: Vantage, 93.
24. *Ibid.*, 94.
25. *Ibid.*
26. Wittner, L. (2012) "Albert Einstein and World Peace." *JBooks.com.* Web. Accessed 18 November.
27. *Ibid.*
28. Einstein, et al. (2007). *Einstein on Politics: His Private Thoughts and Public Stands on Nationalism, Zionism, War, Peace, and the Bomb.* Princeton: Princeton University Press, 240–242.
29. Gittelsohn, R.B., op. cit., 93.
30. Miller, R.M. (1985). *Harry Emerson Fosdick: Preacher, Pastor, Prophet.* New York: Oxford University Press, 76.
31. *Ibid.*, 26.
32. Fosdick, H.E. (1934) "The Unknown Soldier" in *Secrets of Victorious Living.* New York: Harper and Brothers, 76.
33. Gittelsohn, R.B. (1945) *Pacifist to Padre/Pacifist in Uniform/Pacifist No More.* Unpublished manuscript. RBG Files, Box 64, Folder 7, 4.
34. *Ibid.*

Chapter Three

1. Cohen R. (1993). *When the Old Left Was Young.* New York: Oxford University Press, 30.
2. *Ibid.*, 39.
3. *Ibid.*, 36.
4. *Ibid.*, 86.
5. *Ibid.*, 87.
6. *Ibid.*, 88.
7. *Ibid.*
8. *Ibid.*, 79.
9. *Ibid.*, 82.
10. *Ibid.*, 90.
11. Precisely how this conversion came about is the focus of Part II of this book.
12. *Ibid.*, 82.
13. *Ibid.*, 83.
14. *Ibid.*, 95.
15. *Ibid.*
16. *Ibid.*, 97.
17. Gittelsohn, R.B. (1988) *Here Am I, Harnessed to Hope.* New York: Vantage, 10.
18. *Ibid.*, 1–2.
19. *Ibid.*, 2.; Genesis 22:2.
20. *Ibid.*, 2–3.
21. *Ibid.*, 1.
22. *Ibid.*, 3.
23. *Ibid.*, 4.
24. *Ibid.*
25. *Ibid.*
26. *Ibid.*, 5.
27. *Ibid.*
28. *Ibid.*, 5.
29. *Ibid.*, 8.
30. *Ibid.*, 7–8.; Genesis 22.2.
31. Gittelsohn, R.B. "Sermon for Chapel—November 16, 1935," from folder labeled Peace, 1930s. RBG Files, Box 53, Folder 4, 4.
32. *Ibid.*, 4–5.
33. *Ibid.*, 5.
34. *Ibid.*
35. *Ibid.*
36. *Ibid.*, 6.
37. *Ibid.*
38. Gittelsohn, R.B. "The Fast That We Have Chosen," from folder labeled Social Action 1934–1936. RBG Files, Box 61, Folder 6, 1.
39. *Ibid.*
40. *Ibid.*, 2.
41. *Ibid.*
42. *Ibid.*
43. *Ibid.*
44. *Ibid.*
45. *Ibid.*

46. *Ibid.*
47. *Ibid.*, 3.
48. *Ibid.*
49. *Ibid.*
50. *Ibid.*, 3–4.
51. *Ibid.*, 4.
52. *Ibid.*, 5.
53. *Ibid.*, 6.
54. *Ibid.*
55. *Ibid.*, 8.
56. *Ibid.*
57. *Ibid.*

Chapter Four

1. National Federation of Temple Sisterhoods. (1913) *Minutes of First Meeting*, 21 January. http://collections.american jewisharchives.org/ms/ms0073/ms0073. A001.001.pdf. 5 December 2012.
2. *Ibid.*
3. Nadell, P.S., op. cit.
4. National Federation of Temple Sisterhoods. (1931) *Resolution on Peace*, 22 January. http://collections.american jewisharchives.org/ms/ms0073/ms0073. A001.001.pdf. 8 December 2012.
5. Report of the National Committee on Peace, 1 Mar 1933. Women of Reform Judaism. Proceedings of the National Federation of Temple Sisterhoods, 1913–1955. WRJ Files. MS-73, Box 1, Vol. 3, 85–89.
6. Report of the National Committee on Peace, 15 May 1934. Women of Reform Judaism. Proceedings of the National Federation of Temple Sisterhoods, 1913–1955. WRJ Files. MS-73, Box 1, Vol. 3, 63–67.
7. Report of the Executive Secretary, 8 Mar 1935. Women of Reform Judaism. Proceedings of the National Federation of Temple Sisterhoods, 1913–1955. WRJ Files. MS-73, Box 1, Vol. 3, 20.
8. Gittelsohn, R.B. (1935) "Book I: Balancing Our War Books." *The Jew Looks at War And Peace.* Cincinnati: National Federation of Temple Sisterhoods, 2.
9. *Ibid.*, 4.
10. *Ibid.*, 8.
11. Gittelsohn, R.B. (1935) "Book II: Religion on Trial." *The Jew Looks at War And Peace.* Cincinnati: National Federation of Temple Sisterhoods, 3.
12. *Ibid.*, 4.
13. *Ibid.*
14. *Ibid.*
15. *Ibid.*

16. Gittelsohn, R.B. (1935) "Book III: Are Jews Pacifists?" *The Jew Looks at War And Peace.* Cincinnati: National Federation of Temple Sisterhoods, 1.
17. *Ibid.*, 2.
18. *Ibid.*
19. *Ibid.*, 3.
20. *Ibid.*, 5.
21. Gittelsohn, R.B. (1935) "Book IV: Can Jews Afford to Be Pacifists?" *The Jew Looks at War And Peace.* Cincinnati: National Federation of Temple Sisterhoods, 1.
22. *Ibid.*, 2.
23. *Ibid.*, 3.
24. *Ibid.*, 2.
25. *Ibid.*, 5.
26. *Ibid.*
27. *Ibid.*, 6.
28. Gittelsohn, R.B. (1935) "Book V: If Women Wanted Peace." *The Jew Looks at War And Peace.* Cincinnati: National Federation of Temple Sisterhoods, 1.
29. *Ibid.*
30. *Ibid.*, 2.
31. *Ibid.*
32. *Ibid.*, 3.
33. *Ibid.*
34. *Ibid.*
35. *Ibid.*, 4.
36. *Ibid.*
37. *Ibid.*, 5.
38. Report of the National Committee on Peace, 15 December 1936. Women of Reform Judaism. Proceedings of the National Federation of Temple Sisterhoods, 1913–1955. WRJ Files. MS-73, Box 1, Vol. 3, 64.
39. Report of the National Committee on Programs, 15 December 1936. Women of Reform Judaism. Proceedings of the National Federation of Temple Sisterhoods, 1913–1955. WRJ Files. MS-73, Box 1, Vol. 3, 168.

Chapter Five

1. "List of Rabbis." Wikipedia. https:// en.wikipedia.org/wiki/List_of_rabbis#:~: text=Yohanan%20ben%20Zakkai%2C%20 (c.,actually%20be%20called%20%E2%80% 9CRabbi%E2%80%9D. Accessed 8 August 2020.
2. Gittelsohn, R.B. (1988) *Here Am I, Harnessed to Hope.* New York: Vantage, 40.
3. *Ibid.*

4. Golden Jubilee Journal (Rockville Centre, New York) Central Synagogue of Nassau County, 1986, 1.
5. Ibid.
6. Ibid.
7. Gittelsohn, R.B. op. cit., 45.
8. Ibid.
9. Ibid., 46.
10. Ibid.
11. Gittelsohn, R.B. "Rosh Hashonah Eve, 1936," from folder labeled Peace 1930s. RBG Files, Box 53, Folder 4, 4–5.
12. Gittelsohn, R.B. "The Fast That We Have Chosen," from folder labeled Social Action 1934–1936. RBG Files, Box 6, Folder 6, 4.

Chapter Six

1. Golden Jubilee Journal (Rockville Centre, New York) Central Synagogue of Nassau County, 1986, 1.
2. Ibid.
3. Gittelsohn, R.B. "Is There a Road Back?" from folder labeled Peace 1930s. RBG Files, Box 53, Folder 4, 2.
4. Ibid.
5. Ibid., 3.
6. Ibid.
7. Ibid., 4.
8. Ibid., 5.
9. Ibid.
10. Ibid., 6.
11. Ibid.
12. Ibid., 7.

Chapter Seven

1. Cohen, R. (1993). When the Old Left Was Young. New York: Oxford University Press, 135.
2. Ibid., 154.
3. Ibid.
4. Black, C. (2003) Franklin D. Roosevelt, Champion of Freedom. New York: PublicAffairs, 425.
5. Ibid.
6. Ibid.
7. Ibid.
8. Cohen, R. op. cit., 171.
9. Ibid., 173.
10. Ibid.
11. Ibid., 175.
12. Ibid., 184–185.
13. Ibid., 186.

Chapter Eight

1. Gittelsohn, R.B. "Should We Fight for Democracy?" from folder labeled Social Action 1934–1936. RBG Files, Box 53, Folder 4, 2.
2. Ibid.
3. Ibid., 3.
4. Ibid.
5. Ibid.
6. Ibid.
7. Ibid., 4.
8. Ibid.
9. Hensel, H. Struve, and McClung, Richard G. "Profit Limitation Controls Prior to the Present War." Duke Law Review (1943): 209.
10. Ibid.
11. Gittelsohn, R.B. op. cit., 5.
12. Nye, G.P. (1938) "A Bad Bargain for All Parties." The Forum, 276.
13. "May Bill Attacked in Minority Report." (1938) Vassar Miscellany News, 19 March 5.
14. Gittelsohn, R.B. op. cit., 5.
15. Ibid., 6.
16. Ibid.

Chapter Nine

1. Weinberg, G. (1994). A World at Arms. New York: Cambridge University Press, 27.
2. Gittelsohn, R.B. op. cit., 2.
3. Gittelsohn, R.B. "Shabbos Shuvah 5699–1938," from folder labeled Peace 1930s. RBG Files, Box 53, Folder 4, 2.
4. Ibid., 2.
5. Ibid.
6. Sefaria. "A Living Library of Jewish Texts." https//www.sefaria.org/Pirkei_Avot.1.18. Accessed 20 March 2021.
7. Ibid., 3.
8. Ibid., 4.
9. Ibid.
10. Ibid.
11. Ibid.
12. Laquer, W., and Rubin, B. (2001) The Israel-Arab Reader. New York: Penguin, 16.
13. Ibid.
14. Laquer, W., and Rubin, B. op. cit., 42.
15. Ibid.
16. Gittelsohn, R.B. op. cit., 5.
17. Ibid.
18. Ibid., 6.

Chapter Ten

1. Faber, D. (2008) *Munich: The 1938 Appeasement Crisis.* New York: Simon & Schuster, 5–7.
2. Keane, M. (2005) *Dictionary of Modern Strategy and Tactics.* Annapolis: Naval Institute Press, 15.
3. Adams, W.C. (1984) "Opinion and Foreign Policy." *Foreign Service Journal,* 61, May.
4. Gittelsohn, R.B. "Peace with Honor or Dishonor Without Peace: Which Is It?" from folder labeled Peace 1939–1963. RBG Files, Box 53, Folder 5, 1.
5. *Ibid.,* 2.
6. *Ibid.*
7. *Ibid.*
8. *Ibid.,* 3.
9. *Ibid.,*
10. *Ibid.*
11. *Ibid.*
12. *Ibid.,* 4.
13. *Ibid.,* 5.
14. *Ibid.*
15. *Ibid.*
16. *Ibid.*
17. Gittelsohn, R.B. "Peace with Honor or Dishonor Without Peace: Which Is It? Part II" from folder labeled Peace 1939–1963. RBG Files, Box 53, Folder 5, 1.
18. *Ibid.*
19. *Ibid.,* 2.
20. *Ibid.*
21. *Ibid.*
22. *Ibid.,* 3.
23. Caputi, R.J. (1999). *Neville Chamberlain and Appeasement.* Selinsgrove: Susquehanna University Press, 18.
24. *Ibid.,* 19.
25. *Ibid.*
26. Gittelsohn, R.B. op. cit., 4.
27. *Ibid.*
28. *Ibid.*
29. *Ibid.*
30. Caputi, R.J. op. cit., 166.
31. Cockett, R. (1989) "Twilight of the Truth: Chamberlain, Appeasement and the Manipulation of the Press." PhD dissertation, University of London.
32. Gittelsohn, R.B. op. cit., 5.
33. *Ibid.*
34. *Ibid.*
35. *Ibid.*
36. *Ibid.,* 6.
37. *Ibid.*
38. *Ibid.*
39. *Ibid.,* 7.
40. *Ibid.*
41. Weinberg, G.L. (2005) *Visions of Victory.* New York: Cambridge University Press, 8.
42. *Ibid.,* 9.
43. Weinberg, G.L. (2006) *Hitler's Second Book.* New York: Enigma, 47.

Chapter Eleven

1. Laquer, W., and Rubin, B. (2001) *The Israel-Arab Reader.* New York: Penguin, 43.
2. *Ibid.,* 45.
3. *Ibid.,* 44.
4. *Ibid.*
5. Report of the Anglo-American Committee of Enquiry Regarding the Problems of European Jewry and Palestine, April 1946. https://en.wikipedia.org/wiki/Anglo-American_Committee_of_Inquiry, accessed 6 April 2013.
6. Gittelsohn, R.B. "America and the Next War" from folder labeled Peace 1939–1963. RBG Files, Box 53, Folder 5, 5–6.
7. *Ibid.,* 6.
8. Toland, J. (1976). *Adolf Hitler.* New York: Ballantine, 712.
9. Neville Chamberlain speech to Birmingham Unionist Association, March 17,1939.
10. *Ibid.*
11. *Ibid.*
12. Toland, J. op. cit., 710.
13. Nekrich, A.M. and Freeze, G.L. (1997) *Pariahs, Partners, Predators: German-Soviet Relations, 1922–1941.* New York: Columbia University Press, 115.
14. Toland, J. op. cit., 753.
15. Cohen, R. (1993). *When the Old Left Was Young.* New York: Oxford University Press, 279.

Chapter Twelve

1. Toland, J. (1976). *Adolf Hitler.* New York: Ballantine, 718.
2. Lightbody, B. (2004). *The Second World War: Ambitions to Nemesis.* New York: Routledge, 39.
3. Address by Prime Minister Neville Chamberlain in House of Commons, September 3, 1939. https://avalon.law.yale.edu/wwii/gb2.asp, accessed 2 May 2013.
4. Edwards, R. (2006) *White Death:*

Russia's War on Finland 1939–40. London: Weidenfeld & Nicholson, 18.
5. *Ibid.*, 272–273.
6. Golden Jubilee Journal, Central Synagogue of Nassau County. Rockville Center, New York, 1.

Chapter Thirteen

1. Interview with Judy Gittelsohn Fales, 17 March, 2013.
2. Interview with David Gittelsohn, 15 March, 2013.
3. Interview with Donna Gittelsohn, 1 April 2013.
4. Gittelsohn, R.B. (1988) *Here Am I, Harnessed to Hope*. New York: Vantage, 49.
5. *Ibid.*

Chapter Fourteen

1. Gittelsohn, R.B. "Saturday Evening Post Americanism" from folder labeled Capitalism, Socialism, and Communism. RBG Files, Box 38, Folder 7, 1.
2. *Ibid.*
3. *Ibid.*
4. Hibbs, B. "Neo-Liberal Illusion: That Collectivism is Liberty," *Saturday Evening Post*, 10 October 1942.
5. *Ibid.*
6. *Ibid.*
7. *Ibid.*
8. *Ibid.*
9. *Ibid.*
10. Gittelsohn, R.B. op. cit., 2.
11. *Ibid.*
12. *Ibid.*, 3.
13. *Ibid.*
14. *Ibid.*
15. *Ibid.*
16. *Ibid.*
17. *Ibid.*, 4.
18. *Ibid.*
19. *Ibid.*
20. Gittelsohn, R.B. "Saturday Evening Post ,Americanism II" from folder labeled Capitalism, Socialism, and Communism. RBG Files, Box 38, Folder 7, 1.
21. *Ibid.*, 2.
22. Wilkie, W. "Deliver the Materials of War—Define Our Peace Aims." radio speech 26 October 1942.
23. *Ibid.*
24. Gittelsohn, R.B. op. cit., 2.

25. *Ibid.*
26. *Ibid.*
27. *Ibid.*, 3.
28. *Ibid.*
29. *Ibid.*
30. *Ibid.*
31. *Ibid.*
32. *Ibid.*, 4.
33. *Ibid.*
34. *Ibid.*
35. *Ibid.*
36. *Ibid.*
37. "Ben Hibbs" in Kansapedia—Kansas Historical Society. https://www.kshs.org/kansapedia/ben-hibbs/12086rical. Accessed 12 March 2013.
38. Ambrose, S.E. (1994). *D-Day, June 6, 1944: The Climactic Battle of World War II*. New York: Simon & Schuster, 26.

Chapter Fifteen

1. Gittelsohn, R.B. (1945) *Pacifist to Padre/Pacifist in Uniform/Pacifist No More*. Unpublished manuscript. RBG Files, Box 64, Folder 7, 1.
2. Gittelsohn, R.B. (1988) *Here Am I, Harnessed to Hope*. New York: Vantage, 94.
3. Gittelsohn, R.B. (1945) *Pacifist to Padre/Pacifist in Uniform/Pacifist No More*. Unpublished manuscript. RBG Files, Box 64, Folder 7, 2.
4. *Ibid.*, 4.
5. *Ibid.*
6. Shirer, W.L. (1959). *The Rise and Fall of the Third Reich: A History of Nazi Germany*. New York: Simon & Schuster, 884.
7. Gittelsohn, R.B. op. cit., 5.
8. Saperstein, H.I. (2001). *Witness from the Pulpit: Topical Sermons 1933–1980*. Lanham: Lexington, 76.
9. *Ibid.*, 102.
10. Magnes, J.L. (1946). *In the Perplexity of the Times*. Jerusalem: Central, 19.
11. *Ibid.*, 25.
12. Gittelsohn, R.B. op. cit., 83.
13. *Ibid.*, 7.
14. *Ibid.*, 8.
15. Gittelsohn, R.B. (1988) *Here Am I, Harnessed to Hope*. New York: Vantage, 96.
16. Snyder, J. (2009) "Let Us Die Bravely: United States Chaplains in World War II." *Undergraduate Research Journal at UCCS*, Vol. 2.1, Spring.
17. Gittelsohn, R.B. (1945) *Pacifist to*

Padre/Pacifist in Uniform/Pacifist No More. Unpublished manuscript. RBG Files, Box 64, Folder 7, 8.

18. *Ibid.,*10.

19. *Ibid.,*11.

20. Pirkei Avot 1:14.

21. Gittelsohn, R.B. Op. Cit.,12.

22. Pirkei Avot 1:14.

23. Gittelsohn, R.B. (1988) *Here Am I, Harnessed to Hope.* New York: Vantage, 95.

24. Gittelsohn, R.B. (1945) *Pacifist to Padre/Pacifist in Uniform/Pacifist No More.* Unpublished manuscript. RBG Files, Box 64, Folder 7, 14.

25. Drury C.M. (1948) *United States Navy Chaplains 1778-1945.* Washington: U.S. Government Printing Office, 58.

26. *Ibid.,*42–43.

27. *Ibid.,* 58.

28. Gittelsohn, R.B. op. cit., 158.

29. *Ibid.,* 20; Trower, R.H. (2003) "Military Chaplains." University of North Carolina-Wilmington. William Madison Randall Library. Interview 25 February; Wickersham, G.W. (1997). Marine Chaplain 1943–1946. Bennington: Merriam Press, 14.

30. Gittelsohn, R.B. op. cit., 22.

31. "Religion: Seagoing Men of God." (1943) *Time Magazine.* 21 June. http://content.time.com/time/subscriber/article/0,33009,766782,00.html. Accessed 7 August 2012.

32. Gittelsohn, R.B. op. cit., 22.

33. *Ibid.,* 18.

34. *Ibid.,* 24.

35. Trower R.H. "Military Chaplains." University of North Carolina Wilmington. William Madison Randall Library. Interview 25 February 2003.

36. "Religion: Seagoing Men of God." *Time Magazine.* 21 June 1943.

37. Gittelsohn, R.B. op. cit., 25.

38. *Ibid.*

39. *Ibid.,* 27.

Chapter Sixteen

1. Benis, M.F., and Shaw, H.I. (1968) *History of the U.S. Marine Corps Operations in World War II, Volume V: Victory and Occupation.* Washington: U.S. Government Printing Office, 679.

2. Gittelsohn, R.B. (1988) *Here Am I, Harnessed to Hope.* New York: Vantage, 101.

3. Interview with David Gittelsohn, 15 March 2013.

4. Gittelsohn, R.B. (1945) *Pacifist to Padre/Pacifist in Uniform/Pacifist No More.* Unpublished manuscript. RBG Files, Box 64, Folder 7, 29.

5. *Ibid.,* 34.

6. *Ibid.,* 35.

7. *Ibid.,* 39.

8. *Ibid.,* 51.

9. *Ibid.,* 51.

10. Gittelsohn, R.B. (1988) *Here Am I, Harnessed to Hope.* New York: Vantage, 125.

11. Gittelsohn, R.B. (1945) *Pacifist to Padre/Pacifist in Uniform/Pacifist No More.* Unpublished manuscript. RBG Files, Box 64, Folder 7, 147.

12. *Ibid.*

13. *Ibid.,* 158.

14. *Ibid.*

15. *Ibid.,* 159; Gittelsohn, R.B. (1988) *Here Am I, Harnessed to Hope.* New York: Vantage, 142–143.

16. Gittelsohn, R.B. (1945). *Pacifist to Padre/Pacifist in Uniform/Pacifist No More.* Unpublished manuscript. RBG Files, Box 64, Folder 7, 159; Gittelsohn, R.B. (1988). *Here Am I, Harnessed To Hope.* New York: Vantage, 143.

17. "Jews in Army and Navy Request Duty on Christmas to Relieve Non-Jewish Comrades." *Jewish Telegraphic Agency,* 24 December 1943; Gittelsohn, R.B. (1945) *Pacifist to Padre/Pacifist In Uniform/Pacifist No More.* Unpublished manuscript. RBG Files, Box 64, Folder 7, 160.

18. Gittelsohn, R.B. (1945) *Pacifist to Padre/Pacifist In Uniform/Pacifist No More.* Unpublished manuscript. RBG Files, Box 64, Folder 7, 162.

19. Gittelsohn, R.B. (1988) *Here Am I, Harnessed to Hope.* New York: Vantage, 191.

20. Gittelsohn, R.B. (1945) *Pacifist to Padre/Pacifist In Uniform/Pacifist No More.* Unpublished manuscript. RBG Files, Box 64, Folder 7, 133.

21. *Ibid.,* 164.

22. Letter from Yetta Weinberg to Roland Gittelsohn (undated). From folder labeled War, My Experience. RBG Files Box 63, Folder 7.

23. Gittelsohn, R.B. (1945) *Pacifist to Padre/Pacifist In Uniform/Pacifist No More.* Unpublished manuscript. RBG Files, Box 64, Folder 7, 164–165.

Chapter Seventeen

1. Ross, B.D. (1986) *Iwo Jima: Legacy of Valor.* New York: Vintage, 14.
2. Rigg, B.M. (2020) *Flamethrower.* Addison, TX: Fidelis Historia, 554.
3. Ross, B.D. op. cit., 17.
4. *Ibid.*, 13.
5. *Ibid.*, 26.
6. Rigg, B.M. op. cit., 327–28.
7. *Ibid.*, 313.
8. Ross, B.D. op. cit., 163.
9. *Ibid.*, 28.
10. *Ibid.*
11. Bradley, J. (2000). *Flags of Our Fathers.* New York: Bantam, 102.
12. Gittelsohn, R.B. (1988) *Here Am I, Harnessed to Hope.* New York: Vantage, 125.
13. *Ibid.*, 104.
14. Bradley, J. op. cit., 107.

Chapter Eighteen

1. Ross, B.D. (1986) *Iwo Jima: Legacy of Valor.* New York: Vintage Books, 31–32.
2. *Ibid.*, 32.
3. Headquarters letter to Jewish Marines dated 8 August 1944. From folder labeled War, My Experience. RBG Files, Box 63, Folder 7.
4. *Ibid.*
5. *Ibid.*
6. Gittelsohn, R.B. (1988) *Here Am I, Harnessed to Hope.* New York: Vantage, 121.
7. *Ibid.*
8. *Ibid.*
9. *Ibid.*, 105.
10. Gittelsohn, R.B. (1945) *Pacifist to Padre/Pacifist In Uniform/Pacifist No More.* Unpublished manuscript. RBG Files, Box 64, Folder 7, 161.
11. Gittelsohn, R.B. (1988) *Here Am I, Harnessed to Hope.* New York: Vantage, 125.
12. *Ibid.*, 126.
13. Notes entitled "Negroes," dated 29 October 1944 and 25 December 1944. From Folder labeled War, My Experience. RBG Files, Box 63, Folder 7.
14. *Ibid.*
15. Gittelsohn, R.B. op. cit., 126.
16. Gittelsohn, R.B. (1945) *Pacifist to Padre/Pacifist In Uniform/Pacifist No More.* Unpublished manuscript. RBG Files, Box 64, Folder 7, 85.
17. Gittelsohn, R.B. (1988) *Here Am I, Harnessed to Hope.* New York: Vantage, 128.
18. Gittelsohn, R.B. (1945) *Pacifist to Padre/Pacifist In Uniform/Pacifist No More.* Unpublished manuscript. RBG Files, Box 64, Folder 7, 86.
19. *Ibid.*, 87.
20. Gittelsohn, R.B. (1988) *Here Am I, Harnessed to Hope.* New York: Vantage, 128. Gittelsohn is referring to Dale Carnegie, the author of the influential best-seller *How to Win Friends and Influence People.*
21. *Ibid.*, 128–129.
22. Gittelsohn, R.B. (1945) *Pacifist to Padre/Pacifist In Uniform/Pacifist No More.* Unpublished manuscript. RBG Files, Box 64, Folder 7, 89.
23. Moore, D.D. (2004). *G.I. Jews.* Cambridge: Harvard University Press, 27.
24. Brody, S. "American Jews Serve in World War II." Jewish Virtual Library. http://dev.jewishvirtuallibrary.org/cgi-bin/itemPrintMode.pl?Id=4482. Accessed 29 October 2012.
25. Gittelsohn, R.B. (1988) *Here Am I, Harnessed to Hope.* New York: Vantage, 127.
26. "Conference with Bauman, Ecker, and Bradley," dated 9 November 1944. From folder labeled War, My Experience. RBG Files, Box 63, Folder 7.
27. *Ibid.*
28. *Ibid.*
29. *Ibid.*
30. Forster, A. (1947). *Anti-Semitism in the United States in 1947.* New York: Anti-Defamation League of B.nai B'rith, 25.
31. "Conference with Bauman, Ecker, and Bradley," dated 9 November 1944. From Folder labeled War, My Experience. RBG Files, Box 63, Folder 7.
32. Gittelsohn, R.B. (1945) *Pacifist to Padre/Pacifist In Uniform/Pacifist No More.* Unpublished manuscript. RBG Files, Box 64, Folder 7, 152.

Chapter Nineteen

1. Ross, B.D. (1986) *Iwo Jima: Legacy of Valor.* New York: Vintage Books, 39.
2. *Ibid.*, 34.
3. *Ibid.*
4. *Ibid.*, 35.
5. Rigg, B.M. (2020) *Flamethrower.* Addison, TX: Fidelis Historia, 332.
6. Gittelsohn, R.B. (1945) *Pacifist to Padre/Pacifist In Uniform/Pacifist No More.* Unpublished manuscript. RBG Files, Box 64, Folder 7, 165-o.

7. *Ibid.*
8. Ross, B.D. op. cit., 42.
9. Spector R.H. (1985). *Eagle Against the Sun.* New York: Vintage Books, 498.
10. Rigg, B.M. op. cit., 365.
11. *Ibid.*, 350.
12. "Heroism," undated note. From Folder labeled War, My Experience. RBG Files, Box 63, Folder 7.
13. Bradley, J. (2000) *Flags of Our Fathers.* New York: Bantam Books, 147.
14. Spector R.H. op. cit., 498.
15. Rigg, B.M. op. cit., 351.
16. *Ibid.*
17. "Iwo Notes," dated 18 Feb 1945. From Folder labeled War, My Experience. RBG Files, Box 63, Folder 7.
18. Gittelsohn, R.B. (1988) *Here Am I, Harnessed to Hope.* New York: Vantage, 111.
19. *Ibid.*, 105–106.
20. *Ibid.*
21. *Ibid.*
22. *Ibid.*, 106.
23. *Ibid.*
24. *Ibid.*, 106–107.

Chapter Twenty

1. Ross, B.D. (1986) *Iwo Jima: Legacy of Valor.* New York: Vintage Books, 61.
2. *Ibid.*, 62.
3. Gittelsohn, R.B. (1988) *Here Am I, Harnessed to Hope.* New York: Vantage, 108.
4. *Ibid.*
5. *Ibid.*, 110; "General Notes," undated. From Folder labeled War, My Experience. RBG Files, Box 63, Folder 7.
6. Gittelsohn, R.B. op. cit., 109.
7. Gittelsohn, R.B. (1945) *Pacifist to Padre/Pacifist In Uniform/Pacifist No More.* Unpublished manuscript. RBG Files, Box 64, Folder 7, 165-c.
8. Intelligence Section, Amphibious Forces Pacific, and Assistant Chief of Staff, Fleet Marine Forces Pacific. Beach Diagram, Southeastern Beaches, Iwo Jima, 4 July 1944.
9. Bradley, J. (2000). *Flags of Our Fathers.* New York: Bantam Books, 154.
10. "General Notes," undated. From Folder labeled War, My Experience. RBG Files, Box 63, Folder 7.
11. Ross, B.D. op. cit., 69.
12. *Ibid.*, 80.
13. *Ibid.*, 81.

Chapter Twenty-One

1. Ross, B.D. (1986) *Iwo Jima: Legacy of Valor.* New York: Vintage Books, 80.
2. Gittelsohn, R.B. (1988) *Here Am I, Harnessed to Hope.* New York: Vantage, 109–110.
3. Gittelsohn, R.B. (1945) *Pacifist to Padre/Pacifist In Uniform/Pacifist No More.* Unpublished manuscript. RBG Files, Box 64, Folder 7, 165-g.
4. "Personal" (undated). From Folder labeled War, My Experience. RBG Files, Box 63, Folder 7.
5. Delorme R.H. (2003) "Dr. Daniel McCarthy had everything to live for, but gave his life for his country." *Southern Cross,* 11 Dec, 3.
6. "General" (undated). From Folder labeled War, My Experience. RBG Files, Box 63, Folder 7.
7. Gittelsohn, R.B. (1945) *Pacifist to Padre/Pacifist in Uniform/Pacifist No More.* Unpublished manuscript. RBG Files, Box 64, Folder 7, 165-h.
8. *Ibid.*
9. "General" (undated). From Folder labeled War, My Experience. RBG Files, Box 63, Folder 7.
10. *Ibid.*; Gittelsohn, R.B. (1988) *Here Am I, Harnessed to Hope.* New York: Vantage, 109–111.
11. *Ibid.*
12. "Personal" undated. From Folder labeled War, My Experience. RBG Files, Box 63, Folder 7.
13. Gittelsohn, R.B. (1988) *Here Am I, Harnessed to Hope.* New York: Vantage, 111.
14. Ross, B.D. op. cit., 184.
15. *Ibid.*
16. Gittelsohn, R.B. op. cit., 113.
17. Gittelsohn, R.B. (1945) *Pacifist to Padre/Pacifist In Uniform/Pacifist No More.* Unpublished manuscript. RBG Files, Box 64, Folder 7, 165-f.
18. *Ibid.*
19. Ross, B.D. op. cit., 185.
20. Gittelsohn, R.B., op. cit., 165-f–165-g.
21. "General" (undated). From Folder labeled War, My Experience. RBG Files, Box 63, Folder 7.
22. Gittelsohn, R.B., op. cit., 165-i.
23. Gittelsohn, R.B. (1988) *Here Am I, Harnessed to Hope.* New York: Vantage, 113.
24. "General" undated. From Folder labeled War, My Experience. RBG Files, Box 63, Folder 7.

25. Bradley, J. (2000). *Flags of Our Fathers*. New York: Bantam Books, 197.
26. *Ibid.*
27. Ross, B.D. op. cit., 95.
28. *Ibid.* Ross, B.D. op. cit., 95.
29. Bradley, J. op. cit., 202.
30. Ross B.D. op. cit., 96.
31. *Ibid.*
32. *Ibid.*, 99.
33. Bradley, J. op. cit., 207.
34. *Ibid.*, 209.
35. *Ibid.*
36. "General" undated. From Folder labeled War, My Experience. RBG Files, Box 63, Folder 7.
37. Ross B.D. op. cit., 127.
38. *Ibid.*
39. "Humor" undated. From Folder labeled War, My Experience. RBG Files, Box 63, Folder 7.

Chapter Twenty-Two

1. Ross, B.D. (1986) *Iwo Jima: Legacy of Valor*. New York: Vintage Books, 108.
2. *Ibid.*, 109.
3. Gittelsohn, R.B. (1945) *Pacifist to Padre/Pacifist In Uniform/Pacifist No More*. Unpublished manuscript. RBG Files, Box 64, Folder 7, 165-n.
4. *Ibid.*
5. Ross, B.D. op. cit., 150.
6. Rigg, B.M. (2020) *Flamethrower*. Addison, TX: Fidelis Historia, 334.
7. Gittelsohn, R.B. (1988) *Here Am I, Harnessed to Hope*. New York: Vantage, 109.
8. Gittelsohn, R.B. (1945) *Pacifist to Padre/Pacifist In Uniform/Pacifist No More*. Unpublished manuscript. RBG Files, Box 64, Folder 7, 165-b.
9. Gittelsohn, R.B. (1988) *Here Am I, Harnessed to Hope*. New York: Vantage, 113.
10. *Ibid.*, 119.
11. "General" (undated). From Folder labeled War, My Experience. RBG Files, Box 63, Folder 7.
12. *Ibid.*
13. Gittelsohn, R.B. (1988) *Here Am I, Harnessed to Hope*. New York: Vantage, 113–114.
14. Gittelsohn, R.B. (1945) *Pacifist to Padre/Pacifist In Uniform/Pacifist No More*. Unpublished manuscript. RBG Files, Box 64, Folder 7, 165-u.
15. *Ibid.*
16. Gittelsohn, R.B. (1988) *Here Am I, Harnessed to Hope*. New York: Vantage, 114.
17. Bradley, J. (2000). *Flags of Our Fathers*. New York: Bantam Books, 140.
18. "Heroism" undated. From Folder labeled War, My Experience. RBG Files, Box 63, Folder 7.
19. Ross, B.D. op. cit., 185.
20. Bradley, J. op. cit., 344.
21. *Ibid.*, 345.
22. *Ibid.*, 346.
23. "General" undated. From Folder labeled War, My Experience. RBG Files, Box 63, Folder 7.
24. *Ibid.*
25. *Ibid.*
26. Gittelsohn, R.B. (1945) *Pacifist to Padre/Pacifist In Uniform/Pacifist No More*. Unpublished manuscript. RBG Files, Box 64, Folder 7, 165-g.
27. Gittelsohn, R.B. (1988) *Here Am I, Harnessed to Hope*. New York: Vantage, 115.
28. Gittelsohn, R.B. (1945) *Pacifist to Padre/Pacifist In Uniform/Pacifist No More*. Unpublished manuscript. RBG Files, Box 64, Folder 7, 165-l.
29. Gittelsohn, R.B. (1988) *Here Am I, Harnessed to Hope*. New York: Vantage, 115.
30. *Ibid.*
31. "Iwo Humor" undated. From Folder labeled War, My Experience. RBG Files, Box 63, Folder 7.
32. Ross B.D. op. cit., 103.
33. Holcomb R. (2002). *Iwo Jima*. New York: Henry Holt and Company, 106.
34. *Ibid.*

Chapter Twenty-Three

1. Ross, B.D. (1986) *Iwo Jima: Legacy of Valor*. New York: Vintage Books, 283.
2. *Ibid.*, 296.
3. *Ibid.*, 283.
4. "General" undated. From Folder labeled War, My Experience. RBG Files, Box 63, Folder 7.
5. Ross, B.D., op. cit., 284.
6. *Ibid.*, 276–277.
7. Rigg B.M. (2020). *Flamethrower*. Addison TX: Fidelis Historia, 488.
8. *Ibid.*, 489.
9. Ross, B.D. op. cit., 322.

10. Bradley, J. (2000). *Flags of Our Fathers*. New York: Bantam Books, 242.
11. Ross, B.D., op. cit., 321.
12. Gittelsohn, R.B. (1988) *Here Am I, Harnessed to Hope*. New York: Vantage, 144.
13. *Ibid.*
14. *Ibid.*, 145.

Chapter Twenty-Four

1. Gittelsohn, R.B. (1988) *Here Am I, Harnessed to Hope*. New York: Vantage, 131.
2. *Ibid.*
3. The Grapevine. "In the Shadow of Suribachi: Sammy's Story." YouTube, January 22, 2021. youtube.com/watch?v=R-SWu3vdwcFm. Accessed 10 Feb 2021.
4. Marine Corps History Division. "Dedication of the 5th Marine Division Cemetery on Iwo Jima, 1945. YouTube, April 26, 2016. youtube.com/watch?v=0NtcTJAcm90. Accessed 15 Feb 2021.
5. "We had just come through five weeks of miserable hell" undated. From Folder labeled War, My Experience. RBG Files, Box 63, Folder 7.
6. Gittelsohn, R.B. "Brothers all?" *Reconstructionist*. 7 Feb 1947, Vol. 38, 11–12.
7. Rockey, K.E. "Address at the Dedication of the Fifth Marine Division Cemetery at Iwo Jima." *Togetherweserved.com*. Accessed 5 Sept 2012.
8. "The Purest Democracy" undated. From Folder labeled War, My Experience. RBG Files, Box 63, Folder 7.
9. Gittelsohn, R.B. (1988) *Here Am I, Harnessed to Hope*. New York: Vantage, 145.
10. "General" undated. From Folder labeled War, My Experience. RBG Files, Box 63, Folder 7.
11. Gittelsohn, R.B. (1988) *Here Am I, Harnessed to Hope*. New York: Vantage, 145–146.
12. Gittelsohn, R.B. (1945) *Pacifist to Padre/Pacifist In Uniform/Pacifist No More*. Unpublished manuscript. RBG Files, Box 64, Folder 7, 165-q.
13. *Ibid.*
14. Ross, B.D. (1986) *Iwo Jima: Legacy of Valor*. New York: Vintage Books, 336.
15. "General" undated. From Folder labeled War, My Experience. RBG Files, Box 63, Folder 7.
16. Bradley, J. (2000). *Flags of Our Fathers*. New York: Bantam Books, 246.
17. "General" undated. From Folder labeled War, My Experience. RBG Files, Box 63, Folder 7.
18. Gittelsohn, R.B. (1988) *Here Am I, Harnessed to Hope*. New York: Vantage, 117.
19. *Ibid.*, 116.
20. *Ibid.*, 117.
21. *Ibid.*
22. Gittelsohn, R.B. (1945) *Pacifist to Padre/Pacifist In Uniform/Pacifist No More*. Unpublished manuscript. RBG Files, Box 64, Folder 7, 165-e.
23. "Personal" undated. From Folder labeled War, My Experience. RBG Files, Box 63, Folder 7.
24. Gittelsohn, R.B. (1988) *Here Am I, Harnessed to Hope*. New York: Vantage, 118.
25. Gittelsohn, R.B. op. cit., 132.

Chapter Twenty-Five

1. Religion: The Purest Democracy. *Time Magazine*, 30 April 1945.
2. Gittelsohn, R.B. (1988) *Here Am I, Harnessed to Hope*. New York: Vantage, 129.
3. Baird A.C. (1946). "That Men Might Be Free" in *Representative American Speeches*. New York: H.W. Wilson Company, 16–17.
4. *Ibid.*
5. Gittelsohn, R.B. op. cit., 132.
6. *Ibid.*
7. Congressional Record. Vol. 153, No. 85, Wednesday, May 23, 2007; Congressional Record—Senate. June 16, 1997.
8. *Ibid.*, 129.
9. *Ibid.*, 129–130.
10. *Ibid.*, 130.
11. *Ibid.*, 142.
12. "Letter from Mary E. McNeal to Chaplain Roland Gittelsohn" 6 May 1945. From Folder labeled War, My Experience. RBG Files, Box 63, Folder 7.
13. "Letter from Private Walter Mirschinger to Chaplain Roland Gittelsohn" 12 Jun 1945. From Folder labeled War, My Experience. RBG Files, Box 63, Folder 7.
14. "General" undated. From Folder

labeled War, My Experience. RBG Files, Box 63, Folder 7.

15. "Letter from Harold Gross to Chaplain Roland Gittelsohn" undated. From Folder labeled War, My Experience. RBG Files, Box 63, Folder 7.

Chapter Twenty-Six

1. "General" undated. From Folder labeled War, My Experience. RBG Files, Box 63, Folder 7.

2. Gittelsohn, R.B. (1988) *Here Am I, Harnessed to Hope.* New York: Vantage, 101.

3. Letter from Roland Gittelsohn to Julian Morgenstern, 19 October 1945. RBG Files, Box 30, Folder 4.

4. Letter from Roland Gittelsohn to Samuel Wohl, 12 November 1945. RBG Files, Box 30, Folder 4.

5. Braley, B. "Honoring the Life of Rabbi Roland B. Gittelsohn and his Stirring Eulogy on Iwo Jima." *Congressional Record* 155.85, h5688, 23 May 2007.

6. Gittelsohn, R.B. (1988) *Here Am I, Harnessed to Hope.* New York: Vantage, 132.

7. Gittelsohn, R.B. (1945) *Pacifist to Padre/Pacifist In Uniform/Pacifist No More.* Unpublished manuscript. RBG Files, Box 64, Folder 7, 1.

8. *Ibid.,* 166.
9. *Ibid.,* 167.
10. *Ibid.*
11. *Ibid.,* 168.
12. *Ibid.*
13. *Ibid.*
14. *Ibid.*
15. *Ibid.,* 169.
16. *Ibid.*
17. *Ibid.,* 170.
18. *Ibid.*
19. *Ibid.*
20. *Ibid.*
21. *Ibid.,* 170.

22. Cohen, R. (1993). *When the Old Left Was Young.* New York: Oxford University Press, 95.

23. *Ibid.*
24. *Ibid.*

25. Gittelsohn, R.B. (1988) *Here Am I, Harnessed to Hope.* New York: Vantage, 95–96.

26. Lamm, M. (1971) "After the War—Another Look at Pacifism and Selective Conscientious Objection" in *Judaism,* Vol. 20, Issue 4: Fall, 416.

Chapter Twenty-Seven

1. Gittelsohn, R.B. (1945) *Pacifist to Padre/Pacifist In Uniform/Pacifist No More.* Unpublished manuscript. RBG Files, Box 64, Folder 7, 77.
2. *Ibid.,* 97.
3. *Ibid.,* 126.
4. *Ibid.,* 127.
5. *Ibid.,* 127–128.
6. *Ibid.,* 129–130.
7. *Ibid.,* 165-e.
8. *Ibid.,* 165-n.
9. *Ibid.,* i.
10. *Ibid.,* ii.

11. Gittelsohn, R.B. (1988) *Here Am I, Harnessed to Hope.* New York: Vantage, 103.

Chapter Twenty-Eight

1. Gittelsohn, R.B. (1988) *Here Am I, Harnessed to Hope.* New York: Vantage, 85.

2. Dwyer-Ryan, M. et al. *Becoming American Jews: Temple Israel of Boston.* Lebanon, NH: University Press of New England, 104.

3. *Ibid.*
4. Gittelsohn, R.B., op. cit., 191.
5. *Ibid.,* 191.
6. *Ibid.,* 159.

7. "Promoting Progressive Values in Israel." Association of Reform Zionists of America. https://arza.org/promoting-progressive-values-in-israel/. Accessed 30 January 2021.

8. Gittelsohn, R.B., op. cit., 120.
9. *Ibid.,* 205.
10. Dwyer-Ryan, M., et al. op. cit., 136.
11. Gittelsohn, R.B., op. cit., 207.
12. *Ibid.*

13. Clinton, W.J. (1995) "Remarks Commenting on the 50th Anniversary of Iwo Jima in Arlington, Virginia, February 19, 1995." *Public Papers of the Presidents of the United States: William J. Clinton (1995, Book 1),* U.S. Government Publishing Office, 233.

14. Gittelsohn, R.B., "My Cancer and God: A Final Work Unfinished." Reform Judaism Online. https://reformjudaism.org/author/roland-b-gittelsohn. Accessed 20 January 2021.

Epilogue

1. Harris S. (2005) *The End of Faith: Religion, Terror, and the Future of Reason.* New York: W.W. Norton, 199.

2. "USMC Quotes." Heritage Press International. www.usmcpress.com/heritage/usmc_quotations.htm. Accessed 28 April 2021.

3. Gittelsohn, R.B. (1988) *Here Am I-Harnessed to Hope.* New York: Vantage, 221.

Bibliography

Archival Resources

RBG Files: from the Jacob Rader Marcus Center of the American Jewish Archives, Roland Bertram Gittelsohn Papers, 1934–1996. MS-704.

WRJ Files: From the Jacob Rader Marcus Center of the American Jewish Archives, Women of Reform Judaism Records (U.S. Records), 1913–2013. MS-73.

Books and Journal Articles

Adams, William C. (1984) "Opinion and Foreign Policy." *Foreign Service Journal* 61, May.

Ambrose, Stephen E. (1994) *June 6, 1944: The Climactic Battle of World War II*. New York: Simon & Schuster.

Baird, A. Craig. (1946) *Representative American Speeches: 1945-1946*. New York: H.W. Wilson.

Black, Conrad. (2003) *Franklin D. Roosevelt: Champion of Freedom*. New York: Public Affairs.

Bradley, James. (2000) *Flags of Our Fathers*. New York: Bantam.

Braley, Bruce. (2007) "Honoring the Life of Rabbi Roland B. Gittelsohn and His Stirring Eulogy on Iwo Jima." Congressional Record 153.85, h5688, 23 May.

Caputi, Robert J. (1999) *Neville Chamberlain and Appeasement*. Selinsgrove: Susquehanna University Press.

Cockett, Richard. (1989) *"Twilight of the Truth: Chamberlain, Appeasement, and the Manipulation of the Press."* PhD dissertation, University of London.

Cohen, Robert. (1993) *When the Old Left Was Young*. New York: Oxford University Press, 1993.

Delorme, Rita H. (2003) "Dr. Daniel McCarthy Had Everything to Live For, but Gave His Life for His Country." *Southern Cross*. December 11, 3.

Drury, Clifford Merrill. (1948) *United States Chaplains 1775-1945*. Washington: U.S. Government Printing Office.

Dwyer-Ryan, Meaghen, et al. (2009) *Becoming American Jews: Temple Israel of Boston*. Lebanon, NH: University Press of New England.

Edwards, Robert. (2006) *White Death: Russia's War on Finland 1939-40*. London: Weidenfeld & Nicholson.

Einstein, Albert, et al. (2007) *Einstein on Politics: His Private Thoughts and Public Stands on Nationalism, Zionism, War, Peace, and the Bomb*. Princeton: Princeton University Press.

Faber, David. (2008) *Munich: The 1938 Appeasement Crisis*. New York: Simon & Schuster.

Forster, Arnold. (1947) "Anti-Semitism in the United States in 1947." New York: Anti-Defamation League of B'nai B'rith.

Fosdick, Harry Emerson. (1934) *Secrets of Victorious Living*. New York: Harper & Brothers.

Frank, Benis M. and Shaw, Henry I. (1968) *History of U.S. Marine Corps Operations in World War II, Volume V: Victory and Occupation*. U.S. Government Printing Office.

Gittelsohn, Reuben. (1957) *The Little Town That Is No More*. Unpublished manuscript.

Gittelsohn, Roland. (1935) *The Jew Looks at War and Peace*. Cincinnati: National Federation of Temple Sisterhoods.

Gittelsohn, Roland. (1945) *Pacifist to Padre/Pacifist in Uniform/Pacifist No More*. Unpublished manuscript.

Gittelsohn, Roland B. (1988) *Here Am I, Harnessed to Hope*. New York: Vantage.

Grief, Howard. (2008) *The Legal Foundation and Borders of Israel Under International Law*. Jerusalem: Mazo.

Harris, Sam. (2005) *The End of Faith: Religion, Terror, and the Future of Reason*. New York: W.W. Norton.

Hensel, H. Struve, and McClung, Richard G. (1943) "Profit Limitation Controls Prior to the Present War." *Duke Law Review*: 209.

Hibbs, Ben. (1942) "Neo-Liberal Illusion: That Collectivism Is Liberty." *The Saturday Evening Post*. October 10.

Holcomb, Richard. (2002) *Iwo Jima*. New York: Henry Holt.

Keane, Michael. (2005) *Dictionary of Modern Strategy and Tactics*. Annapolis: Naval Institute Press.

Laquer, Walter, and Rubin, Barry. (2001) *The Israel-Arab Reader*. New York: Penguin.

Lightbody, Bradley. (2004) *The Second World War: Ambitions to Nemesis*. New York: Routledge.

Magnus, Judah L. (1946) *In the Perplexity of the Times*. Jerusalem: Central.

Miller, Robert Moats. (1934) *Harry Emerson Fosdick: Preacher, Pastor, Prophet*. New York: Harper.

Moore, Deborah Dash. (2004) *GI Jews*. Cambridge: Harvard University Press.

Morris, Benny. (2000) *Righteous Victims: A History of the Zionist-Arab Conflict, 1881–2001*. New York: Alfred A. Knopf.

Nekrich, Alexandr, and Freeze, Gregory L. (1997) *Pariahs, Partners, Preditors: German-Soviet Relations, 1922–1941*. New York: Columbia University Press.

"Religion: Seagoing Men of God." (1943) *Time Magazine*. June 21.

"Religion: The Purest Democracy." (1945) *Time Magazine*. April 30.

Rigg, Bryan M. (2020) *Flamethrower*. Addison, TX: Fidelis Historia.

Ross, Bill D. (1986) *Iwo Jima: Legacy of Valor*. New York: Vintage.

Saperstein, Harold I. (2001) *Witness from the Pulpit: Topical Sermons 1933–1980*. Lanham: Lexington.

Self, Robert C. (2006) *Britain, America, and the War Department Controversy: The Economic Diplomacy of an Unspecial Relationship, 1917–1941*. New York: Routledge.

Shaw Commission. (1930) *Report of the Commission on the Palestine Disturbances of August 1929. Command Paper 3530*. London: His Majesty's Stationery Office.

Shirer, William L. (1959) *The Rise and the Fall of the Third Reich*. New York: Simon & Schuster.

Snyder, Jeremiah. (2009) "Let Us Die Bravely: United States Chaplains in World War II." *Undergraduate Research Journal at UCCS* Vol. 2, No.1, 24, Spring.

Spector, Ronald H. (1985) *Eagle Against the Sun*. New York: Vintage.

Toland, John. (1976) *Adolf Hitler*. New York: Ballantine.

Weinberg, Gerhard L. (1994) *A World at Arms: A Global History of World War II*. New York: Cambridge University.

Internet Sites Accessed

Avner, Jane. "Cleveland." *Encyclopedia Judaica*. clevelandjewishhistory.net/res/Cleveland-jewish-ej2006.htm. Accessed 24 March 2013.

"Benjamin Gittelsohn. *Encyclopedia of Cleveland History*. Case.edu/ech/articles/g/gittelsohn-benjamin. Accessed 20 October 2012.

Brody, Seymour. "American Jews Serve in World War II." *Jewish Virtual Library*. http://dev.jewishviruallibrary.org/cgi-bin/itemPrintMode.pl?Id=4482. Accessed 29 October 2012.

Cline, Scott. "Jews and Judaism." *Encyclopedia of Cleveland History*. ech-dev.case.edu/cgi/article.pl?id=jj. Accessed 24 March 2013.

Congregation Oer Chodosh Sfard records, 1910–1994. *Western Reserve Historical Society.* wrhs.org. Accessed 20 October 2012.

Gittelsohn, Roland. "My Cancer and God: A Final Work Unfinished." Reform Judaism Online, 1995. reformjudaismonline.org/author/roland-b-gittelson. Accessed 5 January 2021.

Kansas Historical Society. "Ben Hibbs." Kansapedia. Kshs.org/search/index/query:ben%20 hibbs. Accessed 12 March 2013.

Marine Corps Historical Society. "Dedication of the 5th Marine Division Cemetery on Iwo Jima, 1945." YouTube. Youtube.com/watch?v=0NtcTJAcm90. Accessed 15 February 2021.

Nadell, Pamela S. "National Federation of Temple Sisterhoods." *Jewish Women's Archives.* jwa. org/encyclopedia/article/nationsl-federation-of-temple-sistergoods. Accessed 6 December 2012.

Rockey, Keller H. "Address at the Dedication of the Fifth Marine Division Cemetery at Iwo Jima." *Together We Served.* togetherweserved.com. 5 Accessed September 2012.

TheGrapevine. "In the Shadow of Suribachi: Sammy's Story." YouTube. Youtube.com/ watch?v=RSWu3vdwcFM. Accessed 22 January 2021.

Wittner, Lawrence. "Albert Einstein and World Peace." *JBooks.com.* jbooks.com/secularculture/Wittner.htm. Accessed 18 November 2012.

Yoffie, Eric H. "In Memory of Jane Evans." *Union for Reform Judaism.* urj.org. Accessed 7 December 2012.

Index

Numbers in *bold italics* indicate pages with illustrations

255